AI Blueprints

How to build and deploy AI business projects

Dr. Joshua Eckroth

BIRMINGHAM - MUMBAI

AI Blueprints

Acquisition Editors: Frank Pohlmann, Suresh Jain, Andrew Waldron

Project Editor: Veronica Pais

Content Development Editor: Alex Sorrentino

Technical Editor: Saby D'silva

Proofreader: Safis Editing

Indexer: Priyanka Dhadke

Graphics: Tom Scaria

Production Coordinator: Sandip Tadge

First published: December 2018

Production reference: 2281218

Published by Packt Publishing Ltd.
Livery Place
35 Livery Street
Birmingham B3 2PB, UK.

ISBN 978-1-78899-287-9

www.packtpub.com

`mapt.io`

Mapt is an online digital library that gives you full access to over 5,000 books and videos, as well as industry leading tools to help you plan your personal development and advance your career. For more information, please visit our website.

Why subscribe?

- Spend less time learning and more time coding with practical eBooks and Videos from over 4,000 industry professionals
- Learn better with Skill Plans built especially for you
- Get a free eBook or video every month
- Mapt is fully searchable
- Copy and paste, print, and bookmark content

Packt.com

Did you know that Packt offers eBook versions of every book published, with PDF and ePub files available? You can upgrade to the eBook version at `www.Packt.com` and as a print book customer, you are entitled to a discount on the eBook copy. Get in touch with us at `customercare@packtpub.com` for more details.

At `www.Packt.com`, you can also read a collection of free technical articles, sign up for a range of free newsletters, and receive exclusive discounts and offers on Packt books and eBooks.

Foreword

In retrospect, this book has been in the making for years. Stetson University, where I serve as an Assistant Professor of Computer Science, hosted its first annual hackathon in Spring 2016. The student organizers wanted faculty to give some lectures about programming and practical application development. AI was a hot topic then just as it is now, so I reached into my background in AI, including a PhD in the subject and multiple years of teaching an AI course in colleges, to develop a presentation I called *AI/ML IRL*, that is, artificial intelligence and machine learning in real life (*AI/ML IRL, J. Eckroth, sudo HackStetson presentation, 2016*, `https://www2.stetson.edu/~jeckroth/downloads/eckroth-ai-irl-stetson-hackathon-2016.pdf`). I covered current applications of AI, the fears and promises of AI, and concluded with advice about how to use AI in real-world applications. In this presentation may be found the seeds of the AI workflow developed in *Chapter 1*, The AI Workflow, and the discussion of the hype cycle in *Chapter 8, Preparing for Your Future and Surviving the Hype Cycle*.

Around the same time, my colleague and CEO at i2k Connect, Dr. Reid Smith, was awarded the Robert S. Engelmore Memorial Award, sponsored by the *Innovative Applications in Artificial Intelligence conference* and *AI Magazine*. Dr. Smith gave a presentation for this award (*A Quarter Century of AI Applications: What we knew then vs. what we know now, R. G. Smith, Robert S. Engelmore Memorial Lecture Award, presented at the Twenty-Eighth Conference on Innovative Applications of Artificial Intelligence (IAAI-16), Phoenix, AZ, 15 February, 2016*, `http://www.reidgsmith.com/2016-02-15_Engelmore_Lecture.pdf`), where he discussed numerous examples of successful AI applications and the lessons learned.

Dr. Smith and I discussed our separate contributions about the topic of programming AI applications and came together to write the cover article of the Spring 2017 AI Magazine (*Building AI Applications: Yesterday, Today, and Tomorrow*, R. G. Smith and J. Eckroth, *AI Magazine 38(1): 6-22, Spring 2017*, `https://www.aaai.org/ojs/index.php/aimagazine/article/view/2709`). This article examined a series of important deployed applications that made significant use of AI and machine learning. We also showed the increasing interest in AI, which I have updated for *Chapter 5, A Blueprint for Detecting Your Logo in Social Media* when I discuss deep learning. Most importantly, this article introduced some of the essential features of the AI workflow, including some checklist items to pay attention to when developing your own applications.

Jumping back to 2014 momentarily, Frank Pohlmann contacted me to write a book for another publisher. I agreed, and we developed an outline, but as I was just starting at Stetson University, I was swamped with other activities and had to cancel the plan. Three years later, Mr. Pohlmann was now a Managing Acquisition Editor for Packt and contacted me again. All of the developments I described above had occurred in the intervening time and I had more practice managing my time as a professor. The timing was right.

This book is different than any of those prior works. It focuses on programming realistic and useful AI applications with state-of-the-art software libraries and techniques. It also teaches the reader the fundamentals of the techniques we use throughout the book. But this book is the spiritual successor, and the culmination, of several years of thinking, writing, and speaking.

AI Blueprints could not have been written without the encouragement, insights, and close editorial attention from Frank Pohlmann, Reid Smith, and the staff at Packt. Another colleague at i2k Connect, Dr. Eric Schoen, graciously served as the technical reviewer of this work.

His decades of software engineering experience, including more than 30 years at Schlumberger and most recently as their Chief Software Architect, as well as a PhD in AI from Stanford University, helped refine the technical sophistication of the examples and explanations in this book.

As I'm sure every reader knows at some fundamental level, the time is right for AI. It has been for some time and will be for the foreseeable future. This book is designed to help you capture a bit of the magic of AI in your own applications.

Contributors

About the author

Joshua Eckroth is an Assistant Professor of Computer Science at Stetson University, where he teaches AI, big data mining and analytics, and software engineering. He earned his PhD from The Ohio State University in AI and Cognitive Science. Dr. Eckroth also serves as Chief Architect at i2k Connect, which focuses on transforming documents into structured data using AI and enriched with subject matter expertise.

Dr. Eckroth has previously published two video series with Packt, *Python Artificial Intelligence Projects for Beginners* and *Advanced Artificial Intelligence Projects with Python*. His academic publications can be found on Google Scholar.

"I wish to express my gratitude to Dr. Eric Schoen, Director of Engineering at i2k Connect, for taking the time to carefully review each chapter. The rest of my colleagues at i2k Connect also gave me important feedback and new ideas along the way. I also wish to thank my wife for her encouragement and patience in a process that always seems to take longer than expected."

About the reviewer

Eric Schoen is the Chief Technical Officer at i2k Connect, where he has overall responsibility for delivering its AI-powered information discovery platform. He plays a major role in ensuring its implementation, AI science, and processing algorithms are robust enough to enable operation at scale in cloud-based, on-premises, and hybrid installations. Before joining i2k Connect, Eric spent over 30 years at Schlumberger, in both research and engineering functions, most recently as its Chief Software Architect. At Schlumberger, he contributed to a broad range of software, from the company's early pioneering efforts to leverage knowledge-based systems and its GeoFrame and Ocean platforms for reservoir characterization, to its software quality processes and strategies for enterprise-scale architecture for data acquisition, transmission, processing, and delivery. Eric holds a PhD in computer science (AI) from Stanford University.

Packt is searching for authors like you

If you're interested in becoming an author for Packt, please visit `authors.packtpub.com` and apply today. We have worked with thousands of developers and tech professionals, just like you, to help them share their insight with the global tech community. You can make a general application, apply for a specific hot topic that we are recruiting an author for, or submit your own idea.

Table of Contents

Preface

Artificial intelligence (**AI**) is the hot new thing. Though AI has been around for 50 years, recent dramatic advances in the kinds of problems it can solve and the availability of open source software have opened it up to all programmers and organizations. AI technology can magnify the capabilities of an organization and its software, or open entirely new pursuits. For example, in *Chapter 5, A Blueprint for Detecting Your Logo in Social Media*, we show how to use deep learning to detect a company's logos in photos shared publicly on Twitter. Without such an AI tool, these photos would probably never be noticed, and the company would not be able to identify how their products and services connect with individuals' everyday lives. The data is there. Twitter, Reddit, news services, and others have public APIs that expose their continuous feeds of comments, photos, videos, news articles, and more. But nobody has time to look at all of that, and searches and filters do not work on photos. AI completely changes the rules.

My goal with this book is to change your expectation of where AI can be used in your applications, while giving you the power to build your own AI-powered applications. By covering a broad range of applications and technologies, I hope to show that there is not one single kind of AI (such as deep learning), nor a single kind of application.

We cover applications in planning (*Chapter 2, A Blueprint for Planning Cloud Infrastructure*), natural language processing (*Chapter 3, A Blueprint for Making Sense of Feedback* and *Chapter 7, A Blueprint for Understanding Queries and Generating Responses*), recommendation engines (*Chapter 4, A Blueprint for Recommending Products and Services*), deep learning (*Chapter 5, A Blueprint for Detecting Your Logo in Social Media*), logic programming (*Chapter 7, A Blueprint for Understanding Queries and Generating Responses*), and trend and anomaly detection (*Chapter 6, A Blueprint for Discovering Trends and Recognizing Anomalies*).

These applications show AI can help an organization with logistics and automation, customer relations, and marketing. These applications are not designed to replace human workers – instead, each project automates tedious aspects of work and provides new insights to knowledge workers. For example, *Chapter 3, A Blueprint for Making Sense of Feedback* shows how to analyze social media comments and news articles to gather detailed data about sentiment (positive or negative) about certain topics of interest. With this data, marketing experts can gauge whether a marketing campaign was successful, for example, or make an informed judgment about when to introduce a new product.

The time for AI is now. We are presently in an era where the (justified) hype for AI is strong. Consider these hypothetical headlines: "Hospital begins using AI to help with cancer diagnosis," "University uses AI to ensure on-time graduation," "Marketing firm builds AI to better target consumers," "Airline streamlines boarding process with AI." Each headline refers to some improvement, and AI is suggested to be the cause of the improvement. But what if we had replaced "uses AI" or "builds AI" with "adds staff" or "hires firm"? For example, "Airline streamlines boarding process with more gate agents and roped walkways..." It would feel like more of the same, not a revolutionary new approach.

There is something about AI that gives it a mysterious, optimistic, dreamy quality. AI can do anything! And whatever it does, it will be completely novel! Even if AI determined that a streamlined airplane boarding process can be accomplished by more roped walkways, travelers would likely marvel at the result.

"AI found this to be the optimal configuration!" In some sense, the more alien the result, the more likely we are to believe it came from AI and it is indeed optimal.

But they're not wrong. AI *is* different. AI is perpetually new. AI always promises that something we could not do yesterday can now be done with ease. Again, they're not wrong, though the hype can run away with itself sometimes.

I hope this book shows that AI is the future, it is available now, and it is here to stay.

Who this book is for

This book is targeted at software engineers who are familiar with Java and Python and wish to learn how to use artificial intelligence and machine learning in their code. This book is not just a list of techniques and algorithms, however. Every example project includes a detailed discussion of integration and deployment strategies and techniques for continuous evaluation of the AI after it is deployed. The projects and suggested workflow target small/medium businesses and startup companies that wish to introduce advanced capabilities and automation into an existing platform.

What this book covers

Chapter 1, The AI Workflow, introduces the AI workflow, which is a series of four steps in a mature process for building and deploying AI. This chapter also discusses the role of AI in context of a larger software system. The chapter ends with an introduction to each of the projects developed in *Chapter 2, A Blueprint for Planning Cloud Infrastructure* to *Chapter 7, A Blueprint for Understanding Queries and Generating Responses*.

Chapter 2, A Blueprint for Planning Cloud Infrastructure, shows how to use the open source OptaPlanner constraint solver planning engine to create a plan for cloud computing resources.

Given a time and money budget and a set of computing tasks to complete, this chapter develops a Java-based solution for the optimal number of cloud resources to complete the tasks in the shortest time and lowest budget. Benchmarks are detailed to show that the solution is accurate. Each step of the AI workflow is addressed to help readers prepare to deploy the solution.

Chapter 3, A Blueprint for Making Sense of Feedback, shows how to acquire feedback from customers and the general public about a company's products and services, and how to identify the sentiment, or general mood, of the feedback for particular products, services, or categories. The Twitter and Reddit APIs are demonstrated for acquiring feedback.

Two approaches are demonstrated for sentiment analysis: a dictionary-based approach and a method using machine learning with the `CoreNLP` library. The sentiment data is then visualized with `plotly.js` in a dashboard view for real-time updates. Each step of the AI workflow is addressed to help readers prepare to deploy the solution.

Chapter 4, A Blueprint for Recommending Products and Services, shows how to build and deploy a recommendation engine for products and services. Given a history of all user activity (purchases, clicks, ratings), a system is designed that can produce appropriate recommendations for individual users. An overview of the relevant mathematics is included, and the Python `implicit` library is used for building the solution. A continuous evaluation methodology is detailed to ensure the recommender continues to provide appropriate recommendations after it is deployed. Each step of the AI workflow is addressed to help readers prepare to deploy the solution.

Chapter 5, A Blueprint for Detecting Your Logo in Social Media, shows how to build a **convolutional neural network (CNN)** to detect logos in other people's photos. Using the Python library `TensorFlow`, readers are shown how to take an existing pre-trained object recognition model such as Xception and refine it for detecting specific objects using a small training set of images. We also demonstrate the use of YOLO and compare results.

Then the Twitter API code from *Chapter 3, A Blueprint for Making Sense of Feedback* is reused to acquire images from social media, and the detector is run on these images to pick out photos of interest. A short introduction to CNNs and deep learning is included. Each step of the AI workflow is addressed to help readers prepare to deploy the solution.

Chapter 6, A Blueprint for Discovering Trends and Recognizing Anomalies, explains how to discover and track trends on a blog, storefront, or social media platform, as well as recognizing anomalous events that defy the trends. Using statistical models and anomaly detection algorithms, code is developed with the Python library `scikit-learn`. Different approaches are compared to address different use cases. Each step of the AI workflow is addressed to help readers prepare to deploy the solution.

Chapter 7, A Blueprint for Understanding Queries and Generating Responses, shows how to build and deploy an automated helpdesk chatbot. Using the Rasa Python library and Prolog coding, two custom chatbots are developed that examine the user's question and construct an appropriate answer using natural language generation. The Prolog code helps us develop a logical reasoning agent that is able to answer complex questions. Each step of the AI workflow is addressed to help readers prepare to deploy the solution.

Chapter 8, Preparing for Your Future and Surviving the Hype Cycle, examines the current state and near future of artificial intelligence. It examines the hype cycle and the dramatic shifts in popular interest in AI over the years and provides guidance for how to be successful in such unpredictable environments. The chapter includes advice for how to identify new approaches and advances in AI and how to decide whether or not these advances are relevant for real business needs.

What you need for this book

This book uses state-of-the-art techniques and software libraries. For whatever reason, the original development of these libraries is typically done on Linux or macOS machines before being ported to Windows. Thus, it is possible some libraries might be difficult to install on a Windows machine, though Microsoft's Ubuntu on Windows 10 technology is helping close this gap. For example, `TensorFlow` has supported Windows for several years but difficulties installing it remained even in 2017 (https://github.com/tensorflow/tensorflow/issues/42).

Libraries are rapidly changing, so there is little use in detailing installation procedures in this Preface. A list of required libraries for each chapter are provided on this book's code repository: https://github.com/PacktPublishing/ProgrammingAIBusinessApplications. Installation procedures differ for each library and sometimes change as new versions are released. These instructions may be found on the library's linked homepage.

I intentionally chose to use state-of-the-art libraries even though they undergo rapid development and change. This change is usually for the better, but sometimes new versions break existing code or cannot be installed without some effort. However, I felt that it would not be helpful to write a book about old technology. For example, all Python applications in this book use Python 3.6 (or later) even though many may still work with minor changes in a Python 2.7 environment. Likewise, we use TensorFlow 1.10, the latest release at the time of writing. Books with code designed for TensorFlow 0.12, for example, will need significant updates, even though 0.12 was released less than two years ago.

Speaking of TensorFlow, if you have a GPU, you will find the code we develop in *Chapter 5, A Blueprint for Detecting Your Logo in Social Media* to be significantly more efficient, and better (more expensive) GPUs give even more performance gains. Even so, TensorFlow will still work with just a CPU.

Download the example code files

You can download the example code files for this book from your account at http://www.packt.com. If you purchased this book elsewhere, you can visit http://www.packt.com/support and register to have the files emailed directly to you.

You can download the code files by following these steps:

1. Log in or register at http://www.packt.com.
2. Select the **SUPPORT** tab.
3. Click on **Code Downloads & Errata**.
4. Enter the name of the book in the **Search** box and follow the on-screen instructions.

Once the file is downloaded, please make sure that you unzip or extract the folder using the latest version of:

- WinRAR / 7-Zip for Windows
- Zipeg / iZip / UnRarX for Mac
- 7-Zip / PeaZip for Linux

The code bundle for the book is also hosted on GitHub at https://github.com/PacktPublishing/ProgrammingAIBusinessApplications. In case there's an update to the code, it will be updated on the existing GitHub repository.

We also have other code bundles from our rich catalog of books and videos available at https://github.com/PacktPublishing/. Check them out!

Download the color images

We also provide a PDF file that has color images of the screenshots/diagrams used in this book. You can download it here: https://www.packtpub.com/sites/default/files/downloads/9781788992879_ColorImages.pdf.

Conventions used

There are a number of text conventions used throughout this book.

CodeInText: Indicates code words in text, database table names, folder names, filenames, file extensions, pathnames, dummy URLs, user input, and Twitter handles. For example; "Mount the downloaded WebStorm-10*.dmg disk image file as another disk in your system."

A block of code is set as follows:

```
[default]
exten => s,1,Dial(Zap/1|30)
exten => s,2,Voicemail(u100)
exten => s,102,Voicemail(b100)
exten => i,1,Voicemail(s0)
```

When we wish to draw your attention to a particular part of a code block, the relevant lines or items are set in bold:

```
[default]
exten => s,1,Dial(Zap/1|30)
exten => s,2,Voicemail(u100)
exten => s,102,Voicemail(b100)
exten => i,1,Voicemail(s0)
```

Any command-line input or output is written as follows:

```
# cp /usr/src/asterisk-addons/configs/cdr_mysql.conf.sample
    /etc/asterisk/cdr_mysql.conf
```

Bold: Indicates a new term, an important word, or words that you see on the screen, for example, in menus or dialog boxes, also appear in the text like this. For example: "Select **System info** from the **Administration** panel."

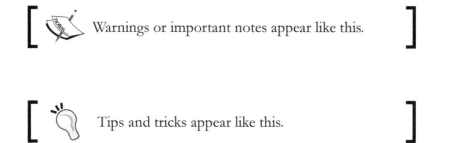

> [Warnings or important notes appear like this.]

> [Tips and tricks appear like this.]

Get in touch

Feedback from our readers is always welcome.

General feedback: If you have questions about any aspect of this book, mention the book title in the subject of your message and email us at customercare@ packtpub.com.

Errata: Although we have taken every care to ensure the accuracy of our content, mistakes do happen. If you have found a mistake in this book we would be grateful if you would report this to us. Please visit, http://www.packt.com/submit-errata, selecting your book, clicking on the Errata Submission Form link, and entering the details.

Piracy: If you come across any illegal copies of our works in any form on the Internet, we would be grateful if you would provide us with the location address or website name. Please contact us at copyright@packt.com with a link to the material.

If you are interested in becoming an author: If there is a topic that you have expertise in and you are interested in either writing or contributing to a book, please visit http://authors.packtpub.com.

Reviews

Please leave a review. Once you have read and used this book, why not leave a review on the site that you purchased it from? Potential readers can then see and use your unbiased opinion to make purchase decisions, we at Packt can understand what you think about our products, and our authors can see your feedback on their book. Thank you!

For more information about Packt, please visit packt.com.

1
The AI Workflow

Like so many technologies before and surely an infinite progression of technologies to come, **artificial intelligence** (**AI**) is the promising idea *du jour*. Due to recent advances in hardware and learning algorithms, new commercial-grade software platforms, and a proliferation of large datasets for training, any software developer can build an intelligent system that *sees* (for example, face recognition), *listens* (for example, writing emails by voice), and *understands* (for example, asking Amazon's Alexa or Google Home to set a reminder). With free off-the-shelf software, any company can have their own army of chatbots, automated sales agents customized to each potential customer, and a team of tireless web bots that scan the media for mentions and photos and videos of a company's products, among other use cases. All of these solutions may be built by regular software developers in regular companies, not just researchers in well-funded institutions.

But any seasoned professional knows that the risk associated with technology is proportional to its newness, complexity, and the number of exclamation points in its marketing copy. Tried-and-true techniques are low risk but might keep a company from taking advantage of new opportunities. AI, like any promise of intelligent automation, must be built and deployed with a specific business outcome in mind. One must have a detailed plan for integrating it into existing workflows and procedures, and should regularly monitor it to ensure the context in which the AI was deployed does not gradually or dramatically change, rendering the AI either useless, or worse, a rogue agent run amok..

This book combines practical AI techniques with advice and strategies for successful deployment. The projects are aimed at small organizations that want to explore new uses of AI in their organizations. Each project is developed to work in a realistic environment and solve a useful task. While virtually all other books, videos, courses, and blogs focus solely on AI techniques, this book helps the reader ensure that the AI makes sense and continues to work effectively.

In this first chapter, we're going to cover:

- The role of AI in software systems
- The details of a unique AI workflow that guides the development
- A brief overview of this book's coding projects

AI isn't everything

"The passion caused by the great and sublime in nature, when those causes operate most powerfully, is astonishment; and astonishment is that state of the soul, in which all its motions are suspended, with some degree of horror. [...] When danger or pain press too nearly, they are incapable of giving any delight and are simply terrible; but at certain distances, and with certain modifications, they may be, and they are delightful, as we every day experience."

– Edmund Burke
(Philosophical Enquiry into the Origin of our Ideas of the Sublime and the Beautiful, 1757)

Edmund Burke's careful study of the distinctions between what is aesthetically pleasing or beautiful versus what is compelling, astonishing, frightening, and sublime is an appropriate metaphor for the promises and the fears engendered by AI. *At certain distances*, that is, with the right design and careful deployment, AI has that quality that makes one marvel at the machine. If borne from a fear of being left behind or deployed haphazardly, if developed to solve a problem that does not exist, AI is a fool's game that can severely damage a company or brand.

Curiously, some of our top thinkers and entrepreneurs appear to be anxious about the careful balance between delight and horror. They have cautioned the world:

"Success in creating AI would be the biggest event in human history [...] Unfortunately; it might also be the last."

– Stephen Hawking
(https://futurism.com/hawking-creating-ai-could-be-the-biggest-event-in-the-history-of-our-civilization/)

"I think we should be very careful about artificial intelligence. If I were to guess at what our biggest existential threat is, it's probably that."

– Elon Musk

(`https://www.theguardian.com/technology/2014/oct/27/elon-musk-artificial-intelligence-ai-biggest-existential-threat`)

"First the machines will do a lot of jobs for us and not be super intelligent. That should be positive if we manage it well. A few decades after that though the intelligence is strong enough to be a concern. I agree with Elon Musk and some others on this and don't understand why some people are not concerned."

– Bill Gates

(`https://www.reddit.com/r/IAmA/comments/2tzjp7/hi_reddit_im_bill_gates_and_im_back_for_my_third/co3r3g8/`)

The fear of AI seems to be rooted in a fear of loss of control. Once the AI is "smart enough," it is thought that the AI will no longer obey our commands. Or it will make its own disastrous decisions and not inform us. Or it will hide critical information from us and make us subjects to its all-powerful will.

But these concerns may be flipped around to benefits: a smart AI can inform us of when we are making a bad decision and prevent embarrassments or catastrophes; it can automate tedious tasks such as making cold calls to open a sales channel; it can aggregate, summarize, and highlight just the right information from a deluge of data to help us make more informed and appropriate decisions. In short, good AI may be distinguished from bad AI by looking at its design, whether there are bugs or faults, its context of use in terms of correct inputs and sanity checks on its outputs, and the company's continuous evaluation methodology to keep track of the performance of the AI after it is deployed. This book aims to show readers how to build good AI by following these practices.

Although this book includes detailed discussion and code for a variety of AI techniques and use cases, the AI component of a larger system is usually very small. This book introduces **planning and constraint solving**, **natural language processing (NLP)**, **sentiment analysis**, **recommendation engines**, **anomaly detection**, and **neural networks**. Each of these techniques is sufficiently exciting and complex to warrant textbooks, PhDs, and conferences dedicated to their elucidation and study. But they are a very small part of any deployed software system.

Consider the following diagram, showing some everyday concerns of a modern software developer:

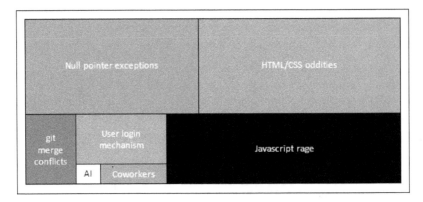

Although probably the most interesting part of a project, the AI component is often the least troublesome part of software development. As we will see throughout this book, AI techniques are often contained in a single project module or class or function. The performance of the AI component depends almost entirely on the appropriateness of the inputs and correct handling and cleanup of the outputs.

For example, an AI component that determines the sentiment, positive or negative, of a tweet or product review is relatively straightforward to implement, particularly with today's AI software libraries (though the code in the library is quite complex). On the other hand, acquiring the tweets or reviews (likely involving authentication and rate limiting), formatting and cleaning the text (especially handling odd Unicode characters and emojis), and saving the output of sentiment analysis into a database for summarization and real-time visualization takes far more work than the "intelligent" part of the whole process.

But the AI is the most interesting part. Without it, there is no insight and no automation. And particularly in today's hyped environment with myriad tools and techniques and best practices, it is easy to get this part wrong. This book develops an AI workflow to help ensure success in building and deploying AI.

The AI workflow

Building and deploying AI should follow a workflow that respects the fact that the AI component fits in the larger context of pre-existing processes and use cases. The AI workflow may be characterized as a four step process:

1. Characterize the problem, goal, and business case
2. Develop a method for solving the problem

3. Design a deployment strategy that integrates the AI component into existing workflows

4. Design and implement a continuous evaluation methodology

To help you ensure the AI workflow is followed, we offer a checklist of considerations and questions to ask during each step of the workflow.

Characterize the problem

Given the excitement around AI, there is a risk of adding AI technology to a platform just for the sake of not missing out on the next big thing. However, AI technology is usually one of the more complex components of a system, hence the hype surrounding AI and the promise of advanced new capabilities it supposedly brings. Due to its complexity, AI introduces potentially significant *technical debt*, that is, code complexity that is hard to manage and becomes even harder to eliminate. Often, the code must be written to message inputs to the AI into a form that meets its assumptions and constraints and to fix outputs for the AI's mistakes.

Engineers from Google published an article in 2014 titled *Machine Learning: The High-Interest Credit Card of Technical Debt* (https://ai.google/research/pubs/pub43146), in which they write:

> *In this paper, we focus on the system-level interaction between machine learning code and larger systems as an area where hidden technical debt may rapidly accumulate. At a system level, a machine learning model may subtly erode abstraction boundaries. It may be tempting to re-use input signals in ways that create unintended tight coupling of otherwise disjoint systems. Machine learning packages may often be treated as black boxes, resulting in large masses of "glue code" or calibration layers that can lock in assumptions. Changes in the external world may make models or input signals change behavior in unintended ways, ratcheting up maintenance cost and the burden of any debt. Even monitoring that the system as a whole is operating as intended may be difficult without careful design.*
>
> *Machine Learning: The High-Interest Credit Card of Technical Debt, D. Sculley, G. Holt, D. Golovin, E. Davydov, T. Phillips, D. Ebner, V. Chaudhary, and M. Young, presented at the SE4ML: Software Engineering for Machine Learning (NIPS 2014 Workshop), 2014*

They proceed to document several varieties of technical debt that often come with AI and **machine learning (ML)** technology and suggest mitigations that complement those covered in our AI workflow.

AI should address a business problem that is not solvable by conventional means. The risk of technical debt is too high (higher than many other kinds of software practices) to consider adding AI technology without a clear purpose.

The problem being addressed with AI should be known to be *solvable*. For example, until recent advances found in Amazon Echo and Google Home, speech recognition in a large and noisy room was not possible. A few years ago, it would have been foolish to attempt to build a product that required this capability.

The AI component should be well-defined and bounded. It should do one or a few tasks, and it should make use of established algorithms, such as those detailed in the following chapters. The AI should not be treated as an amorphous intelligent concierge that solves any problem, specified or unspecified. For example, our chatbot case study in *Chapter 7, A Blueprint for Understanding Queries and Generating Responses*, is intentionally designed to handle a small subset of possible questions from users. A chatbot that attempts to answer all questions, perhaps with some kind of continuous learning based on the conversations users have with it, is a chatbot that has a high chance of embarrassing its creators, as was the case with Microsoft's Tay chatbot (https://blogs.microsoft.com/blog/2016/03/25/learning-tays-introduction/).

In summary, the AI should solve a business problem, it should use established techniques that are known to be able to solve the problem, and it should have a well-defined and bounded role within the larger system.

Checklist

- The AI solves a clearly stated business problem
- The problem is known to be solvable by AI
- The AI uses established techniques
- The role of the AI within the larger system is clearly defined and bounded

Develop a method

After characterizing the problem to be solved, a method for solving the problem must be found or developed. In most cases, a business should not attempt to engage in a greenfield research project developing a novel way to solve the problem. Such research projects carry significant risk since an effective solution is not guaranteed within a reasonable time. Instead, one should prefer existing techniques.

This book covers several existing and proven techniques for a variety of tasks. Many of these techniques, such as **planning engines**, **natural language part-of-speech tagging**, and **anomaly detection,** are much less interesting to the AI research community than some newer methods, such as **convolutional neural networks (CNN)**. But these older techniques are still quite useful. These techniques have "disappeared in the fabric," to use a phrase Dr. Reid Smith, Fellow of the **Association for the Advancement of Artificial Intelligence** (**AAAI**), and I wrote in an article for *AI Magazine* titled, *Building AI Applications: Yesterday, Today, and Tomorrow* in 2017 (`https://www.aaai.org/ojs/index.php/aimagazine/article/view/2709`) (*Building AI Applications: Yesterday, Today, and Tomorrow*, R. G. Smith and J. Eckroth, *AI Magazine, vol. 38, no. 1, pp. 6–22, 2017*). What is sometimes called the "AI Effect" is the notion that whatever has become commonplace is no longer AI but rather everyday software engineering (`https://en.wikipedia.org/wiki/AI_effect`). We should measure an AI technique's maturity by how "boring" it is perceived to be, such as boring, commonplace heuristic search and planning. *Chapter 2, A Blueprint for Planning Cloud Infrastructure*, solves a real-world problem with this kind of boring but mature AI.

Finally, when developing a method, one should also take care to identify computation and data requirements. Some methods, such as **deep learning**, require a significant amount of both. In fact, deep learning is virtually impossible without some high-end **graphics processing units** (**GPU**) and thousands to millions of examples for training. Often, open source libraries such as `CoreNLP` will include highly accurate pre-trained models so the challenge of acquiring sufficient data for training purposes can be avoided. In *Chapter 5, A Blueprint for Detecting Your Logo in Social Media*, we demonstrate a means of customizing a pre-trained model for a custom use case with what is known as "transfer learning."

Checklist

- The method does not require significant new research
- The method is relatively mature and commonplace
- The necessary hardware resources and training data are available

Design a deployment strategy

Even the most intelligent AI may never be used. It is rare for people to change their habits even if there is an advantage in doing so. Finding a way to integrate a new AI tool into an existing workflow is just as important to the overall AI workflow as making a business case for the AI and developing it. Dr. Smith and I wrote:

> *Perhaps the most important lesson learned by AI system builders is that success depends on integrating into existing workflows — the human context of actual use. It is rare to replace an existing workflow completely. Thus, the application must play nicely with the other tools that people use. Put another way, ease of use delivered by the human interface is the "license to operate." Unless designers get that part right, people may not ever see the AI power under the hood; they will have already walked away.*
>
> *Building AI Applications: Yesterday, Today, and Tomorrow, R. G. Smith and J. Eckroth, AI Magazine, vol. 38, no. 1, Page 16, 2017*

Numerous examples of bad integrations exist. Consider Microsoft's "Clippy," a cartoon character that attempted to help users write letters and spell check their document. It was eventually removed from Microsoft Office (https://www.theatlantic.com/technology/archive/2015/06/clippy-the-microsoft-office-assistant-is-the-patriarchys-fault/396653/). While its assistance may have been useful, the problem seemed to be that Clippy was socially awkward, in a sense. Clippy asked if the user would like help at nearly all the wrong times:

> *Clippy suffered the dreaded "optimization for first-time use" problem. That is, the very first time you were composing a letter with Word, you might possibly be grateful for advice about how to use various letter-formatting features. The next billion times you typed "Dear..." and saw Clippy pop up, you wanted to scream.*
>
> (https://www.theatlantic.com/technology/archive/2008/04/-quot-clippy-quot-update-now-with-organizational-anthropology/8006/)

In a more recent example, most smartphone users do not use Apple Siri or Google Home, especially not in public (*What can I help you with?: Infrequent users' experiences of intelligent personal assistants*, B. R. Cowan, N. Pantidi, D. Coyle, K. Morrissey, P. Clarke, S. Al-Shehri, D. Earley, and N. Bandeira, presented at the *19th International Conference on Human-Computer Interaction with Mobile Devices and Services, New York, New York, USA, 2017, pp. 43–12*). Changing social norms in order to increase adoption of a product is a significant marketing challenge. On the other hand, to "google" something, which clearly involves AI, is a sufficiently entrenched activity that it is defined as a verb in the Oxford English Dictionary ("Google, v.2'" OED Online, January 2018, Oxford University Press, http://www.oed.com/view/Entry/261961?rskey=yiwSeP&result=2&isAdvanced=false). Face recognition and automatic tagging on Facebook have been used by millions of people. And we click product recommendations on Amazon and other storefronts without a second thought. We have many everyday workflows that have evolved to include AI.

As a general rule, it is easier to ask users to make a small change to their habits if the payoff is large; and it is hard or impossible to ask users to make a large change to their habits or workflow if the payoff is small.

In addition to considering the user experience, effective deployment of AI also requires that one considers its placement within a larger system. What kinds of inputs are provided to the AI? Are they always in the right format? Does the AI have assumptions about these inputs that might not be met in extreme circumstances? Likewise, what kinds of outputs does the AI produce? Are these outputs always within established bounds? Is anything automated based on these outputs? Will an email be sent to customers based on the AI's decisions? Will a missile be fired?

As discussed in the preceding section, *AI isn't everything*, often a significant amount of code must be written *around* the AI component. The AI probably has strong assumptions about the kind of data it is receiving. For example, CNNs can only work on images of a specific, fixed size – larger or smaller images must be squished or stretched first. Most NLP techniques assume the text is written in a particular language; running part-of-speech tagging with an English model on a French text will produce bogus results.

If the AI gets bad input, or even if the AI gets good input, the results might be bad. What kind of checks are performed on the output to ensure the AI does not make your company look foolish? This question is particularly relevant if the AI's output feeds into an automated process such as sending alerts and emails, adding metadata to photos or posts, or even suggesting products. Most AI will connect to some automated procedure since the value added by AI is usually focused on its ability to automate some task. Ultimately, developers will need to ensure that the AI's outputs are accurate; this is addressed in the final step in the workflow, *Design and implement a continuous evaluation*. First, however, we provide a checklist for designing a deployment strategy.

Checklist

- Plan a user experience, if the AI is user-facing, that fits into an existing habit or workflow, requiring very little change by the user
- Ensure the AI adds significant value with minimal barriers to adoption
- List the AI's assumptions or requirements about the nature (format, size, characteristics) of its inputs and outputs
- Articulate boundary conditions on the AI's inputs and outputs, and develop a plan to either ignore or correct out-of-bounds and bogus inputs and outputs
- List all the ways the AI's outputs are used to automate some task, and the potential impact bad output may have on that task, on a user's experience, and on the company's reputation

Design and implement a continuous evaluation

The fourth and final stage of the workflow concerns the AI after it is deployed. Presumably, during development, the AI has been trained and tested on a broad range of realistic inputs and shown to perform admirably. And then it is deployed. Why should anything change?

No large software, and certainly no AI system, has ever been tested on all possible inputs. Developing "adversarial" inputs, that is, inputs designed to break an AI system, is an entire subfield of AI with its own researchers and publications (https://en.wikipedia.org/wiki/Adversarial_machine_learning). Adversarial inputs showcase the limits of some of our AI systems and help us build more robust software.

However, even in non-adversarial cases, AI systems can degrade or break in various ways. According to The Guardian, YouTube's recommendation engine, which suggests the next video to watch, has begun showing extremist content next to kid-friendly videos. Advertisers for the benign videos are reasonably upset about unexpected brand associations with such content (https://www.theguardian.com/technology/2017/mar/25/google-youtube-advertising-extremist-content-att-verizon). Particularly when the AI is trained using a large corpus of example data, the AI can pick out statistical regularities in the data that do not accurately reflect our society. For example, some AI has been shown to be racist (https://www.theguardian.com/inequality/2017/aug/08/rise-of-the-racist-robots-how-ai-is-learning-all-our-worst-impulses). The quality of the training set is usually to blame in these situations. When mature adults examine the data, they are able to bring a lifetime of experience to their interpretation. They understand that the data can be skewed due to various reasons based on a host of possible systemic biases in data collection, among other factors. However, feeding this data into an AI may well produce a kind of sociopathic AI that has no lifetime of experience to fall back on. Rather, the AI trusts the data with absolute assuredness. The data is all the AI knows unless additional checks and balances are added to the code.

The environments in which AI is deployed almost always change. Any AI deployed to humans will be subjected to an environment in constant evolution. The kinds of words used by people leaving product reviews will change over time ("far out," "awesome," "lit," and so on (https://blog.oxforddictionaries.com/2014/05/07/18-awesome-ways-say-awesome/)), as will their syntax (that is, Unicode smilies, emojis, "meme" GIFs). The kinds of photos people take of themselves and each other have changed from portraits, often taken by a bystander, to selfies, thus dramatically altering the perspective and orientation of faces in photos.

Any AI that becomes part of a person's workflow will be manipulated by that person. The user will attempt to understand how the AI behaves and then will gradually adjust the way they use the AI in order to get maximum benefit from it.

Fred Brooks, manager of IBM's System/360 effort and winner of the Turing Award, observed in his book *The Mythical Man-Month* that systems, just before deployment, exist in a *metastable* modality – any change to their operating environment or inputs could cause the system to collapse to a less functional state:

> *"Systems program building is an entropy-decreasing process, hence inherently metastable. Program maintenance is an entropy-increasing process, and even its most skillful execution only delays the subsidence of the system into unfixable obsolescence."*

> *The Mythical Man-Month: Essays on Software Engineering, Anniversary Edition, F.P. Brooks, Jr., Addison Wesley, 2/E. 1995, Page 123*

Perhaps there is no escape from the inevitable obsolescence of every system. However, one could presumably delay this fate by continuously monitoring the system after it is deployed and revise or retrain the system in light of new data. This new data can be acquired from the system's *actual* operating environment rather than its *expected* operating environment, which is all one knows before it is deployed.

The following checklist may help system builders to design and implement a continuous evaluation methodology.

Checklist

- Define performance metrics. These are often defined during system building and may be reused for continuous evaluation.

- Write scripts that automate system testing according to these metrics. Create "regression" tests to ensure the cases the system solved adequately before are still solved adequately in the future.

- Keep logs of all AI inputs and outputs if the data size is not unbearable or keep aggregate statistics if it is. Define alert conditions to detect degrading performance; for example, to detect whether the AI system is unusually producing the same output repeatedly.

- Consider asking for feedback from users and aggregate this feedback in a place that is often reviewed. Read *Chapter 3, A Blueprint for Making Sense of Feedback,* for a smart way to handle feedback.

Overview of the chapters

The projects detailed in chapters 2 through 7 showcase multiple AI use cases and techniques. In each chapter, the AI workflow is addressed in the context of the specific project. The reader is encouraged not only to practice with the techniques and learn new coding skills but also to critically consider how the AI workflow might apply to new situations that are beyond the scope of this book.

Chapter 2, A Blueprint for Planning Cloud Infrastructure, shows how AI can be used in a planning engine to provide suggestions for optimal allocation of cloud computing resources. Often, AI and ML require significant computational time for training or processing. Today, cloud computing is a cost-effective option for these large computing jobs. Of course, cloud computing carries a certain cost in money and time. Depending on the job, tasks may be run in parallel on multiple cloud instances, thus significantly reducing time, but possibly increasing costs depending on how long the tasks take to start up on each instance.

This chapter shows how to use the open source **OptaPlanner** constraint solver planning engine to create a plan for cloud computing resources. This chapter develops a Java-based solution for the optimal number of cloud resources to complete the tasks in the shortest time and lowest budget. Benchmarks are detailed to show that the solution is accurate.

Chapter 3, A Blueprint for Making Sense of Feedback, shows how to acquire feedback from customers and the general public about a company's products and services, and how to identify the sentiment, or general mood, of the feedback for particular products, services, or categories. The Twitter and Reddit APIs are demonstrated for acquiring feedback. Two approaches are demonstrated for sentiment analysis: a dictionary-based approach and a method using ML with the `CoreNLP` library. The sentiment data is then visualized with **plotly.js** in a dashboard view for real-time updates.

Chapter 4, A Blueprint for Recommending Products and Services, shows how to build and deploy a recommendation engine for products and services. Given a history of all user activity (purchases, clicks, ratings), a system is designed that can produce appropriate recommendations for individual users. An overview of the relevant mathematics is included, and the Python `implicit` library is used for building the solution. A continuous evaluation methodology is detailed to ensure the recommender continues to provide appropriate recommendations after it is deployed.

Chapter 5, A Blueprint for Detecting Your Logo in Social Media, shows how to build a CNN to detect certain objects, such as products and logos, in other people's photos. Using the Python library `TensorFlow`, readers are shown how to take an existing pre-trained object recognition model such as **Xception** and refine it for detecting specific objects using a small training set of images. Then the Twitter and Reddit API codes from *Chapter 3, A Blueprint for Making Sense of Feedback*, are reused to acquire images from social media, and the detector is run on these images to pick out photos of interest. A short introduction to CNNs and deep learning is included.

Chapter 6, A Blueprint for Discovering Trends and Recognizing Anomalies, explains how to discover and track trends on a blog, storefront, or social media platform. Using statistical models and anomaly detection algorithms, the code is developed with the Python library `scikit-learn`. Different approaches in ML are compared to address different use cases.

Chapter 7, A Blueprint for Understanding Queries and Generating Responses, explains how to use the `Rasa` Python library and Prolog to build two custom chatbots that examine the user's question and construct an appropriate answer using natural language generation. The Prolog code helps us develop a logical reasoning agent that is able to answer complex questions. Each step of the AI workflow is addressed to help readers prepare to deploy the solution.

The final part of this book, *Chapter 8, Preparing for Your Future and Surviving the Hype Cycle*, examines the various highs and lows of interest in AL and ML over the last several decades. A case is made that AI has continued to improve and grow over all this time, but often the AI is behind the scenes or accepted as standard practice and thus not perceived as exciting. However, as long as a business case continues to exist for the AI solutions and the AI workflow is followed, the hype cycles should not impact the development of an effective solution. The chapter ends with advice on how to identify new approaches and advances in AI and how to decide whether or not these advances are relevant for real business need.

Summary

In this chapter, we saw that AI can play a crucial role in a larger system, a role that enables new functionality that can form the basis of a product or service. However, in practice, the AI component is actually quite small when compared to the code and time spent on surrounding issues such as the user interface, handling messy input and correcting bad outputs, and all the issues intrinsic to working in software teams larger than one. In any event, the AI component is also often the most complex part of an intelligent software system, and special care must be taken to get it right. We've introduced an AI workflow that ensures that the benefits of building and deploying AI have a hope of outweighing the costs of initial development and continued monitoring and maintenance. This chapter also introduced the projects that make up the bulk of this book.

In the next chapter, we follow the AI workflow with an AI cloud resource planning project that will prove to be useful in several other projects.

2
A Blueprint for Planning Cloud Infrastructure

Electronic computing was once so rarefied and expensive that few people had ever seen such a machine. Elaborate public displays such as IBM's Selective Sequence Electronic Calculator (*The IBM Selective Sequence Electronic Calculator*, *Columbia University Computing History*, http://www.columbia.edu/cu/computinghistory/ssec.html), placed behind glass on the ground floor of their New York headquarters in 1948, attest to the esteemed introduction of computing. Yet, through the most remarkable technological progression of human history, computing power has grown while hardware size and power usage have shrunk in equally spectacular orders of magnitude – today, chips less than a billionth the size have more computing power than the original electro-mechanical marvels, and equally, machines nominally the size of a refrigerator have billions of times the speed and memory.

Originally, computing resources were rented from large firms such as IBM, UNIVAC, and Honeywell, but eventually, businesses purchased and installed commodity servers on-premises as a cost-saving measure. Now, ironically, computing power and network connectivity are so cheap that businesses again find it more cost effective to rent from big companies such as Amazon, Google, and Microsoft.

But no business is willing to throw money around. Now that computing is again rented, every minute counts. Cloud providers allow (virtual) machines to be created and destroyed on demand. Cloud providers also have many configurations available, ranging from cheap but slow machines to specialized high-performance machines for specialized workloads. The price and performance of cloud machines continually change as hardware and software improve and cloud providers compete in an innovative and low-margin market. Buying machine time up-front in fixed quantities can also reduce cost. Deciding how many machines and what kinds are needed to complete some task within some budget is virtually impossible to do by hand – perhaps AI can help us?

Given some collection of independent tasks to complete, how do we decide which and how many machines are needed to complete them in the smallest amount of time and within a certain monetary budget? The answer: use a constraint solver!

In this chapter, we will cover:

- The characteristics of a cloud infrastructure planning problem
- A technique for solving the problem using the free and open source constraint solver OptaPlanner
- Deployment scripts and a method for evaluating the accuracy of the planner

The problem, goal, and business case

In accordance with the AI workflow developed in the previous chapter, we will first identify the problem, goal, and business case of cloud infrastructure planning. This ensures our efforts are not in vain, that is, we are applying AI toward a useful purpose with a measurable payoff.

Cloud computing is commonly used for hosting long-running services such as databases, load-balancing, and "bursty" workloads, such as sudden web traffic. Costs are usually expressed by cloud providers in monthly or yearly terms. However, cloud computing is also useful for one-off batch processing for AI. Many AI techniques require significant preprocessing of large data sets and long training phases. The processing is typically longer than a bursty workload, but the virtual machines are no longer needed when the processing is complete. In some cases, the preprocessing and/or training may be done on multiple machines in parallel.

Naturally, cloud providers have tools to help an engineer calculate the costs of various configurations and run times. The major cloud providers, that is, **Amazon Web Services**, **Microsoft Azure**, and **Google Cloud Platform**, compete to keep these costs as low as possible for their various machine configurations. Apparently, as a kind of competitive necessity, each of these cloud providers has multiple different possible machine configurations, with corresponding prices ranging from $0.100/hour (Amazon m4.large) to $3.060/hour (Amazon c5.18xlarge). For the cloud provider, the different configurations are mostly just tweaks to the configurations of the virtual machines – it is easy to create new machine variations with more or fewer CPU cores and RAM. However, for the engineer pricing out a solution, the abundance of choice is surely disheartening: how can we know we are using the optimal (cheapest, fastest) configuration for our data processing needs?

By "disheartening," we refer to the fact that Google Cloud Platform provides 26 different machine types, Microsoft Azure provides 93, and Amazon Web Services 102.

Their respective cost calculators are no more sophisticated than grade-school handheld calculators: they just multiply the number of machines × hours × cost/hour to obtain overall cost. The following screenshot shows a portion of Amazon's cost calculator:

Compute: Amazon EC2 Instances:						
	Description	Instances	Usage	Type	Billing Option	Monthly Cost
⊖	Machine 1	3	5 Hours/Month ⬍	Linux on m4.large	On-Demand (No Cor ⬤	$ 1.50
⊖	Machine 2	1	3 Hours/Month ⬍	Linux on m3.xlarge	On-Demand (No Cor ⬤	$ 0.80
⊖	Machine 3	7	18 Hours/Month ⬍	Linux on t2.medium	On-Demand (No Cor ⬤	$ 5.88
⊕	Add New Row					

Figure 1: A portion of Amazon's cost calculator

An engineer's fundamental question may be stated as follows: *How much computing power do I really need, and how much will it cost to finish the job?* A cost calculator yields only one half of the answer: *How much will it cost?* Techniques from AI will help us find the other answer: *How much computing power do I really need?* Even better, AI can search for *optimal* (or near-optimal) cost and/or time to complete the job.

With such a planning engine, an engineer can set up an appropriate cloud computing configuration. Doing so could save time or money or both. There is a clear business case for this kind of technology.

Our planning problem will center on a large image processing task. The **Panoramic Survey Telescope and Rapid Response System (Pan-STARRS1)** data archive provides public access to thousands of wide-field astronomical images taken by the Institute for Astronomy at the University of Hawaii (http://panstarrs. stsci.edu/). We have downloaded more than 25,000 images, totaling 868 GB and spanning more than two trillion pixels. Our processing task is to detect circles (stars) in every image and record their location in **right ascension, declination (RA/Dec)** coordinates, the typical coordinates for astronomical objects.

The time-consuming parts of this task are downloading the images from Amazon's S3 storage, where we have previously uploaded them; and dilating, eroding, thresholding, and detecting circles in the images. This data processing task comes from a *Big Data Mining and Analytics* course at Stetson University, DeLand, Florida. Details about the task are explained in the context of a course assignment in the article, *A course on big data analytics, Eckroth, J., Journal of Parallel and Distributed Computing, 118(1), 2018* (https://www.sciencedirect.com/science/article/ pii/S0743731518300972). In that article, we demonstrate that using a high-end GPU gives faster results if a GPU-optimized circle detection algorithm is used, but just performing dilation, erosion, and thresholding on the GPU takes more time than just using a CPU due to the overhead of uploading and downloading the image from the GPU's memory. As always, benchmarking small example cases is necessary for predicting the performance of larger jobs.

We will use Amazon's **Elastic Compute Cloud** (EC2) instance types m4.large, m4.xlarge, c4.large, c4.xlarge, and c4.2xlarge. Our planner will determine how many machines of each type are needed, and which subset of images each machine should process. Our image processing program is written in C++ using the OpenCV 3 library. The **GNU Parallel** tool (*Tange, O., GNU Parallel - The Command-Line Power Tool, ;login: The USENIX Magazine, pp. 42-47, 2011*) will run this program in parallel, splitting the images into groups and running as many processes in parallel as CPU cores in the virtual machine. Our planner will estimate the cost and generate a sequence of commands that we can use to run the multi-machine processing job. These commands use Amazon's **AWS Command Line Interface** tool, known as **AWS CLI**, to create the respective instances, start the processing tasks, and shut down the instances.

In order to supply the planner with sufficient information to find a cheap and efficient configuration of machines and assign each machine one or more subsets of images to process, we will need to know some characteristics about each machine type:

- The cost of the cloud machine in $/minute
- The startup time of the machine (booting, installing a couple packages, uploading the image processing program)
- The time required to download and process one subset of images with GNU Parallel (each image subset contains 100 images)

The time required for starting the machines and processing a subset of images must be found experimentally. These measurements are included in the source code, described in detail in the following sections.

Method – constraint solvers

The problem of cloud infrastructure planning may be solved with a **constraint satisfaction engine**, also known as a **constraint solver**. Constraint solving is a search process that attempts to minimize (or maximize) certain metrics while respecting certain constraints. There are many algorithmic methods for finding solutions that meet all the constraints and simultaneously minimize or maximize certain metrics. These methods include **branch-and-bound**, **tabu search**, **simulated annealing**, and **genetic algorithms**. It is worth noting that except in relatively simplistic cases, the optimal solution (as opposed to near-optimal) cannot be found efficiently, where "efficiently" refers to thousands of seconds as compared to thousands of years. We will develop a cloud infrastructure planner that searches for a good solution, but it might not be optimal.

In order to use a constraint solver, we need to know the following about our problem:

- **Constraints**: The characteristics of valid and invalid solutions (hard constraints), and the metrics to optimize (soft constraints).
- **Planning entities and planning variables**: The things that are subject to changes in order to construct a solution. In an object-oriented design, planning entities are the objects subject to changes, and planning variables are the fields in these objects that are actually changed.
- **Planning solution**: A means of collecting or arranging planning entities into a solution that can be evaluated according to the hard and soft constraints.

A constraint solver abstractly works as follows:

1. Start by creating a set of instances of the planning entities with particular values in the planning variables. The variables may be set by some intelligent heuristic or set randomly. Collect these planning entities into a planning solution.
2. Evaluate the planning solution. If it breaks any hard constraints, throw it out and start again.
3. Take the best planning solution found so far (according to the soft constraints) and modify it. Change one or more planning variables in one or more planning entities to create a new planning solution.
4. Evaluate this new solution. If it breaks hard constraints, throw it out.
5. Repeat step 3 until we run out of time or no better solution can be found after a certain number of attempts.

Further reading about constraint solvers may be found at AITopics (`https://aitopics.org/class/Technology/Information%20Technology/Artificial%20Intelligence/Representation%20&%20Reasoning/Constraint-Based%20Reasoning`) and the popular AI textbook, *Artificial Intelligence: A Modern Approach, Russel, S. and Norvig, P., 3rd Ed., Pearson, 2009 (Chapter 4, Beyond Classical Search)*.

OptaPlanner

Though many constraint solver packages are available, we will use Red Hat's OptaPlanner (`https://www.optaplanner.org/`) for this project for several reasons: it is free and open source; it supports a wide variety of planning problems with hard, soft, and even "medium" constraints; it supports a wide variety of search algorithms, and it is actively developed and maintained.

OptaPlanner runs on the **Java Virtual Machine**, and it officially supports coding in Java, Kotlin, and Scala. We will use Java here. It uses common object-oriented design patterns and Java tools. It can run standalone, as we will do here, or may be deployed in Java EE compliant application servers. OptaPlanner also includes a web-based GUI for defining planning entities, variables, and constraints. In short, it is "enterprise ready."

It is worth noting that OptaPlanner's documentation (`https://docs.optaplanner.org/7.6.0.Final/optaplanner-docs/html_single/index.html`) includes a "cloud balancing" example. That example is a version of *bin packing*, in which a fixed set of resources are available (cloud virtual machines) with certain capacities (CPU and RAM), and a set of tasks need to be assigned to these machines. The problem is to assign tasks to the machines so that the machines are not overloaded (their CPU and/or RAM are not exceeded) and each task is assigned to exactly one machine.

Their goal is to minimize the number of machines that have assigned tasks. Our cloud infrastructure planning problem is different. In our case, machines do not have limited resources; instead, they have performance characteristics and costs. These costs are not fixed but rather a function of the time the machines are in use. Furthermore, we wish to minimize both time and cost, while ensuring cost does not exceed a certain fixed threshold. Our problem belongs to the class of problems known as *job shop scheduling*.

Now we will look at our implementation. The code is organized according to this filesystem hierarchy:

- `src/main/java/pub/smartcode/simplecloudplanner`
  - `Main.java`
  - `CloudPlanner.java`
  - `Machine.java`
  - `Task.java`
  - `Scorer.java`

- `resources/simpleCloudPlannerConfig.xml`

We will use **Maven** for dependency management. OptaPlanner is available in Maven:

```xml
<dependency>
  <groupId>org.optaplanner</groupId>
  <artifactId>optaplanner-core</artifactId>
  <version>7.5.0.t018</version>
</dependency>
```

As can be seen in the filesystem hierarchy shown previously, our planner only needs a handful of classes. For simple use cases, OptaPlanner needs the following classes:

- A `Main` class that loads OptaPlanner-specific configuration, creates the planning entities, runs the solver, and saves or prints the solution.

- A class representing a planning solution, that is, a collection of planning entities. For us, this is the `CloudPlanner` class.

- A class representing each different kind of planning entity. This class should have at least one planning variable. For us, this is the `Task` class. A `Task` object will represent a processing task to be performed in the cloud. The planning variable in the `Task` class is the machine that the Task will run on.

- Various "problem fact" classes, if applicable. A problem fact is something that can be assigned to a planning variable. Problem facts are often physical resources such as people, planes, or in our case, cloud machines. Our `Machine` class is a kind of problem fact. Each `Task` will be assigned to one `Machine` object, specified in the planning variable in `Task`.

- A class that contains a method for scoring planning solutions. The method should return a hard/soft score (that is, constraint) object. Our `Solver` class plays this role.

Each class will be detailed in turn. First, we will look at the simple configuration file, `simpleCloudPlannerConfig.xml`, that OptaPlanner uses to find the various required classes mentioned previously:

```xml
<?xml version="1.0" encoding="UTF-8"?>
<solver>
  <scanAnnotatedClasses>
    <packageInclude>
      pub.smartcode.simplecloudplanner
    </packageInclude>
  </scanAnnotatedClasses>
  <scoreDirectorFactory>
    <easyScoreCalculatorClass>
      pub.smartcode.simplecloudplanner.Scorer
    </easyScoreCalculatorClass>
  </scoreDirectorFactory>
  <termination>
    <secondsSpentLimit>10</secondsSpentLimit>
  </termination>
</solver>
```

This configuration tells OptaPlanner to find the planning entity, planning variables, and problem facts in the source files under the `pub.smartcode.simplecloudplanner` package. We will use source annotations to indicate these specific attributes. Also, the configuration refers to the class that contains the scoring method (`pub.smartcode.simplecloudplanner.Scorer`). Lastly, we set a time limit (10 seconds) for planning since experimentation showed a good solution is often found quickly and waiting longer does not produce a better solution.

For the next step, we will examine the problem fact and planning entity classes: `Machine` and `Task`, respectively. These are the most straightforward classes as they represent simple concrete ideas.

Here are the fields of `Machine.java` (the parts not shown are the obvious getters and setters and constructor):

```
public class Machine {
    private double cost;              // in dollars/minute
    private double startupTime;       // in minutes
    private String configuration;     // machine type, e.g., c4.large
    private int id;
```

We will have a `Machine` object for each different kind of cloud machine we wish to use. As we will see soon, the `Main` class will create a sufficient number of `Machine` objects to cover our planning needs. Not all `Machine` objects necessarily will be used (not all will be assigned tasks).

The planning entity, which we call `Task`, has a few interesting fields. We need to know how long a task takes to complete on each different kind of machine (field `Map<String, Double> machineTimings`). We also need to know which `Machine` object the task has been assigned to (field `Machine machine`). Besides the obvious getters, setters, and constructor, our `Task.java` file must include some annotations that inform OptaPlanner that `Task` is a planning entity and the `machine` field is the planning variable. We annotate the `getMachine()` method to indicate the planning variable. The problem facts that may be selected and assigned to the planning variable are also indicated in the annotation. The annotation says that problem facts come from `machineRange`, which is defined in our planning solution class, `CloudPlanner`:

```
@PlanningEntity
public class Task {
    private String taskType;
    private int id;
    private Map<String, Double> machineTimings;
    private Machine machine;

    @PlanningVariable(valueRangeProviderRefs = {"machineRange"})
    public Machine getMachine() {
```

```
        return machine;
    }
}
```

Now we can look at the planning solution class, `CloudPlanner`. An annotation indicates it is a planning solution, and the `taskList` field holds the solution (machine-task assignments). The getter for this field is annotated as a provider of planning entities. The `machineList` field holds all available machines, created in the `Main` class, and annotated as the source of problem facts (used by the `Task` class shown previously). Finally, the planning solution holds the score of the solution it represents. Each solution is evaluated with a `HardSoftScore` evaluator, detailed in the following code block:

```
@PlanningSolution
public class CloudPlanner {
    private List<Machine> machineList;
    private List<Task> taskList;
    private HardSoftScore score;

    @ValueRangeProvider(id = "machineRange")
    @ProblemFactCollectionProperty
    public List<Machine> getMachineList() {
        return machineList;
    }

    @PlanningEntityCollectionProperty
    public List<Task> getTaskList() {
        return taskList;
    }

    @PlanningScore
    public HardSoftScore getScore() {
        return score;
    }
}
```

Next, we define the scoring function. OptaPlanner supports various techniques for defining scores and thereby defining constraints. We use a "hard-soft" score to distinguish between a hard score or constraint, in our case a strict limit on a budget ($2), and a soft score, in our case a calculation that measures the cost and efficiency of the plan. A hard-soft score is represented as a pair of integers. OptaPlanner seeks to maximize both scores. The hard score is always preferred over the soft score: if OptaPlanner can find a new plan that increases the hard score, it will keep that plan even if the soft score drops. If we wish to minimize a value (such as cost or time), we use a negative number so that OptaPlanner's preference for maximizing results is actually minimizing the value (closer to 0).

A hard constraint may be specified by giving a hard score below 0 if the constraint is not met, and a hard score equal to 0 if the constraint is met. This way, OptaPlanner will prefer to change the hard score to 0 if possible; otherwise, if it is already 0, it will focus on maximizing the soft score.

Our soft score is somewhat complex. We want to minimize total run time, taking into account that the machines will be running their processing jobs in parallel since each virtual machine is independent, while minimizing the total number of virtual machines (Amazon has limits on the number of machines that can be active at a time), all while minimizing the total cost. To achieve this three-part minimization, we will establish desired values (say, 60 minutes processing time, 10 machines, and $1.50 cost), and then compute ratios between the plan's actual values and the desired values. This way, we can combine metrics with different units (minutes, machine count, dollars) into a single unified metric since ratios are unit-less. We will find the maximum ratio, that is, the worst ratio (over time, over machine count, over cost), and return the negation of this ratio as the soft score. When OptaPlanner seeks to maximize the soft score, it will, in-effect, be minimizing whichever measurement is farthest from the desired values: processing time, machine count, or cost.

Finally, since hard and soft scores must be integers, we sometimes multiply our measures by 1,000 or 10,000 before converting to integers. This ensures we have sufficiently high precision in the integer conversions from the original floating-point metrics.

In light of the preceding explanation of our hard-soft scores, the `Scorer` class has a straightforward implementation:

```
public class Scorer implements EasyScoreCalculator<CloudPlanner> {
  public HardSoftScore calculateScore(CloudPlanner cloudPlanner) {
    // accumulate data about the tasks running on each machine
    Map<Machine, List<Task>> machineTasks = new HashMap<Machine,
List<Task>>();
    // go through each task
    for(Task task : cloudPlanner.getTaskList()) {
      if(task.getMachine() != null) {
        if (!machineTasks.containsKey(task.getMachine())) {
          machineTasks.put(task.getMachine(),new
LinkedList<Task>());
        }
        machineTasks.get(task.getMachine()).add(task);
      }
    }

    // Now compute how long each machine will run
    Map<Machine, Double> machineRuntimes = new HashMap<Machine,
```

```
Double>();
    // go through each machine
    for(Machine machine : machineTasks.keySet()) {
      double time = machine.getStartupTime();
      for(Task task : machineTasks.get(machine)) {
        time += task.getMachineTiming(machine.getConfiguration());
      }
      machineRuntimes.put(machine, time);
    }

    // Find max machine time (all machines run in parallel),
    // and find total cost
    double maxRuntime = 0.0;
    double totalCost = 0.0;
    for(Machine machine : machineRuntimes.keySet()) {
      if(machineRuntimes.get(machine) > maxRuntime) {
        maxRuntime = machineRuntimes.get(machine);
      }
      totalCost += machineRuntimes.get(machine) *
machine.getCost();
    }

    // round-off double values to ints for scoring

    // hard score: refuse to spend more than $2;
    // times 1000 for higher precision
    int hardScore = 0;
    if(totalCost > 2.0) {
      hardScore = (int) (-totalCost * 1000);
    }

    // soft score: prefer completion in < 60 mins
    // and prefer to use no more than 10 machines
    // and prefer to spend about $1.50 or less;
    // times 10000 for higher precision
    Double[] ratios = {1.0, maxRuntime/60.0,
machineRuntimes.keySet().size()/10.0, totalCost/1.50};
    double maxRatio = Collections.max(Arrays.asList(ratios));
    // prefer lower values in maxRatio, so maximize 1.0-maxRatio
    int softScore = (int)(10000 * (1.0 - maxRatio));

    return HardSoftScore.valueOf(hardScore, softScore);
  }
}
```

Finally, we have the `Main` class, which sets up the `Machine` objects with their performance and price characteristics, and the `Task` objects, which give the subset of images to process (indicated by `imageid` and ranging from 1322 to 1599) and the time to process an image subset on each type of machine. Then the OptaPlanner solver is executed, and the resulting plan is printed:

```
public class Main {
  public static void main(String[] args) {

    List<Machine> machineList = new ArrayList<Machine>();

    // AWS EC2 pricing: https://aws.amazon.com/ec2/pricing
    // (on-demand pricing used here, time units = minutes)
    // create 20 of each (not all will necessarily be used);
    // don't create more than AWS limits allow
    int machineid = 0;
    for(int i = 0; i < 20; i++) {
      // startup: 218.07 secs
      machineList.add(new Machine(0.100/60.0, 3.6, "m4.large",
machineid));
      machineid++;
      // startup: 155.20 secs
      machineList.add(new Machine(0.200/60.0, 2.6, "m4.xlarge",
machineid));
      machineid++;
      // startup: 135.15 secs
      machineList.add(new Machine(0.100/60.0, 2.3, "c4.large",
machineid));
      machineid++;
      // startup: 134.28 secs
      machineList.add(new Machine(0.199/60.0, 2.3, "c4.xlarge",
machineid));
      machineid++;
      // startup: 189.66 secs
      machineList.add(new Machine(0.398/60.0, 3.2, "c4.2xlarge",
machineid));
      machineid++;
    }

    // generate tasks; in our case, image ids
    int taskid = 1;
    ArrayList<Task> tasks = new ArrayList<Task>();
    for(int imageid = 1322; imageid <= 1599; imageid++) {
```

```
        Task t = new Task(String.valueOf(imageid), taskid, null);

        // benchmark: time to complete a task on each machine
        // (time units = minutes)

        // three runs: 2:42.80 2:36.34 2:37.15
        t.setMachineTiming("m4.large", 2.65);

        // three runs: 1:43.98 1:32.22 1:31.21
        t.setMachineTiming("m4.xlarge", 1.60);

        // three runs: 2:21.64 2:41.51 2:35.87
        t.setMachineTiming("c4.large", 2.55);

        // three runs: 1:37.34 1:25.28 1:27.68
        t.setMachineTiming("c4.xlarge", 1.50);

        // three runs: 1:12.32 1:02.30 1:01.89
        t.setMachineTiming("c4.2xlarge", 1.09);

        tasks.add(t);
        taskid++;
    }

    SolverFactory<CloudPlanner> solverFactory =
SolverFactory.createFromXmlResource("simpleCloudPlannerConfig.xml"
);
    Solver<CloudPlanner> solver = solverFactory.buildSolver();

    CloudPlanner unsolvedCloudPlanner = new CloudPlanner();
    unsolvedCloudPlanner.setMachineList(machineList);
    unsolvedCloudPlanner.setTaskList(tasks);

    CloudPlanner solvedCloudPlanner =
solver.solve(unsolvedCloudPlanner);

    System.out.println("Best plan:");
    for(Task task : solvedCloudPlanner.getTaskList()) {
      System.out.println(task + " - " + task.getMachine());
    }
    System.out.println("---");
    double totalCost = 0.0;
    double maxTime = 0.0;
```

```java
    Map<Machine, List<Task>> machineTasks = new HashMap<Machine,
List<Task>>();
        // go through each task
        for(Task task : solvedCloudPlanner.getTaskList()) {
            if(task.getMachine() != null) {
                if (!machineTasks.containsKey(task.getMachine())){
                    machineTasks.put(task.getMachine(), new
LinkedList<Task>());
                }
                machineTasks.get(task.getMachine()).add(task);
            }
        }
        // go through each machine
        for(Machine machine : machineTasks.keySet()) {
            double time = machine.getStartupTime();
            for(Task task : machineTasks.get(machine)) {
                time += task.getMachineTiming(machine.getConfiguration());
            }
            double cost = time * machine.getCost();
            System.out.format("Machine time for %s: " + "%.2f min (cost:
$%.4f), tasks: %d\n", machine, time, cost,
machineTasks.get(machine).size());
            totalCost += cost;
            // save the time of the longest-running machine
            if(time > maxTime) { maxTime = time; }
        }
        System.out.println("---");
        System.out.println("Machine count: " +
machineTasks.keySet().size());
        System.out.format("Total cost: $%.2f\n", totalCost);
        System.out.format("Total time (run in parallel): %.2f\n",
maxTime);
    }
}
```

Build the code with Maven on the command line: `mvn package`. Then run the code as follows:

```
java -jar target/SimpleCloudPlanner-1.0-SNAPSHOT-launcher.jar
```

The resulting plan is found in 10 seconds (due to our hard cut-off in runtime specified in `simpleCloudPlannerConfig.xml`). The plan found a way to complete all tasks using 10 machines of various types, giving faster machines more subsets of images than slower machines, and finishing the job in an estimated 59.25 minutes and costing $1.50.

Changes in the soft score over the 10 seconds of planning are visualized in the following figure. Each change is due to the planner experimenting with variations in the plan. At the 10 second cut-off, whichever plan had the best score would be chosen. Thus, the figure indicates we probably could have stopped the planner after about 4.5 seconds and arrived at an equally good (or identical) final plan. The following figure is produced by parsing the logging output produced by the planner:

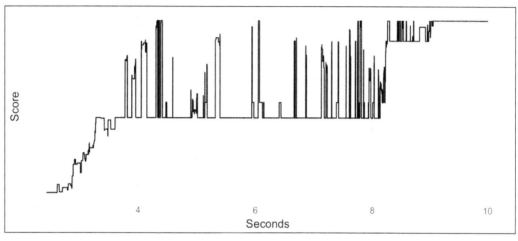

Figure 2: Changes in the soft score over the duration of the planner's search time

The specific machine types and number of tasks in the final plan are as follows. Note that the machines' startup times are accounted for in the machines' total times and costs. The specific image processing task assignments for each machine are not shown due to limited space:

1. c4.large: 50.75 min (cost: $0.0846), tasks: 19
2. c4.large: 55.85 min (cost: $0.0931), tasks: 21
3. c4.large: 58.40 min (cost: $0.0973), tasks: 22
4. c4.xlarge: 54.80 min (cost: $0.1818), tasks: 35
5. c4.xlarge: 56.30 min (cost: $0.1867), tasks: 36
6. c4.2xlarge: 43.53 min (cost: $0.2887), tasks: 37
7. m4.large: 56.60 min (cost: $0.0943), tasks: 20
8. m4.large: 59.25 min (cost: $0.0987), tasks: 21
9. m4.xlarge: 53.80 min (cost: $0.1793), tasks: 32
10. m4.xlarge: 58.60 min (cost: $0.1953), tasks: 35

Deployment strategy

The cloud infrastructure planner can be used to plan virtually any cloud processing task, as long as the tasks are independent. We did not include any code that checks for interdependencies of tasks, such as task A must complete before task B. For independent tasks, the planner can keep track of the time each task will take on each type of cloud machine and find a near-optimal plan given certain time and cost constraints and preferences. For an organization that expects to have continual cloud computing needs, the planner may be deployed as a service that may be consulted at any time.

As described above, OptaPlanner solutions may be deployed in Java enterprise environments such as **WildFly** (formerly known as **JBoss**). A simple web-frontend may be built that allows engineers to specify the various types of virtual machines, the processing tasks, and benchmark measurements for how long each processing task takes on each variety of machine.

Most plans will involve several cloud machines. The plan found in our example above involves 10 machines, and each machine has between 19 and 37 tasks assigned to it. Naturally, nobody wishes to create and manage these cloud machines manually. As much as possible, it should all be automated and scripted. Depending on the environment in which the planner is deployed, automation may be realized in a variety of forms. The script may take the form of XML commands that are interpreted by another tool and executed in the cloud environment. In our case, we will build Linux shell scripts for creating the cloud machines and running the tasks.

No matter what form the automation takes, be sure to have a "human in the loop" evaluating the script before executing it. It is unwise to trust a constraint solver to always select a reasonable plan (for example, using 10 machines for about an hour) and never accidentally develop a pathological plan (for example, using 3,600 machines for 10 seconds). A constraint solver will attempt to optimize for whatever the hard and soft constraints specify. A small error in coding these constraints can have surprising consequences.

For the Linux shell script approach, we use Amazon's AWS CLI. First, it must be configured with an access key that is associated with our AWS account:

```
$ aws configure
AWS Access Key ID [*******************]:
AWS Secret Access Key [*******************]:
Default region name [us-east-1]:
Default output format [None]: text
```

We choose to output data as text so that we can use the outputs in further shell commands. We could also output JSON, but then we will need a command line tool such as **jq** to handle the JSON.

Now that AWS is configured, we can use it to create a cloud machine:

```
$ aws ec2 run-instances --image-id ami-3179bd4c --count 1 \
> --instance-type m4.large --key-name SmartCode
> --associate-public-ip-address --subnet-id subnet-xxxxxx \
> --security-group-ids sg-xxxxxx \
> --tag-specifications "ResourceType=instance,Tags=
[{Key=MachineId,Value=100}]"
```

This command creates an m4.large instance. Ahead of time, we created a custom Linux disk image with Ubuntu and OpenCV 3 installed, specified in the `--image-id` parameter. We also use the "tag" feature to associate a `MachineId` tag with the value 100 so that we can later retrieve information about this instance using this tag. Our automation scripts will give each instance a different machine id so we can tell them apart. In fact, the `Machine` class above has a field specifically for this purpose. For example, the following command uses the `MachineId` tag to get the IP address of a specific machine:

```
$ aws ec2 describe-instances --query \
> Reservations[].Instances[].NetworkInterfaces[]
.Association.PublicIp \
> --filters Name=tag:MachineId,Values=100
```

Once a cloud machine has started, we have a few steps to get it fully configured for our data processing task:

- Make the `.aws` directory (used by the AWS command-line tool)
- Copy AWS CLI credentials and configuration from the host
- Install AWS CLI and GNU Parallel
- Copy the C++ code and compile
- Copy the `run.sh` script

The machine startup time described previously measures the time to boot the machine and get SSH access as well as the time to complete these five steps. The `run.sh` script is unique to our data processing task. It first downloads the images from S3 and then runs the C++ program with GNU Parallel on the subset of images it just downloaded. Then it proceeds to the next subset, and so on.

The `setup-and-run.sh` script for each machine is called with the various tasks (image subset ids) assigned to it by the planner. For example, machine #1 with 19 tasks is called as follows:

```
$ bash ./setup-and-run.sh c4.large 1 \
> 1337 1345 1350 1358 1366 1372 1375 1380 1385 1429 \
> 1433 1463 1467 1536 1552 1561 1582 1585 1589 &
```

This script creates the machine with a specific id (in this case, id 1) and then calls `run.sh` on the machine with the image subset ids provided by the planner (1337, 1345, and so on)

Altogether, the various scripts allow us to take the output of the planner and directly execute those commands in a terminal to start the cloud machines, complete the processing task, and shut down the machines.

The deployment strategies of a cloud infrastructure planner may differ depending on the needs of the organization, but in any case, some kind of automation must be available to actually execute the plans.

Continuous evaluation

Cloud computing infrastructure providers compete on cost, performance, and features. Their offerings are gradually cheaper, quicker to start up and more efficient with CPU- or disk- or network-intense workloads, and support more exotic hardware such as GPUs. Due to these inevitable changes and market dynamics, it is important to evaluate the accuracy of the planner over time continuously.

The accuracy of the planner depends on a few factors. First, the various supported machine instance types (for example, m4.large, c4.large, etc.) may change over time. The costs per hour may change. And the performance characteristics may change: the machines may start up faster, or they may handle the same processing task more or less efficiently. In our example planning application, all of these numbers were coded directly in the `Main` class, but a traditional database may be used to store this information in order to facilitate easy updates.

Continuous evaluation in a production environment should include active benchmarking: for every task completed on a cloud machine of a certain type, a record should be made in a database of the time-to-completion for that task and machine. With this information, each run of the planner can recompute the average time to complete the task on various cloud machine instance types to enable more accurate estimates.

We have not yet asked a critical question about our planner. *Was it at all accurate?* The planner estimated that the image processing job would require 59.25 minutes to complete, including the time required to start and configure the cloud machines. In other words, it predicted that from the point that the various `setup-and-run.sh` scripts were executed (all in parallel for the 10 planned machines), to the time the job was finished and all machines terminated, would be 59.25 minutes. In actuality, the time required for this entire process was 58.64 minutes, an error of about 1%.

Interestingly, a little naiveté about a cloud provider's offerings can have big consequences. The t2.* instance types on AWS (`https://docs.aws.amazon.com/AWSEC2/latest/UserGuide/t2-instances.html`), and the B-series machines on Microsoft's Azure (`https://techcrunch.com/2017/09/11/azure-gets-bursty/`), are designed for bursty performance. If we run a benchmark of the image processing task for a single subset of 100 images, we will see a certain (high) performance. However, if we then give one of those same machines a long list of image processing tasks, eventually the machine will slow down. These machine types are cheaper because they only offer high performance at short intervals. This cannot be detected in a quick benchmark; it can only be detected after a long processing task has been underway for some time. Or, one could read all documentation before attempting anything:

> *T2 instances are designed to provide a baseline level of CPU performance with the ability to burst to a higher level when required by your workload.*
>
> (`https://docs.aws.amazon.com/AWSEC2/latest/UserGuide/t2-instances.html`)

When a job that is predicted to take about an hour drags on for two, three, or more hours, one begins to suspect that something is wrong. The following figure shows a graph of CPU utilization on a t2.* instance. It is clear from the graph that either the image processing code has something seriously wrong, or the cloud provider is enforcing no more than 10% CPU utilization after about 30 minutes of processing.

These are the kinds of subtleties that require some forewarning and demonstrate the importance of continuous evaluation and careful monitoring:

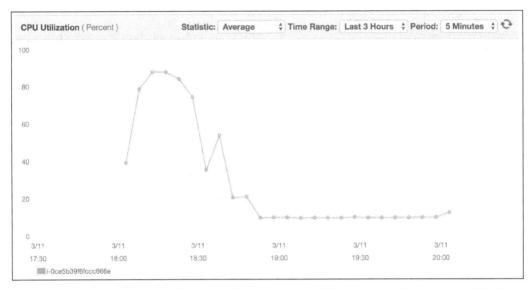

Figure 3: Bursty performance of Amazon's t2.* instance types. CPU was expected to have been utilized 100% at all times. Other instance types such as m4.* and c4.* perform as expected, that is, non-bursty.

Summary

This chapter showed the design, implementation, deployment, and evaluation of a cloud infrastructure planner. Using constraint solving technology from OptaPlanner, we developed a tool that is capable of planning a cloud machine configuration and task assignments for a large data processing task. We showed that some preliminary benchmarks are required to inform the planner how long a processing job takes on each different kind of cloud machine. We also showed how to produce plans that meet certain monetary or time constraints. The planner produces a script containing commands that automate the creation and configuration of the cloud machines and start the processing jobs. The planner predicts the time required to complete the entire job, and our evaluation showed that its prediction was highly accurate in practice.

Finally, we discussed potential methods for deploying the planner in enterprise environments and techniques for continuously evaluating the planner's accuracy after it is deployed.

3
A Blueprint for Making Sense of Feedback

Being smart, in business or otherwise, depends on acquiring and learning from feedback. For example, after deploying a new service, a business can start to understand why the service is or is not generating revenue by analyzing feedback from users and the recipients of marketing campaigns. One could also discover the overall sentiment of an idea such as "self-driving cars" in order to plan engagement with a new or emerging market. But no one has time to find, read, and summarize hundreds to millions of comments, tweets, articles, emails, and more. If done on a large scale, intelligent automation is required.

The first step in making sense of feedback is acquiring the feedback. Unlike previous generations' dependence on paper surveys sent via mail or randomized polling by phone, today's organizations can tap into the firehose of social media to learn what people think of their products and services. Open-access social media platforms, such as Twitter and Reddit, are bringing an entirely new paradigm of social interaction. With these platforms, people are willing to publicly document their thoughts and feelings about a wide variety of matters. Conversations that used to occur solely over small gatherings of friends and confidants are now broadcasted to the entire world.

So much text is written and published on these platforms each day that it takes some data mining skills to extract comments that are relevant to a particular organization. For example, the generic search term `artificial intelligence` and hashtag `#artificialintelligence` together yield about 400 messages per hour on Twitter. Larger events, such as the 2014 World Cup finals, can produce tweets at extraordinary rates (10,312 per second in the case of the World Cup), as shown from CampaignLive (`https://www.campaignlive.co.uk/article/ten-twitter-facts-social-media-giants-10th-birthday/1388131`). With an enterprise account, Twitter provides access to a random 10% of tweets, known as the Decahose (`https://developer.twitter.com/en/docs/tweets/sample-realtime/overview/decahose`), which provides a stream in the neighborhood of 50 to 100 million tweets per day.

Likewise, as of 2015, Reddit receives about two million comments per day (`https://www.quora.com/How-many-comments-are-made-on-reddit-each-day`). Of course, not every person expresses their every thought and emotion on Twitter or Reddit. But these two venues are too abundant to ignore their popularity on the web.

In this chapter, we will develop code that examines tweets and comments obtained from the Twitter and Reddit APIs. We will also include news articles obtained from News API (`https://newsapi.org/`), a service that crawls 30,000 publications and reports articles in specified time ranges that contain specified keywords. Since full access to these massive streams of random thoughts, opinions, and news articles is generally unobtainable to all but the largest organizations (and governments), we will need to search and filter the streams for particular tweets and comments and articles of interest. Each of these APIs support search queries and filters. For our demonstration, we will use the search terms related to "self-driving cars" and "autonomous vehicles" to get a sense of the mood about that new AI technology.

Acquiring feedback is only one-third of the battle. Next, we need to analyze the feedback to discover certain features. In this chapter, we will focus on estimating the *sentiment* of the feedback, that is, whether the feedback is positive, negative, or neutral. The last third of making sense of feedback is summarizing and visualizing the sentiment in aggregate form. We will develop a live chart that shows a real-time picture of the sentiment related to our search terms.

In this chapter, we will cover:

- Background on natural language processing (NLP) and sentiment analysis
- The Twitter, Reddit, and News APIs and open source Java libraries for accessing those APIs
- The CoreNLP library for NLP
- A deployment strategy that involves continuously watching Twitter and Reddit and showing the results of sentiment analysis with a real-time chart
- A technique for continuously evaluating the accuracy of the AI code

The problem, goal, and business case

According to the AI workflow developed in *Chapter 1, The AI Workflow*, the first step in building and deploying an AI project is to identify the problem that the AI will solve. The problem should be related to a business concern and have a well-defined goal. Equally, the problem should also be known to be solvable by existing AI technologies, thus ensuring a team does not engage in an uncertain research effort that may never yield results.

In most organizations, user feedback is a valuable source of information about the success and deficiencies of a product or service. Except in rare and possibly apocryphal cases, such as Apple's Steve Jobs, who supposedly never engaged in market research or focus groups ("*people don't know what they want until you show it to them,*" https://www.forbes.com/sites/chunkamui/2011/10/17/five-dangerous-lessons-to-learn-from-steve-jobs/#1748a3763a95), user feedback can help refine or repair designs. Sampling the populace's opinion about general ideas or burgeoning industries, such as self-driving vehicles, can also be a valuable source of information about the public's general mood.

The goal of our analysis of feedback will be to find the average sentiment about our search terms. The sentiment may range from very negative to very positive. We would also like to know how many comments and articles include the search terms to get a sense of volume of interest and to gauge the strength of the information (just a few negative voices is very different than a torrent of negative voices). Finally, we want to see this data on a live dashboard that gives a quick overview of the sentiment over time. The dashboard will be just one source of information for decision-makers – we do not plan to automate any procedures as a result of the sentiment analysis. Thus, the AI is constrained and will likely not cause catastrophic failures if the AI is buggy and the sentiment analysis is inaccurate.

Sentiment analysis is a mature and proven branch of artificial intelligence and NLP in particular. As we will see in the following section, libraries are available that perform sentiment analysis of a given text with just a few function calls – all the difficult work is hidden behind a simple API.

Method – sentiment analysis

Sentiment analysis is achieved by labeling individual words as positive or negative, among other possible sentiments such as happy, worried, and so on. The sentiment of the sentence or phrase as a whole is determined by a procedure that aggregates the sentiment of individual words. Consider the sentence, *I didn't like a single minute of this film.* A simplistic sentiment analysis system would probably label the word *like* as positive and the other words as neutral, yielding an overall positive sentiment. More advanced systems analyze the "dependency tree" of the sentence to identify which words are modifiers for other words. In this case, *didn't* is a modifier for *like*, so the sentiment of *like* is reversed due to this modifier. Likewise, a phrase such as, *It's definitely not dull*, exhibits a similar property, and *...not only good but amazing* exhibits a further nuance of the English language.

It is clear a simple dictionary of positive and negative words is insufficient for accurate sentiment analysis. The presence of modifiers can change the polarity of a word. Wilson and others' work on sentiment analysis (*Recognizing contextual polarity in phrase-level sentiment analysis, Wilson, Theresa, Janyce Wiebe*, and *Paul Hoffmann*, published in *Proceedings of the conference on human language technology and empirical methods in natural language processing, pp. 347-354, 2005*) is foundational in the dependency tree approach. They start with a lexicon (that is, a collection) of 8,000 words that serve as "subjectivity clues" and are tagged with polarity (positive or negative).

Using just this dictionary, they achieved 48% accuracy in identifying the sentiment of about 3,700 phrases. To improve on this, they adopted a two-step approach. First, they used a statistical model to determine whether a subjectivity clue is used in a neutral or polar context. When used in a neutral context, the word can be ignored as it does not contribute to the overall sentiment. The statistical model for determining whether a word is used in a neutral or polar context uses 28 features, including the nearby words, binary features such as whether the word *not* appears immediately before, and part-of-speech information such as whether the word is a noun, verb, adjective, and so on.

Next, words that have polarity, that is, those that have not been filtered out by the neutral/polar context identifier, are fed into another statistical model that determines their polarity: positive, negative, both, or neutral. 10 features are used for polarity classification, including the word itself and its polarity from the lexicon, whether or not the word is being negated, and the presence of certain nearby modifiers such as *little, lack,* and *abate*. These modifiers themselves have polarity: neutral, negative, and positive, respectively. Their final procedure achieves 65.7% percent accuracy for detecting sentiment. Their approach is implemented in the open source OpinionFinder (`http://mpqa.cs.pitt.edu/opinionfinder/opinionfinder_2/`).

A more modern approach may be found in Stanford's open source CoreNLP project (`https://stanfordnlp.github.io/CoreNLP/`). CoreNLP supports a wide range of NLP processing such as sentence detection, word detection, part-of-speech tagging, named-entity recognition (finding names of people, places, dates, and so on), and sentiment analysis. Several NLP features, such as sentiment analysis, depend on prior processing including sentence detection, word detection, and part-of-speech tagging.

As described in the following text, a sentence's dependency tree, which shows the subject, object, verbs, adjectives, and prepositions of a sentence, is critical for sentiment analysis. CoreNLP's sentiment analysis technique has been shown to achieve 85.4% accuracy for detecting positive/negative sentiment of sentences. Their technique is state-of-the-art and has been specifically designed to better handle negation in various places in a sentence, a limitation of simpler sentiment analysis techniques as previously described.

CoreNLP's sentiment analysis uses a technique known as **recursive neural tensor networks (RNTN)** (*Recursive deep models for semantic compositionality over a sentiment treebank, Richard Socher, Alex Perelygin, Jean Y. Wu, Jason Chuang, Christopher D. Manning, Andrew Y. Ng*, and *Christopher Potts*, published in *Proceedings of the 2013 Conference on Empirical Methods in Natural Language Processing, pp. 1631-1642, 2013*). The basic procedure is as follows. First, a sentence or phrase is parsed into a binary tree, as seen in *Figure 1*. Every node is labeled with its part-of-speech: NP (noun phrase), VP (verb phrase), NN (noun), JJ (adjective), and so on. Each leaf node, that is, each word node, has a corresponding **word vector**. A word vector is an array of about 30 numbers (the actual size depends on a parameter that is determined experimentally). The values of the word vector for each word are learned during training, as is the sentiment of each individual word. Just having word vectors will not be enough since we have already seen how sentiment cannot be accurately determined by looking at words independently of their context.

The next step in the RNTN procedure collapses the tree, one node at a time, by calculating a vector for each node based on its children. The bottom-right node of *Figure 1*, the NP node with children *own* and *crashes*, will have a vector that is the same size of the word vectors but is computed based on those child word vectors. The computation multiplies each child word vector and sums the results. The exact multipliers to use are learned during training. The RNTN approach, unlike prior but similar tree collapsing techniques, uses a single combiner function for all nodes.

Ultimately, the combiner function and the word vectors are learned simultaneously using thousands of example sentences with the known sentiment.

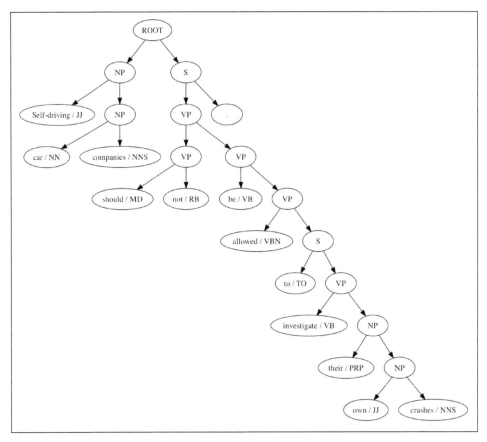

Figure 1: CoreNLP's dependency tree parse of the sentence,
"Self-driving car companies should not be allowed to investigate their own crashes"

The dependency tree from the preceding figure has 12 leaf nodes and 12 combiner nodes. Each leaf node has an associated word vector learned during training. The sentiment of each leaf node is also learned during training. Thus, the word *crashes*, for example, has a neutral sentiment with 0.631 confidence, while the word *not* has negative sentiment with 0.974 confidence. The parent node of *allowed* and the phrase *to investigate their own crashes* has a negative sentiment, confidence 0.614, even though no word or combiner node among its descendants have anything but neutral sentiment. This demonstrates that the RNTN learned a complex combiner function that operates on the word vectors of its children and not just a simple rule such as, *If both children are neutral, then this node is neutral, or if one child is neutral, but one is positive, this node is positive, ...*

The sentiment values and confidence of each node in the tree is shown in the output of CoreNLP shown in the following code block. Note that sentiment values are coded:

- 0 = very negative
- 1 = negative
- 2 = neutral
- 3 = positive
- 4 = very positive

```
(ROOT|sentiment=1|prob=0.606
  (NP|sentiment=2|prob=0.484
    (JJ|sentiment=2|prob=0.631 Self-driving)
    (NP|sentiment=2|prob=0.511
      (NN|sentiment=2|prob=0.994 car)
      (NNS|sentiment=2|prob=0.631 companies)))
  (S|sentiment=1|prob=0.577
    (VP|sentiment=2|prob=0.457
      (VP|sentiment=2|prob=0.587
        (MD|sentiment=2|prob=0.998 should)
        (RB|sentiment=1|prob=0.974 not))
      (VP|sentiment=1|prob=0.703
        (VB|sentiment=2|prob=0.994 be)
        (VP|sentiment=1|prob=0.614
          (VBN|sentiment=2|prob=0.969 allowed)
          (S|sentiment=2|prob=0.724
            (TO|sentiment=2|prob=0.990 to)
            (VP|sentiment=2|prob=0.557
              (VB|sentiment=2|prob=0.887 investigate)
              (NP|sentiment=2|prob=0.823
                (PRP|sentiment=2|prob=0.997 their)
                (NP|sentiment=2|prob=0.873
                  (JJ|sentiment=2|prob=0.996 own)
                  (NNS|sentiment=2|prob=0.631 crashes))))))))))
    (.|sentiment=2|prob=0.997 .)))
```

We see from these sentiment values that *allowed to investigate their own crashes* is labeled with negative sentiment. We can investigate how CoreNLP handles words such as *allowed* and *not* by running through a few variations. These are shown in the following table:

Sentence	Sentiment	Confidence
They investigate their own crashes.	Neutral	0.506

They are *allowed* to investigate their own crashes.	Negative	0.697
They are *not allowed* to investigate their own crashes.	Negative	0.672
They are *happy* to investigate their own crashes.	Positive	0.717
They are *not happy* to investigate their own crashes.	Negative	0.586
They are *willing* to investigate their own crashes.	Neutral	0.507
They are *not willing* to investigate their own crashes.	Negative	0.599
They are *unwilling* to investigate their own crashes.	Negative	0.486
They are *not unwilling* to investigate their own crashes.	Negative	0.625

Table 1: Variations of a sentence with CoreNLP's sentiment analysis

It is clear from Table 1 that the phrase *investigate their own crashes* is not contributing strongly to the sentiment of the whole sentence. The verb, whether it be *allowed*, *happy*, or *willing*, can dramatically change the sentiment. The modifier *not* can flip the sentiment, though curiously *not unwilling* is still considered negative. Near the end of this chapter, we will address how to determine, on an ongoing basis, whether the sentiment analysis is sufficiently accurate.

We should be particularly careful to study CoreNLP's sentiment analysis with sentence fragments and other kinds of invalid English that is commonly seen on Twitter. For example, the Twitter API will deliver phrases such as, *Ford's self-driving car network will launch 'at scale' in 2021 - Ford hasn't been shy about...* with the ... in the actual tweet. CoreNLP labels this sentence as negative with confidence 0.597.

CoreNLP was trained on movie reviews, so news articles, tweets, and Reddit comments may not match the same kind of words and grammar found in movie reviews. We might have a *domain mismatch* between the training domain and the actual domain. CoreNLP can be trained on a different dataset but doing so requires that thousands (or ten's or hundred's of thousands) of examples with known sentiment are available. Every node in the dependency tree of every sentence must be labeled with a known sentiment. This is very time-consuming. The authors of CoreNLP used **Amazon Mechanical Turk** to recruit humans to perform this labeling task.

We should note, however, that Twitter is a popular subject of sentiment analysis. For example, sentiment on Twitter has been analyzed to identify the "mood" of the United States depending on the time of day (*Pulse of the Nation: U.S. Mood Throughout the Day inferred from Twitter, Alan Mislove, Sune Lehmann, Yong-Yeol Ahn, Jukka-Pekka Onnela,* and *J. Niels Rosenquist,* https://mislove.org/twittermood/). Twitter sentiment has also been used to predict the stock market (*Twitter mood predicts the stock market, Bollen, Johan, Huina Mao,* and *Xiaojun Zeng, Journal of Computational Science 2(1), pp. 1-8, 2011*); presumably, this data source is still used by some hedge funds.

In this chapter, we will develop a project that uses CoreNLP to determine sentiment for statements made in a variety of sources. A more accurate approach would require training CoreNLP or a similar system on example phrases from our data feeds. Doing so is very time-consuming and often not in the scope-of-work of a short-term AI project. Even so, details for training a sentiment analysis model for CoreNLP in a different domain are provided later in this chapter.

Deployment strategy

In this project, we will develop a live sentiment detector using articles and comments about autonomous vehicles gathered from traditional online news sources as well as Twitter and Reddit. Aggregate sentiment across these sources will be shown in a plot. For simplicity, we will not connect the sentiment detector to any kind of automated alerting or response system. However, one may wish to review techniques for detecting anomalies, that is, sudden changes in sentiment, as developed in *Chapter 6, A Blueprint for Discovering Trends and Recognizing Anomalies*.

We will use Java for the backend of this project and Python for the frontend. The backend will consist of the data aggregator and sentiment detector, and the frontend will host the live plot. We choose Java for the backend due to the availability of libraries for sentiment analysis (CoreNLP) and the various APIs we wish to access. Since the frontend does not need to perform sentiment analysis or API access, we are free to choose a different platform. We choose Python in order to demonstrate the use of the popular Dash framework for dashboards and live plots.

A high-level view of the project is shown in *Figure 2*. The **sentiment analysis** box represents the Java-based project we will develop first. It uses the Twitter, Reddit, and News APIs, making use of the corresponding libraries, hbc-core, JRAW, and Crux. The latter library, Crux, is used to fetch the original news stories provided by the News API. Crux finds the main text of an article while stripping out advertisements and comments. The News API itself uses typical HTTP requests and JSON-encoded data, so we do not need to use a special library for access to that API. The various APIs will be queried simultaneously and continuously in separate threads.

After retrieving the text and detecting its sentiment with CoreNLP, the results are saved into an SQLite database. We use SQLite instead of a more powerful database, such as MySQL or SQL Server, just for simplicity. Finally, we develop an independent program in Python with the Dash library (from the makers of plotly.js) that periodically queries the database, aggregates the sentiment for the different sources, and shows a plot in a browser window.

This plot updates once per day, but could be configured to update more frequently (say, every 30 seconds) if your data sources provide sufficient data:

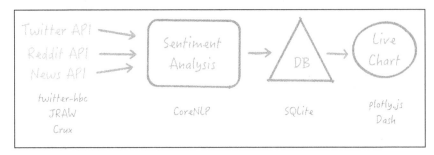

Figure 2: High-level view of the components and libraries used in this project

First, we develop the backend. Our Java project will use the following Maven dependencies:

- **CoreNLP**: https://mvnrepository.com/artifact/edu.stanford.nlp/ stanford-corenlp, v3.9.1

- **CoreNLP models**: https://mvnrepository.com/artifact/edu. stanford.nlp/stanford-corenlp, v3.9.1 with additional Maven dependency tag:

    `<classifier>models</classifier>`

- **Gson**: https://mvnrepository.com/artifact/com.google.code.gson/ gson, v2.8.2

- **Twitter API**: https://mvnrepository.com/artifact/com.twitter/hbc-core, v2.2.0

- **Reddit API**: https://mvnrepository.com/artifact/net.dean.jraw/ JRAW, v1.0.0

- **SQLite JDBC**: https://mvnrepository.com/artifact/org.xerial/ sqlite-jdbc, v3.21.0.1

- **HTTP Request**: https://mvnrepository.com/artifact/com.github. kevinsawicki/http-request, v6.0

- **Crux**: Crux is not yet in the Maven repository so it will need to be installed locally according to the instructions on their project page: https://github. com/karussell/snacktory

The project is structured into a few separate classes:

- SentimentMain: This contains the main() method, which creates the database (if it does not exist), initializes CoreNLP (the SentimentDetector class), and starts the TwitterStream, RedditStream, and NewsStream threads.

- `SentimentDetector`: Detects sentiment of a given text, saves the result to the database.

- `TwitterStream`: Uses the Twitter API (`hbc-core` library) to monitor Twitter for given search terms continuously; detects sentiment on each matching tweet.

- `RedditStream`: Uses the Reddit API (`JRAW` library) to search for certain terms periodically, then extracts the matching post and all comments; all extracted text is sent for sentiment detection.

- `NewsStream`: Uses the News API (`HTTP Request` and `Crux` libraries) to search for articles containing certain terms periodically; article body is extracted with `Crux` from the original source, and this text is sent for sentiment detection.

Since the various APIs and libraries need some configuration parameters, such as API keys and query terms, we will use a Java properties file to hold this information:

```
sqlitedb = sentiment.db
twitter_terms = autonomous vehicle, self-driving car
twitter_consumer_key = ...
twitter_consumer_secret = ...
twitter_token = ...
twitter_token_secret = ...
reddit_user = ...
reddit_password = ...
reddit_clientid = ...
reddit_clientsecret = ...

reddit_terms = autonomous vehicle, self-driving car
news_api_key = ...
news_api_terms = autonomous vehicle, self-driving car
```

The `SentimentMain` class' `main()` method loads the properties file, establishes the database, and starts the background feedback acquisition threads. We see that the SQLite table contains the original text of each sentence, the source (News API, Twitter, or Reddit), the date found, and the sentiment computed by CoreNLP, composed of the sentiment name (`Positive`, `Negative`, and so on), numeric value (`0-4`, `0` for `Very Negative`, `4` for `Very Positive`), and confidence score (between `0.0` and `1.0`):

```
public static void main( String[] args ) throws Exception
{
  Properties props = new Properties();
  try
  {
    props.load(new FileInputStream("config.properties"));
  }
```

```
catch(IOException e)
{
  System.out.println(e);
  System.exit(-1);
}

  Connection db = DriverManager.getConnection("jdbc:sqlite:" +
props.getProperty("sqlitedb"));
  String tableSql = "CREATE TABLE IF NOT EXISTS sentiment (\n" +
"id text PRIMARY KEY,\n" +
" datefound DATE DEFAULT CURRENT_DATE,\n" +
"source text NOT NULL,\n" + "msg text NOT NULL,\n" +
"sentiment text NOT NULL,\n" + "sentiment_num int NOT NULL,\n" +
" score double NOT NULL\n" + ");";
  Statement stmt = db.createStatement();
  stmt.execute(tableSql);

  Gson gson = new Gson();

  SentimentDetector sentimentDetector = new SentimentDetector(db);

  TwitterStream twitterStream =
new TwitterStream(sentimentDetector, gson, props);
  Thread twitterStreamThread = new Thread(twitterStream);
  twitterStreamThread.start();

  RedditStream redditStream =
new RedditStream(sentimentDetector, props);
  Thread redditStreamThread = new Thread(redditStream);
  redditStreamThread.start();

  NewsStream newsStream =
new NewsStream(sentimentDetector, gson, props);
  Thread newsStreamThread = new Thread(newsStream);
  newsStreamThread.start();

  twitterStreamThread.join();
  redditStreamThread.join();
  newsStreamThread.join();
}
```

The `SentimentDetector` class contains the functionality for detecting sentiment with CoreNLP as well as the procedures for saving the analyzed sentences into the database. In order to explain our code for detecting sentiment, we will first examine the processing pipeline of CoreNLP.

CoreNLP processing pipeline

Like many NLP tools, CoreNLP uses a pipeline metaphor for its processing architecture. In order to detect sentiment of a body of text, the system must know the individual words, parts-of-speech, and dependency trees of the sentences in the body of text. This information is computed in a specific order. First, a body of text must be split into **tokens**, that is, words and punctuation. Before **tokenization**, a body of text is just a sequence of bytes. Depending on the language, tokenization may be simple or complex. For example, English text is relatively straightforward to tokenize since words are separated by spaces. However, Chinese text is more challenging to tokenize since words are not always split by spaces, and machine learning tools may be required to segment 雨天地面积水 into 雨 (rainy) 天 (day) 地面 (ground) 积水 (accumulated water) instead of any other pairing, since "each consecutive two characters can be combined as a word," producing a different meaning (*Gated recursive neural network for Chinese word segmentation, Chen, Xinchi, Xipeng Qiu, Chenxi Zhu, and Xuanjing Huang,* published in *Proceedings of the 53rd Annual Meeting of the Association for Computational Linguistics and the 7th International Joint Conference on Natural Language Processing (Volume 1: Long Papers), pp. 1744-1753, 2015.*).

Once split into tokens, the text is then split into individual sentences, as all future steps only work on a single sentence at a time. Next, for each sentence, the part-of-speech of each word is identified. Given these part-of-speech labels, a dependency tree can be built, as shown previously in *Figure 1*. Finally, this tree can be used with recursive neural networks to identify sentiment, as explained previously.

CoreNLP's processing pipeline attaches **annotations** to the text at each stage. Future stages in the pipeline may refer to these annotations, such as part-of-speech tags, to do their work. CoreNLP supports more processing stages than we need for sentiment analysis, including named entity recognition and gender detection. We indicate our required processing stages in our Java properties file, and initialize the CoreNLP library with these **annotators**:

```
Properties props = new Properties();
props.setProperty(
"annotators", "tokenize, ssplit, pos, parse, sentiment");
pipeline = new StanfordCoreNLP(props);
```

The annotators are known as `tokenize` for word tokenization, `ssplit` for sentence splitting, `pos` for part-of-speech tagging, `parse` for dependency tree parsing, and `sentiment` for sentiment analysis.

Now, given a body of text, we can run the annotation pipeline and retrieve information from the resulting fully annotated text. This process begins by creating an `Annotation` object with the text, and then running the pipeline:

```
Annotation annotation = new Annotation(txt);
pipeline.annotate(annotation);
```

Once annotated, we can retrieve the different kinds of annotations by specifying the relevant annotation class. For example, we can obtain the sentences:

```
List<CoreMap> sentences =
annotation.get(CoreAnnotations.SentencesAnnotation.class);
```

Next, we iterate through the sentences and, for each sentence, we retrieve the sentiment. Note, the sentiment annotation consists of a string applied to the whole sentence. The whole sentence may be annotated as `Positive`, for example:

```
String sentiment =
sentence.get(SentimentCoreAnnotations.SentimentClass.class);
```

In order to save space in the database, we choose not to save the sentence and its sentiment if the sentiment is neutral or the sentiment detector is not confident about its decision. Furthermore, we wish to save a numeric value for the sentiment, `0-4`, rather than the phrases `Very Negative` to `Very Positive`. This numeric value will make it easier to graph average sentiment over time.

We could easily convert the various string sentiments to numeric values (for example, `Very Negative` to `0`) with a series of conditions. But we will need to look deeper in the CoreNLP annotations to retrieve the confidence score. Doing so will also give us the numeric value (`0-4`), so we will avoid the exhaustive conditions for that conversion.

Technically, every node in the dependency tree of the sentence is annotated with a sentiment value and confidence score. An example tree with scores (labeled as probabilities) was shown previously. We can obtain this tree and read the root confidence score with the following steps. First, we retrieve the tree:

```
Tree sentimentTree =
sentence.get(SentimentCoreAnnotations.SentimentAnnotatedTree
.class);
```

Next, we obtain the numeric value of the predicted sentiment, 0-4:

```
// 0 = very negative, 1 = negative, 2 = neutral,
// 3 = positive, and 4 = very positive
Integer predictedClass =
RNNCoreAnnotations.getPredictedClass(sentimentTree);
```

This value will be used as an index into a matrix of confidence scores. The matrix simply holds the confidence scores for each sentiment, with 1.0 being the highest possible score. The highest score indicates the most confident sentiment prediction:

```
SimpleMatrix scoreMatrix =
RNNCoreAnnotations.getPredictions(sentimentTree);
```

```
double score = scoreMatrix.get(predictedClass.intValue(), 0);
int sentiment_num = predictedClass.intValue();
```

Finally, we save the sentence, its source, and its sentiment value and confidence in the database only if `score > 0.3` and `sentiment_num != 2` (Neutral).

Twitter API

The `TwitterStream`, `RedditStream`, and `NewsStream` classes run as simultaneous threads that continuously monitor their respective sources for new stories and comments. They are each implemented differently to meet the requirements of their respective APIs, but they all share access to the `SentimentDetector` object in order to detect and save the sentiment detections to the database.

We're going to use the official Twitter `hbc` Java library for Twitter access. We must provide the library search terms to filter the Twitter *firehose* to specific kinds of tweets. Authentication is achieved with an API key associated with our user account and application.

The library setup is a straightforward use of the Twitter `hbc` library:

```java
public class TwitterStream implements Runnable
{
  private BlockingQueue<String> msgQueue;
  private Client client;
  public TwitterStream(...)
  {
    msgQueue = new LinkedBlockingQueue<String>(100000);
    Hosts hosts = new HttpHosts(Constants.STREAM_HOST);
    StatusesFilterEndpoint endpoint =
new StatusesFilterEndpoint();

    List<String> terms =
Lists.newArrayList(props.getProperty("twitter_terms")
.split("\\s*,\\s*"));
    endpoint.trackTerms(terms);

    Authentication auth =
new OAuth1(props.getProperty("twitter_consumer_key"),
props.getProperty("twitter_consumer_secret"),
props.getProperty("twitter_token"),
props.getProperty("twitter_token_secret"));
    ClientBuilder builder = new ClientBuilder()
.name("SmartCode-Client-01").hosts(hosts).authentication(auth)
.endpoint(endpoint)
.processor(new StringDelimitedProcessor(msgQueue));
```

```
      client = builder.build();
      client.connect();

  }
```

Since we want our `TwitterStream` to run as a thread, we'll implement a `run()` method that grabs a single tweet at a time from the streaming client, forever:

```
public void run() {
  try
  {
    while (!client.isDone())
    {
      String msg = msgQueue.take();
      Map<String, Object> msgobj = gson.fromJson(msg, Map.class);
      String id = (String)msgobj.get("id_str");
      String text = (String) msgobj.get("text");
      String textClean = cleanupTweet(text);
      if(!sentimentDetector.alreadyProcessed(id))
      {
        sentimentDetector.detectSentiment(id,
textClean, "twitter", false, true);
      }
    }
  }
  catch(InterruptedException e)
  {
    client.stop();
  }
}
```

We see in this code snippet that the tweet is manipulated before running sentiment detection. Tweets can be syntactically cryptic, deviating significantly from natural language. They often include hashtags (`#foobar`), mentions (`@foobar`), retweets (`RT: foobar`), and links (`https://foobar.com`).

As we discussed previously, the CoreNLP sentiment detector (and tokenizer and part-of-speech detector, and so on) was not trained on tweets; rather it was trained on movie reviews, written in common English form. Thus, Twitter-specific syntax and numerous abbreviations, emojis, and other quirks somewhat unique to tweets will not be handled correctly by CoreNLP. We cannot easily avoid all of these problems, but we can at least clean up some of the obvious syntactical elements. We expect that specific hashtags, mentions, retweet markers, and URLs do not significantly contribute to the overall sentiment of a tweet. We define a function called `cleanupTweet` that uses a few **regular expressions** to strip out all of the Twitter-specific syntax:

```
private String cleanupTweet(String text) {
   return text.replaceAll("#\\w+", "")
.replaceAll("@\\w+", "")
.replaceAll("https?:[^\\s]+", "")
.replaceAll("\\bRT\\b", "")
.replaceAll(" : ", "").replaceAll("\\s+", " ");
}
```

The GATE platform

It is worth noting that the GATE platform (General Architecture for Text Engineering, https://gate.ac.uk/), from the University of Sheffield, has improved CoreNLP's tokenizer and part-of-speech tagger specifically for English tweets. They modified the tokenizer to include the following features, quoted from their documentation (*Tools for Social Media Data*, https://gate.ac.uk/sale/tao/splitch17.html):

- *URLs and abbreviations (such as "gr8" or "2day") are treated as a single token.*

- *User mentions (@username) are two tokens, one for the @ and one for the username.*

- *Hashtags are likewise two tokens (the hash and the tag) but see below for another component that can split up multi-word hashtags.*

- *"Emoticons" such as :-D can be treated as a single token. This requires a gazetteer of emoticons to be run before the tokenizer; an example gazetteer is provided in the Twitter plugin. This gazetteer also normalizes the emoticons to help with classification, machine learning, etc. For example, :-D, and 8D are both normalized to :D.*

Their system also "uses a spelling correction dictionary to correct mis-spellings and a Twitter-specific dictionary to expand common abbreviations and substitutions." Furthermore, their tokenizer can also break apart multi-word hashtags:

Since hashtags cannot contain white space, it is common for users to form hashtags by running together a number of separate words, sometimes in "camel case" form but sometimes simply all in lower (or upper) case, for example, "#worldgonemad" (as search queries on Twitter are not case-sensitive).

> *The "Hashtag Tokenizer" PR attempts to recover the original discrete words from such multi-word hashtags. It uses a large gazetteer of common English words, organization names, locations, etc. as well as slang words and contractions without the use of apostrophes (since hashtags are alphanumeric, words like "wouldn't" tend to be expressed as "wouldn't" without the apostrophe). Camel-cased hashtags (#CamelCasedHashtag) are split at case changes.*

We elected not to include GATE's processing chain for simplicity, but we highly recommend GATE for any project that makes use of tweets.

Reddit API

We retrieve Reddit posts and comments using the JRAW library. Like TwitterStream, our RedditStream runs as a thread in the background and therefore implements the Runnable interface. Like Twitter, we specify some search terms in the Java properties file:

```
public class RedditStream implements Runnable {
  private RedditClient reddit;
  private SentimentDetector sentimentDetector;
  private ArrayList<String> terms;

  public RedditStream(SentimentDetector sentimentDetector,
Properties props)
  {
    this.sentimentDetector = sentimentDetector;
    UserAgent userAgent = new UserAgent(...);
    Credentials credentials = Credentials.script(
props.getProperty("reddit_user"),
props.getProperty("reddit_password"),
props.getProperty("reddit_clientid"),
props.getProperty("reddit_clientsecret"));
    NetworkAdapter adapter = new OkHttpNetworkAdapter(userAgent);
    reddit = OAuthHelper.automatic(adapter, credentials);

    terms = Lists.newArrayList(props.getProperty("reddit_terms")
.split("\\s*,\\s*"));
  }
```

The run() method searches the Reddit API every 10 minutes for our specific terms (the 10-minute interval can be changed to any interval you wish). It attempts to skip any posts and comments it has already seen by querying the database for existing entries with the same post/comment id. Due to extensive object-oriented modeling of Reddit entities by JRAW, we omit the code for querying and retrieving posts and comments.

The code is somewhat elaborate because search results are retrieved as pages (requiring a loop to iterate over each page), each page contains multiple submissions (requiring a loop), and each submission might have a tree of comments (requiring a custom tree iterator). We do not need to clean up the text of the posts and comments because, in most cases, these are written in regular English (unlike tweets).

News API

The News API (`https://newsapi.org/`) provides article titles, short summaries, and URLs for articles matching search terms and a specified date range. The News API harvests articles from more than 30,000 news sources. The actual article content is not provided by the API, as the News API does not possess a license for redistribution of the news organizations' copyrighted content. The titles and summaries provided by the News API are insufficient to gauge the sentiment of the article, so we will write our own code that fetches the original news articles given the URLs returned by a search for our keywords on the News API.

Just like `TwitterStream` and `RedditStream`, `NewsStream` will implement `Runnable` so that the crawling process can run on a separate thread. We will add logging to this class to give us extra information about whether our article fetching code is working, and we use a date formatter to tell the News API to search for articles published today. We will delay one day between the searches since articles are published less frequently than tweets or Reddit posts:

```
public class NewsStream implements Runnable {

    private SentimentDetector sentimentDetector;
    private Gson gson;
    private String apiKey;
    private ArrayList<String> searchTerms;
    private Logger logger;
    private SimpleDateFormat dateFormat;

    public NewsStream(SentimentDetector sentimentDetector,
Gson gson, Properties props)
    {
        this.sentimentDetector = sentimentDetector;
        this.gson = gson;
        apiKey = props.getProperty("news_api_key");
        searchTerms =
Lists.newArrayList(props.getProperty("news_api_terms")
.split("\\s*,\\s*"));
        this.logger = Logger.getLogger("NewsStream");
        this.dateFormat = new SimpleDateFormat("yyyy-MM-dd");
    }
```

The News API expects a typical HTTP GET request and returns JSON. We are going to use the `HTTP Request` library to simplify HTTP requests, and Google's Gson for JSON parsing:

```java
public void run()
{
  try
  {
    while (true)
    {
      for (String searchTerm : searchTerms)
      {
        Date todayDate = new Date();
        String today = dateFormat.format(todayDate);
        HttpRequest request = HttpRequest.get(
"https://newsapi.org/v2/everything", true, "apiKey", apiKey, "q",
searchTerm, "from", today, "sortBy", "popularity")
.accept("application/json");
        if (request.code() == 200)
        {
          String json = request.body();
```

At this point, we have the JSON search results from the News API. We next convert the JSON to Java objects with Gson:

```java
Map<String, Object> respmap = gson.fromJson(json, Map.class);
ArrayList<Map<String, Object>> articles =
(ArrayList<Map<String, Object>>) respmap.get("articles");
```

Then we iterate through each article that matched our query:

```java
for (Map<String, Object> article : articles) {
  String url = (String) article.get("url");
```

Now we need to retrieve the actual article from the original source. Naturally, we do not want to extract sentiment from a raw HTML page, which is the result of simply requesting the URL. We only want the article text, stripping out ads, comments, and headers and footers.

The `Crux` library (derived from Snacktory, which itself was derived from goose and jreadability) is designed to extract just the main body text from any web page. It uses a variety of heuristics and special cases acquired over years of development (including lessons learned from the prior libraries it derives from). Once we extract the article text with `Crux`, we pass it off, in full, to the sentiment detector, which will then break it down into paragraphs and sentences and detect sentiment for each sentence:

```
HttpRequest artRequest =
HttpRequest.get(url).userAgent("SmartCode");
if (artRequest.code() == 200)
{
  String artHtml = artRequest.body();
  Article crux =
ArticleExtractor.with(url, artHtml).extractContent().article();
  String body = crux.document.text();
  sentimentDetector.detectSentiment(url, body, "newsapi",false,
true);
}
```

After processing each article returned from the News API query, the thread sleeps for one day before searching News API again.

Dashboard with plotly.js and Dash

The Java project described in the preceding section continuously monitors several sources for news and comments about autonomous vehicles/self-driving cars. The sentiment (Very Negative up to Very Positive) of every sentence or tweet found in these sources is recorded in an SQLite database. Because we do not expect the overall sentiment of autonomous vehicles to change rapidly, we choose to look at the results on a daily basis. However, if we were monitoring a more active topic, for example, tweets about a sporting event, we may wish to examine the results every hour or minute.

To get a quick overview of the aggregate sentiment from our three sources over the last several days, we use Dash, from the makers of plotly.js, to plot the sentiment in a continuously updating webpage. Dash is a Python library for creating dashboards that uses plotly.js to draw the plots. If you have your own website already, you can just use plotly.js to draw plots without using Dash. We will need to query an SQLite database, so some kind of backend server is required since in-browser JavaScript will not be able to query the database.

First, our Python code will import the requisite libraries and load a pointer to the database:

```
import dash
from dash.dependencies import Input, Output
import dash_core_components as dcc
import dash_html_components as HTML
import plotly.graph_objs as go
import datetime
import plotly
import sqlite3
```

```
import math

db = sqlite3.connect('../sentiment/sentiment.db')
cursor = db.cursor()
```

Next, we create a `Dash` object and specify a layout. We will have a title at the top of the page ("Sentiment Live Feed"), then the live-updating graph that updates once per hour (so that we see within the hour when the new data has been added for the day), followed by a list of individual sentences and their sentiment below the graph. This list helps us check, at a glance, if the sentiment detector is working as expected and if the various sources are providing relevant sentences:

```
app = dash.Dash("Sentiment")
app.css.append_css({'external_url':
'https://codepen.io/chriddyp/pen/bWLwgP.css'})

app.layout = html.Div(
  html.Div([
    html.H4('Sentiment Live Feed'),
    dcc.Graph(id='live-update-graph'),
    dcc.Interval(
      id='interval-component',
      interval=60*60*1000, # in milliseconds
      n_intervals=0
    ),
    html.Table([
      html.Thead([html.Tr([
        html.Th('Source'),
        html.Th('Date'),
        html.Th('Text'),
        html.Th('Sentiment')])]),
    html.Tbody(id='live-update-text')])
  ])
)
```

The graph will be updated by a function call that is scheduled by the "interval-component" mentioned in the previous code snippet, that is, once per hour:

```
@app.callback(Output('live-update-graph', 'figure'),
[Input('interval-component', 'n_intervals')])
def update_graph_live(n):
```

In order to update the graph, we first must query the database for all the data we wish to show in the graph. We will store the results in Python data structures before we build the graph components:

```
cursor.execute(
"select datefound, source, sentiment_num from sentiment")
data = {}
while True:
  row = cursor.fetchone()
  if row == None:
    break
  source = row[1]
  if source not in data:
    data[source] = {}
  datefound = row[0]
  if datefound not in data[source]:
    data[source][datefound] = []
  data[source][datefound].append(row[2])
```

Next, we prepare the data for two different graphs. On the top will be the average sentiment from each source, per day. On the bottom will be the number of sentences found from each source (sentences with the non-neutral sentiment, that is):

```
figdata = {'sentiment': {}, 'count': {}}
for source in data:
  figdata['sentiment'][source] = {'x': [], 'y': []}
  figdata['count'][source] = {'x': [], 'y': []}
  for datefound in data[source]:
    sentcnt = 0
    sentsum = 0
    for sentval in data[source][datefound]:
      sentsum += sentval
      sentcnt += 1
    figdata['sentiment'][source]['x'].append(datefound)
    figdata['sentiment'][source]['y'].append(sentsum /
float(len(data[source][datefound])))
    figdata['count'][source]['x'].append(datefound)
    figdata['count'][source]['y'].append(sentcnt)
```

Now we make a plotly figure with two subplots (one above the other):

```
fig = plotly.tools.make_subplots(rows=2, cols=1,
vertical_spacing=0.2, shared_xaxes=True,
subplot_titles=('Average sentiment',
'Number of positive and negative statements'))
```

The top plot, identified by position row 1 column 1, contains the average data:

```
for source in sorted(figdata['sentiment'].keys()):
  fig.append_trace(go.Scatter(
x = figdata['sentiment'][source]['x'],
```

```
y = figdata['sentiment'][source]['y'],
xaxis = 'x1', yaxis = 'y1', text = source, name = source), 1, 1)
```

The bottom plot, identified by position row 2 column 1, contains the count data:

```
for source in sorted(figdata['count'].keys()):
  fig.append_trace(go.Scatter(
x = figdata['count'][source]['x'],
y = figdata['count'][source]['y'], xaxis = 'x1', yaxis = 'y2',
text = source, name = source, showlegend = False), 2, 1)
```

Finally, we set the y-axis range for the top plot to 0-4 (Very Negative to Very Positive) and return the figure:

```
fig['layout']['yaxis1'].update(range=[0, 4])
return fig
```

The table below the plot must also be updated on a periodic basis. Only the most recent 20 sentences are shown. Its code is simpler due to the simple nature of the table:

```
@app.callback(Output(
'live-update-text', 'children'),
[Input('interval-component', 'n_intervals')])
def update_text(n):
  cursor.execute("select datefound, source, msg,
sentiment from sentiment order by datefound desc limit 20")
  result = []
  while True:
    row = cursor.fetchone()
    if row == None:
      break
    datefound = row[0]
    source = row[1]
    msg = row[2]
    sentiment = row[3]
    result.append(html.Tr([html.Td(source), html.Td(datefound),
html.Td(msg), html.Td(sentiment)]))

  return result
```

Lastly, we just need to start the application when the Python script is executed:

```
if __name__ == '__main__':
  app.run_server()
```

The resulting dashboard is shown in *Figure 3*:

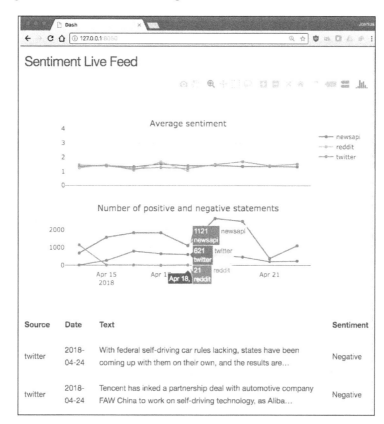

Figure 3: Live-updating dashboard showing average sentiment and some individual sentiments from various sources for the search terms "autonomous vehicles" and "self-driving cars"

Continuous evaluation

Once deployed, there are several ways in which this system may prove to be inaccurate or degrade over time:

1. The streaming services (the Twitter API, Reddit API, and/or News API) might eventually fail to provide new posts and comments, due to rate limits, lost connections, or other issues.

2. The sentiment detector might be inaccurate; this may be consistent (consistently lower or higher sentiment than the true sentiment), inconsistent (seemingly random decisions about sentiment), or degrading (sentiment becomes less accurate over time due to some change in the format of the inputs provided by the APIs).

3. Feedback, in the form of tweets and posts and comments, related to our search terms may degrade over time; the search terms may be used in more unrelated stories over time, or the popular terms to refer to our subject of interest may change over time. For example, what was once known as unmanned aerial vehicles (UAVs) are now more commonly called "drones."

The system built in this chapter already contains some features that help mitigate these potential issues:

1. By referring to the second plot, which shows counts of sentences with sentiment found in the various sources, we can easily notice that a source has failed to produce content for a period of time. Our code also includes some (limited) exception handling to restart failed streaming connections. Note, there is one drawback to our solution detailed in the preceding text. Our system only saves sentences in the database if they have a non-neutral sentiment. This was done to save space in the database. However, if the sentiment detector is inaccurate or otherwise produces neutral sentiment far more often than it should, the sentences will not be saved, and it will appear that the source is failing to produce content.

2. We noted in the preceding section that the CoreNLP sentiment detector is trained on movie reviews, which might not match the syntax and word usage found in tweets, Reddit posts and comments, and news articles. It takes considerable effort to retrain the CoreNLP sentiment detector on more representative examples. We show how to do so in the following text. However, our system does help us spot, at a glance, whether the sentiment detector is accurate, at least in a vague sense. We can look at the list of the most recent sentences and their sentiment in the dashboard. If something seems bogus on this list, we can look further into the issue. Also, see the following example comparing dictionary-based sentiment analysis with CoreNLP to compute accuracy scores.

3. If word usage changes over time or, for whatever reason, the kinds of content returned by the APIs for our search query changes over time, we might be able to notice by a change in the average sentiment or the number of sentences obtained from the sources. We could also possibly notice a change in the kinds of sentences shown below the graphs and the topics those sentences discuss. However, this potential issue is the most difficult to detect at a glance since it would require a periodic review of the full content provided by the streaming sources.

We can evaluate, in an ad hoc manner, the accuracy of CoreNLP with a handful of sentences. We will also compare a simple dictionary-based sentiment detector, in which we count the number of positive and negative adjectives found in the sentence; these adjectives come from the SocialSent project (*Inducing Domain-Specific Sentiment Lexicons from Unlabeled Corpora, Hamilton, William L., Kevin Clark, Jure Leskovec,* and *Dan Jurafsky, ArXiv preprint (arxiv:1606.02820), 2016*):

Sentence	True Sentiment	CoreNLP Sentiment	Dictionary Sentiment
Presenting next week to SF Trial Lawyers Association.	Neutral	Negative	Neutral
Electric and autonomous vehicle policy wonks who are worried about suburban sprawl, idling cars: worry about a problem that exists today.	Negative	Negative	Neutral
But we are always working to make cars safer.	Positive	Positive	Positive
The 5 Most Amazing AI Advances in Autonomous Driving via …	Positive	Negative	Neutral
Ohio advances in autonomous and connected vehicle infrastructure	Positive	Negative	Neutral
Lyft is one of the latest companies to explore using self-driving car technology.	Positive	Positive	Neutral
This screams mega lawsuit the first time an accident does occur.	Negative	Negative	Neutral
In addition, if a ball or (anything similar) were to roll into the street, a self-driving car would probably slow down anyway.	Neutral	Negative	Neutral
Uber Exec Ron Leaves an Autonomous-Vehicle Unit in Turmoil	Negative	Negative	Neutral
Learning from aviation to makes self-driving cars safer is a good idea.	Positive	Positive	Positive
This is happening more and more and more, and it is becoming truly harmful.	Negative	Positive	Negative
If the glorious technological future that Silicon Valley enthusiasts dream about is only going to serve to make the growing gaps wider and strengthen existing unfair power structures, is it something worth striving for?	Negative	Positive	Neutral

Assuming the column "True Sentiment" is accurate, CoreNLP's number of correct predictions is just 6/12 (50%), and the dictionary-based approach's accuracy is 5/12 (42%). Worse, in four cases, CoreNLP predicted an opposite sentiment (predicted Negative when the true sentiment was Positive, or vice versa), while the dictionary-based approach had no instances of opposite predictions. We see that the dictionary-based approach is less likely to get a positive or negative sentiment, preferring neutral sentiment, since it is searching for a relatively small number of sentiment adjectives (about 2,000 words).

To get a more precise measure of the accuracy of CoreNLP or any other approach requires that we label the true sentiment (according to our judgment) of many sentences randomly sampled from the texts provided by our streaming sources. Even better would be to do this exercise repeatedly to detect any changes in the style or syntax of the texts that may impact the sentiment detector. Once this has been done some number of times, one may then have a sufficient amount of training data to retrain CoreNLP's sentiment detector to better match the kinds of sentences found in our sources.

Retraining CoreNLP sentiment models

The accuracy of our sentiment analysis code depends on the quality of the sentiment model. There are three factors that influence the quality of a model:

1. How closely do the model's training examples match our own data?
2. How accurate are the training examples' labels?
3. How accurately does the machine learning algorithm identify the sentiment of the training examples?

CoreNLP provides the original training examples for their sentiment analysis model (`https://nlp.stanford.edu/sentiment/code.html`). These training examples consist of movie reviews. We can investigate each of these questions by examining CoreNLP's training data.

First, let's examine the training examples and see how well they match our Twitter, Reddit, and news data. Each example in the training data is represented as a tree of sentiment values. Each single word (and punctuation) is a leaf in the tree and has a sentiment score. Then words are grouped together, and that bundle has another score, and so on. The root of the tree has the score for the whole sentence. For example, consider this entry in the training data, *A slick, engrossing melodrama*:

```
(4
  (3
    (3
      (2 (2 A) (3 slick))
      (2 ,))
    (3 (4 engrossing) (2 melodrama)))
  (2 .))
```

The word *A* has a sentiment of 2 (`Neutral`), *slick* has a sentiment of 3 (`Positive`), and the combined *A slick* has a sentiment of 2 (`Neutral`), and so on (*engrossing* is `Positive`, *melodrama* is `Neutral`, the whole sentence is `Very Positive`).

If we examine more of the training examples provided by CoreNLP, we see that they are all movie reviews and they are generally complete, grammatically correct English sentences. This somewhat matches our News API content but does not match our Twitter data. We would have to create our own phrases for the training examples by taking real phrases found in our data.

We can also examine the training data to see if we agree with the sentiment labels. For example, perhaps you disagree that *melodrama* has a Neutral sentiment – perhaps you think it should be Negative (0 or 1). Examining each entry in the training set takes considerable time, but it can be done.

In order to change the training data to our own examples, we would first have to use CoreNLP's sentence parser to create the tree structure. This structure can be obtained for your own sentences by running:

```
java -cp ejml-0.23.jar:stanford-corenlp-3.9.1.jar:stanford-corenlp-3.9.1-
models.jar -Xmx8g \
  edu.stanford.nlp.pipeline.StanfordCoreNLP \
  -annotators tokenize,ssplit,parse -file mysentences.txt
```

The output of this command includes trees such as the following:

```
(ROOT
  (NP
    (NP (NNP Ohio))
    (NP
      (NP (NNS advances))
      (PP (IN in)
        (NP
          (ADJP (JJ autonomous)
            (CC and)
            (JJ connected))
          (NN vehicle) (NN infrastructure))))))
```

Next, we can replace the part-of-speech tags (ROOT, NP, JJ, CC, and so on) with desired sentiment scores (0-4).

To do this for a large number of examples (CoreNLP has 8,544 sentences in its training set) would require considerable effort. This is why most people just use pre-developed models rather than build their own. Even so, it is important to know how to build your own models should the need arise.

Once a large number of phrases are labeled with sentiment scores in this way, the phrases should be split into training, testing, and development files. The training file is used to train the model.

The testing file is used to test the model at the end of training; it is important that the testing examples are not used during training to measure how well the model works on new data (like we get in the real world). Finally, the development file is used to test the model as it is training; again, this file should not include any examples from the training file. While training, the machine learning algorithms evaluate how well they are performing by using the partially trained model against the development set. This provides an on-going accuracy score. Also, at the end of training, the code will test the final model against the test file to get a final accuracy score.

We can run training on these files with the following command:

```
java -cp ejml-0.23.jar:stanford-corenlp-3.9.1.jar \
  -mx8g edu.stanford.nlp.sentiment.SentimentTraining \
  -numHid 25 -trainPath train.txt -devPath dev.txt \
  -train -model mymodel.ser.gz
```

Training can take some time (several hours). The final accuracy, using CoreNLP's original movie review dataset, is described by two numbers. First, the system predicted 41% of sentiments correct. This number measures the predictions of the overall phrase or sentence, not counting individual word sentiments (which it also predicts in order to predict the sentiment of the overall phrase). This accuracy seems low because it measures whether the system got the exact sentiment correct (values 0-4). The second measure is an "approximate" measure which checks how often the system gets the overall sentiment correct: positive or negative (ignoring phrases that were neutral in the original test data). For this measure, it achieves 72% accuracy.

It is difficult to say whether these accuracy scores are "good enough" for any particular use case. We have seen that the CoreNLP movie reviews sentiment model might not be good enough for analyzing tweets and social media comments. However, these scores do allow us to identify whether we are making improvements whenever we add more examples to a training data set and retrain the model.

Summary

This chapter demonstrated one method for making sense of feedback, specifically, a method for acquiring tweets and posts and news articles about a topic and identifying the overall sentiment (negative or positive) of the general population's feeling about the topic. We chose "autonomous vehicles" and "self-driving cars" for our search terms in order to get a sense of how people feel about this burgeoning technology, particularly in light of recent news (some good, some bad) at the time of writing.

Our method used the Twitter, Reddit, and News APIs, running as independent threads that continuously acquire new tweets and posts and comments. The text is then sent to the CoreNLP library for sentiment detection. CoreNLP first breaks down the text into individual sentences and then detects the sentiment of each sentence. We next save each sentence with a non-neutral sentiment in an SQLite database, along with the date and source. In order to visualize the current sentiment, we also built a live-updating web dashboard with a plot of average sentiment per day per source and a total number of sentences per day per source. We added a table to this dashboard that shows a sampling of the recent sentences and their sentiment in order to gauge whether the system is working properly quickly. Finally, we discussed ways to evaluate the system on an ongoing basis, including a quick comparison of CoreNLP versus a simple dictionary-based sentiment detector.

4
A Blueprint for Recommending Products and Services

Many, if not most, businesses today have an online presence that promotes and often sells products and services. Most people will find these sites by searching on Google, or other search engines. In this case, we will be using Google as an example, but users will typically be directed by Google to a particular page on the business website, where users might also go back to Google to find related products. For example, an amateur photographer might find a camera on one website and a lens on another, and possibly not realize the company that sells the camera also sells an array of lenses. It is a challenge for these businesses to ensure repeat business when a third-party search engine controls a user's shopping experience.

Recommendation systems can help businesses keep customers on their sites by showing users related products and services. Related items include those that are similar to the item being viewed as well as items related to the user's interests or purchase history. Ideally, the recommendation system would be sufficiently smart enough that users would have no need or interest in searching again for a different site. Recommendations could be determined by examining a user's purchase history, product ratings, or even just page views.

Recommendation systems are helpful not only for online commerce but also for a number of other online experiences. Consider a music streaming service such as Spotify. Each time a user plays a track, the system can learn the kinds of artists that the user prefers and suggest related artists. The related artists could be determined by the similarity in terms of musical attributes, as demonstrated best by Pandora Radio, another music streaming site, or by similarity to other users and the artists they prefer. If the user is new, related artists can be determined just from other users' preferences. In other words, the system can see that *The Beatles* and *The Who* are similar because users who listen to one often listen to the other.

There are two ways to recommend an item. Let's suppose we know the user, and we know what the user is viewing, for example, a particular camera or a particular blues musician. We can generate recommendations by examining the item's (camera's or musician's) properties and the user's stated interests. For example, a database could help generate recommendations by selecting lenses compatible with the camera or musicians in the same genre or a genre that the user has selected in their profile. In a similar context, items can be found by examining the items' descriptions and finding close matches with the item the user is viewing. These are all a kind of **content-based recommendation** (*Content-based recommendation systems, Pazzani, Michael J., and Daniel Billsus, The Adaptive Web, pp. 325-341, Springer, Berlin, Heidelberg, 2007,* `https://link.springer.com/chapter/10.1007%2F978-3-540-72079-9_10`).

The second type of recommendation is known as **collaborative filtering**. It goes by this name because the technique uses feedback from other users to help determine the recommendation for this user (*Item-based collaborative filtering recommendation algorithms, Sarwar, Badrul, George Karypis, Joseph Konstan, and John Riedl, in Proceedings of the 10th international conference on World Wide Web, pp. 285-295, ACM, 2001,* `https://dl.acm.org/citation.cfm?id=372071`). Other users may contribute ratings, likes, purchases, views, and so on. Sometimes, websites, such as Amazon, will include a phrase such as, *Customers who bought this item also bought....* Such a phrase is a clear indication of collaborative filtering. In practice, collaborative filtering is a means for predicting how much the user in question will like each item, and then filtering down to the few items with the highest-scoring predictions.

There are many techniques for generating both content-based and collaborative filtering recommendations. We will cover simple versions of the current best practice, **BM25 weighting** (*The Probabilistic Relevance Framework: BM25 and Beyond, Robertson, Stephen, and Hugo Zaragoza, Information Retrieval Vol. 3, No. 4, pp. 333-389, 2009,* `https://www.nowpublishers.com/article/Details/INR-019`), to better compare items and users with vastly different activity, **efficient nearest neighbor search** to find the highest scoring recommendations, and **matrix factorization** to predict a user's preference for every item and to compute item-item similarities.

Recommendation systems may be evaluated in multiple ways, but ultimately the goal is to sell more products and increase engagement. Simple A/B testing, in which recommendations are randomly turned on or off, can tell us whether the recommendation system is providing value. Offline evaluations may also be performed. In this case, historical data is used to train the system, and a portion of the data is kept aside and not used for training. Recommendations are generated and compared to the held-out data to see if they match actual behavior. For real-time evaluations, online evaluation is an option. We will demonstrate online evaluation in which every purchase is checked against the recommendations generated for the user. The system is evaluated by looking at the number of purchases that were also recommended at the time the purchase occurred.

In this chapter, we will cover:

- The methods needed for generating content-based and collaborative filtering recommendations
- The `implicit` Python library, by Ben Frederickson (`https://github.com/benfred/implicit`), which is used for building recommendation systems
- The `faiss` Python library, by Facebook AI Research (`https://github.com/facebookresearch/faiss`), which is used for efficient nearest neighbor search
- An HTTP-based API that is used for recording user activity such as purchases and generating recommendations
- A technique that can be used for online evaluation of the recommendation system's accuracy

Usage scenario – implicit feedback

There are many scenarios in which recommendation systems may be utilized; one such example is Amazon's online store. On the front page, Amazon recommends featured products developed in-house (for example, their Alexa voice-controlled assistant), "deals" specific for the user, items "inspired by your wish list," various thematic lists of recommended items (for example, "recommendations for you in sports and outdoors"), and then more traditional recommendations based on the customer's overall purchase history. Presumably, these recommendations are based on product ratings from other users, product popularity, time between purchases (in Amazon's recommendation system, buying two products close in time makes their relatedness stronger (*Two decades of recommender systems at Amazon.com, Smith, Brent,* and *Greg Linden, IEEE Internet Computing Vol. 21, no. 3, pp. 12-18, 2017,* `https://ieeexplore.ieee.org/abstract/document/7927889/`), the customer's own behavior (purchases, ratings, clicks, wish lists), behavior of other users with interests similar to the customer, or Amazon's current marketing focus (for example, Alexa, Whole Foods, Prime), and so on. It would not be outlandish to claim Amazon as the top storefront with the most sophisticated storefront marketing techniques. Whatever recommendation systems may be described in a book chapter are a small component of the overall marketing strategy of a massive storefront such as Amazon's.

Since this chapter's main focus is to address the main features of recommendation systems, we will focus on a universal scenario. This scenario utilizes the least amount of information possible to build a recommendation system. Rather than product ratings, which are a kind of "explicit" feedback in which users make a specific effort to provide information, we will rely on the content (title, product details) of the item as well as "implicit" feedback.

This kind of feedback does not require the user to do anything extra. **Implicit feedback** consists of clicks, purchases, likes, or even mouse movements. For simplicity, in this chapter, we will focus on purchases to determine which items are preferred and to recommend items to a user by identifying those items that are often purchased by other users with similar purchase histories.

With implicit feedback, we have no way to model negative feedback. With explicit ratings, a low rating can indicate that a user does not prefer the product and these negative ratings can help the recommendation system filter out bad recommendations. With implicit feedback, such as purchase history, all we know is that a user did or did not (yet) purchase an item. We have no way to know if a user did not purchase an item (yet) because the user wishes not to purchase the item, the user just does not know enough about the item, or they wish to purchase the item but just have not yet done so and will do so at a later date.

This simple and straightforward usage scenario will allow us to develop a universal recommendation system. As we will see in the *Deployment strategy* section, we will develop a small HTTP server that will be notified every time a user purchases an item. It will periodically update its recommendation model and provide item-specific and user-specific recommendations upon request. For simplicity's sake, we will not use a database or require special integration into an existing platform.

Content-based recommendations

Previously, we saw that there are two kinds of recommendations, content-based (*Content-based recommendation systems, Pazzani, Michael J.,* and *Daniel Billsus, The Adaptive Web, pp. 325-341, Springer, Berlin, Heidelberg, 2007,* `https://link.springer.com/chapter/10.1007%2F978-3-540-72079-9_10`) and collaborative filtering (*Item-based collaborative filtering recommendation algorithms, Sarwar, Badrul, George Karypis, Joseph Konstan,* and *John Riedl,* in *Proceedings of the 10th international conference on World Wide Web, pp. 285-295, ACM, 2001,* `https://dl.acm.org/citation.cfm?id=372071`). A content-based recommendation finds similar items to a given item by examining the item's properties, such as its title or description, category, or dependencies on other items (for example, electronic toys require batteries). These kinds of recommendations do not use any information about ratings, purchases, or any other user information (explicit or implicit).

Let's suppose we wish to find similar items by their titles and descriptions. In other words, we want to examine the words used in each item to find items with similar words. We will represent each item as a vector and compare them with a distance metric to see how similar they are, where a smaller distance means they are more similar.

We can use the **bag-of-words** technique to convert an item's title and description into a vector of numbers. This approach is common for any situation where text needs to be converted to a vector. Furthermore, each item's vector will have the same dimension (same number of values), so we can easily compute the distance metric on any two item vectors.

The bag-of-words technique constructs a vector for each item that has as many values as there are *unique* words among *all* the items. If there are, say, 1,000 unique words mentioned in the titles and descriptions of 100 items, then each of the 100 items will be represented by a 1,000-dimension vector. The values in the vector are the counts of the number of times an item uses each particular word. If we have an item vector that starts <3, 0, 2, ...>, and the 1,000 unique words are *aardvark, aback, abandoned, ...* then we know the item uses the word *aardvark* 3 times, the word *aback* 0 times, the word *abandoned* 2 times, and so on. Also, we often eliminate "stop words," or common words in the English language, such as *and, the,* or *get,* that have little meaning.

Given two item vectors, we can compute their distance in multiple ways. One common way is **Euclidean distance**: $d = \sqrt{\sum (x_i - y_i)^2}$, where x_i and y_i refer to each value from the first and second items' vectors. Euclidean distance is less accurate if the item titles and descriptions have a dramatically different number of words, so we often use **cosine similarity** instead. This metric measures the angle between the vectors. This is easy to understand if our vectors have two dimensions, but it works equally well in any number of dimensions. In two dimensions, the angle between two item vectors is the angle between the lines that connect the 0,0 and the item vector values, <*x,y*>. Cosine similarity is calculated as $d = (\sum x_i * y_i)/(\|x\|\|y\|)$, where x and y are *n*-dimensional vectors and $\|x\|$ and $\|y\|$ refer to the *magnitude* of a vector, that is, its distance from the origin, $\|x\| = \sqrt{(\sum x_i^2)}$. Unlike Euclidean distance, *larger* values are better with cosine similarity because a larger value indicates the angle between the two vectors is smaller, so the vectors are closer or more similar to each other (recall that the graph of cosine starts at 1.0 with angle 0.0). Two identical vectors will have a cosine similarity of 1.0. The reason it is called the cosine similarity is because we can find the actual angle by taking the inverse cosine of d: $\Theta = \cos^{-1} d$. We have no reason to do so since d works just fine as a similarity value.

Now we have a way of representing each item's title and description as a vector, and we can compute how similar two vectors are with cosine similarity. Unfortunately, we have a problem. Two items will be considered highly similar if they use many of the same words even if those particular words are very common. For example, if all video items in our store have the word *Video* and *[DVD]* at the end of their titles, then every video might be considered similar to every other. To resolve this problem, we want to penalize (reduce) the values in the item vectors that represent common words.

A popular way to penalize common words in a bag-of-words vectors is known as **Term Frequency-Inverse Document Frequency (TF-IDF)**. We recompute each value by multiplying a weight that factors in the commonality of the word. There are multiple variations of this reweighting formula, but a common one works as follows.

Each value x_i in the vector is changed to $\hat{x}_i = x_i * \left(1 + \log \dfrac{N}{F(x_i)}\right)$, where N is the number of items (say, 100 total items) and $F(x_i)$ gives the count of items (out of the 100) that contain the word x_i. A word that is common will have a smaller $N/F(x_i)$ factor so its weighted value $\hat{x}_i$ will be smaller the original x_i. We use the log () function to ensure the multiplier does not get excessively large for uncommon words. It's worth noting that $N/F(x_i) \geq 1$, and in the case when a word is found in every item ($N = F(x_i)$, so $\log \dfrac{N}{F(x_i)} = 0$), the 1+ in front of the log() ensures the word is still counted by leaving x_i unchanged.

Now we have properly weighted item vectors and a similarity metric, the last task is to find similar items with this information. Let's suppose we are given a query item; we want to find three similar items. These items should have the largest cosine similarity to the query item. This is known as a nearest neighbor search. If coded naively, the nearest neighbor search requires computing the similarity from the query item to every other item. A better approach is to use a very efficient library such as Facebook's `faiss` library (`https://github.com/facebookresearch/faiss`). The `faiss` library precomputes similarities and stores them in an efficient index. It can also use the GPU to compute these similarities in parallel and find nearest neighbors extremely quickly. Ben Frederickson, author of the `implicit` library we will be using for finding recommendations, has compared the performance of nearest neighbor searches with the naive approach and `faiss`, among other libraries (`https://www.benfrederickson.com/approximate-nearest-neighbours-for-recommender-systems/`). His results show the naive approach can achieve about 100 searches per second, while `faiss` on the CPU can achieve about 100k per second, and `faiss` on a GPU can achieve 1.5 million per second.

There is one last complication. The bag-of-words vectors, even with stop words removed, is very large, and it is not uncommon to have vectors with 10k to 50k values, given how many English words may be used in an item title or description. The `faiss` library does not work well with such large vectors. We can limit the number of words, or a number of "features," with a parameter to the bag-of-words processor. However, this parameter keeps the most common words, which is not necessarily what we want; instead, we want to keep the most important words. We will reduce the size of the vectors to just 100 values using matrix factorization, specifically the **singular-value decomposition (SVD)**. Matrix factorization will be explained in the following section on collaborative filtering.

With all this in mind, we can use some simple Python code and the `scikit-learn` library to implement a content-based recommendation system. In this example, we will use the Amazon review dataset, aggressively deduplicated version, which contains 66 million reviews of 6.8 million products, gathered from May 20, 1996, to July 23, 2014 (`http://jmcauley.ucsd.edu/data/amazon/`).

 Due to memory constraints, we will process only the first 3.0 million products.

For content-based recommendation, we will ignore the reviews and will just use the product title and descriptions. The product data is made available in a JSON file, where each line is a separate JSON string for each product. We extract the title and description and add them to a list. We'll also add the product identifier (asin) to a list. Then we feed this list of strings into the `CountVectorizer` function of `scikit-learn` for constructing the bag-of-words vector for each string; following on, we'll then recalculate these vectors using TF-IDF, before reducing the size of the vectors using SVD. These three steps are collected into a `scikit-learn` pipeline, so we can run a single `fit_transform` function to execute all of the steps in sequence:

```
pipeline = make_pipeline(
CountVectorizer(stop_words='english', max_features=10000),
TfidfTransformer(), TruncatedSVD(n_components=128))
product_asin = []
product_text = []

with open('metadata.json', encoding='utf-8') as f:
  for line in f:
    try:
      p = json.loads(line)
      s = p['title']
      if 'description' in p:
        s += ' ' + p['description']
      product_text.append(s)
      product_asin.append(p['asin'])
    except:
      pass
d = pipeline.fit_transform(product_text, product_asin)
```

The result, d, is a matrix of all of the vectors. We next configure `faiss` for efficient nearest neighbor search. Recall that we wish to take our bag-of-words vectors and find similar items to a given item using cosine similarity on these vectors. The three most similar vectors will give us our content-based recommendations:

```
gpu_resources = faiss.StandardGpuResources()
```

```
index = faiss.GpuIndexIVFFlat(
gpu_resources, ncols, 400, faiss.METRIC_INNER_PRODUCT)
```

Note that `faiss` may also be configured without a GPU:

```
quantizer = faiss.IndexFlat(ncols)
index = faiss.IndexIVFFlat(
quantizer, ncols, 400, faiss.METRIC_INNER_PRODUCT)
```

Then we *train* `faiss` so that it learns the distribution of the values in the vectors and then *add* our vectors (technically, we only need to train on a representative subset of the full dataset):

```
index.train(d)
index.add(d)
```

Finally, we can find the nearest neighbor by *searching* the index. A search can be performed on multiple items at once, and the result is a list of distances and item indexes. We will use the indexes to retrieve each item's asin and title/description. For example, suppose we want to find a neighbor of a particular item:

```
# find 3 neighbors of item #5
distances, indexes = index.search(d[5:6], 3)
for idx in indexes[0]:
  print((product_asin[idx], product_text[idx]))
```

After processing 3.0 million products, here are some example recommendations. Italicized recommendations are less than ideal:

Product	3 Nearest neighbors	Similarity
The Canterbury Tales (Puffin Classics)	The Canterbury Tales (Signet Classics)	0.109
	Geoffrey Chaucer: Love Visions (Penguin Classics)	0.101
	The English House: English Country Houses & Interiors	0.099
Oracle JDeveloper 10g for Forms & PL/SQL Developers: A Guide to Web Development with Oracle ADF (Oracle Press)	Developing Applications with Visual Basic and UML	0.055
	Web Design with HTML and CSS Digital Classroom	0.055
	Programming the Web with ColdFusion MX 6.1 Using XHTML (Web Developer Series)	0.054
Dr. Seuss's ABC (Bright & Early Board Books)	Elmo's First Babysitter	0.238
	The Courtesan	0.238
	Moonbear's books	0.238

It is clear that this approach mostly works. Content-based recommendations are an important kind of recommendation, particularly for new users who do not have a purchase history. Many recommendation systems will mix in content-based recommendations with collaborative filtering recommendations. Content-based recommendations are good at suggesting related items based on the item itself, while collaborative filtering recommendations are best for suggesting items that are often purchased by the same people but otherwise have no intrinsic relation, such as camping gear and travel guidebooks.

Collaborative filtering recommendations

With content-based recommendations, as described in the preceding section, we only use the items' properties, such as their titles and descriptions, to generate recommendations of similar items. We demonstrated these kinds of recommendations with Amazon product data. The fact that users on Amazon are actually buying and reviewing the products makes no difference in content-based recommendations.

Collaborative filtering recommendations utilize *only* user activity. We can still find items similar to a specific item, but this time the similar items are found by finding items that are purchased or rated highly by users who also rated or purchased the item in question. Perhaps more importantly, we can also find recommendations for a particular user. Finding recommendations for a particular user is not possible with content-based recommendations. We can do this by finding similar users, based on rating or purchase history, and then determining which other items those similar users rate highly or purchase.

As described previously in our usage scenario, we will not use item ratings but rather only purchase history. This is a form of implicit user feedback since we are assuming that the user prefers the product by virtue of buying it, and we have no negative feedback (items the user does not prefer) since we do not look at a user's product ratings and reviews if they even exist.

We can represent this implicit feedback for each user as a vector of purchase counts, where each column in the vector represents an item. Thus, in an online store that has, say, 1,000 items, each user will be represented as a vector with 1,000 elements. If we collect these user vectors together, we get a user-item matrix, where each row represents a user, and each column represents an item. If we have M users and N items, the matrix will have dimensions $M \times N$.

BM25 weighting

Using raw purchase counts for each user-item cell in the matrix introduces a similar problem to what we saw with the bag-of-words vectors. Users who purchase a lot of items, and items that are very popular, will have very large values in the matrix. Users with lots of purchases across a wide range of products do not actually give much information about how items relate to each other. Likewise, items that are very popular, such as bestselling books or music, are relatively generic and appeal to many users. We do not want *The Da Vinci Code* to be related to every other item just because it is popular.

We could use TF-IDF in exactly the same way we did with word vectors. However, a variant of TF-IDF has proven to be more successful for recommendation systems. Known as BM25 (BM stands for "best match," and 25 is the particular algorithm variant), the formula has similar properties to TF-IDF but extra parameters that allow us to customize it to our particular needs. Each value in the vector is updated as follows:

$$\hat{x}_i = \left(x_i * \frac{K_1 + 1}{K_1 * w_i + x_i} \right) * \log\left(\frac{N}{1 + D} \right),$$

where:

$$w_i = (1 - B) + B * \left(\frac{d_i}{\bar{d}} \right)$$

$K_i \geq 0$ and $0 \leq B \leq 1$ are the parameters, N is the total number of items, D is the number of distinct items this user has ever purchased, d_i is the number of times this item was purchased by any user, and $\bar{d}$ is the average number of times an item is purchased across all items in D. The first component is a modified form of the "term frequency" part of TF-IDF, and the second part (with the log()) corresponds to the "inverse document frequency" part of TF-IDF. Everything else being equal, when an item is purchased more often by a user, it has a higher value in the vector (the TF part), but that value is lowered if the user has purchased lots of items (the IDF part). The weight w_i adjusts the contribution of the TF part if lots of users have purchased this item. When *B=0*, the weight w_i goes to 0 so the fraction with x_i collapses to just *K1+1* and this constant multiplies by the IDF. As *B* grows up to 1, the item's value in the user vector decreases to look more like the average popularity of the item, discounting the user's specific preference for the item. The *K1* parameter adjusts how much the item's average popularity has an impact.

If *K1=0*, the user's preference for the item (x_i) is completely ignored, leaving only the IDF portion (like when *B=0*). As *K1* increases (up to ∞), the user's preference for the item starts to dominate until (at $K1 = \infty$) the weight w_i and *B* parameter have no effect, leaving just x_i. Common values for these parameters are *K1=1.2* and *B=0.5*. Note that BM25 weighting gives 0s wherever $x_i = 0$, so the weighting function does not change the sparsity of the matrix.

Appropriate values for *K1* and *B* depend on the dataset. We will demonstrate how to experimentally find these values using a database of movie ratings in the *Continuous evaluation* section.

Matrix factorization

Consider our user-items matrix, dimensions *M×N*, perhaps on the order of millions of users and millions of items. This matrix is likely very sparse, meaning it is mostly 0s. It would take considerable time to find the top 3 or 10 similar items or similar users with such a large matrix. Another issue to consider is that there may be so much diversity in the users' purchase activities that, except for bestsellers, most items will be purchased by only a few users. For example, suppose a store has hundreds of mystery novels for sale, and suppose there is a group of users who each purchased one of these novels, but never purchased the same novel as any other user. Likewise, suppose these users have no other purchases in common, then the cosine similarity will see that they have no purchases in common and declare them to be totally dissimilar. However, it is clear to us that the users are similar in their love of mysteries, so we should be able to at least recommend to each user some of the novels they have not yet purchased.

In essence, we want our system to know about "mystery novels" as a concept or genre, and recommend products based on these genres. We call such variables "latent factors." They can be computed by supposing a specific number of such factors exist, say 50, and then transforming the large user-item matrix into a smaller matrix (actually, a pair of matrices) based on these 50 factors. These two matrices can be multiplied to reproduce (a close approximation to) the original user-item matrix. Using a technique called matrix factorization, we can find these two new matrices, sizes *M×F* and *N×F*, where *F* is the desired number of latent factors (commonly *F=50* or *F=100*), so that they multiply (after transposing the second matrix) to produce a close approximation to the original matrix. This factorization is shown diagrammatically in *Figure 1*.

The new matrices represent the *M* users as vectors of *F* factor weights, and the *N* items as vectors of *F* factor-weights. In other words, both users and items are now represented in terms of the strength of their relationships to each factor or genre.

Presumably, therefore, a user who loves mysteries will have a high weight on that factor, and likewise, the various mystery novels will have high weights on that same factor:

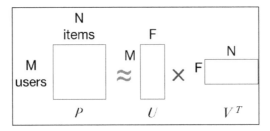

Figure 1: Matrix factorization of the user-item matrix, $P \approx UV^T$

Suppose we name the original user-items matrix P (dimensions $M \times N$ for M users and N items), the new user-factor matrix, U (dimensions $M \times F$ for M users and F factors), and the new item-factor matrix, V (dimensions $N \times F$ for N users and F factors), whose transpose, V^T (dimensions $F \times N$), will allow us to multiply U and V. Then the original P matrix can be reconstructed using normal matrix multiplication, that is, each value in the reconstruction of P, which we can call $\hat{P}$, can be computed as the dot-product of the corresponding row and column in U and V^T, respectively:

$$p_{ij} \approx \sum_{0 \leq f \leq F} u_{if} * v_{fj}$$

Appropriate values for the U and V matrices can yield a good approximation, that is, each $\hat{P}_{ij}$ in the reconstructed matrix is close or exactly the original value in the user-items matrix, P_{ij}. We can compute the overall error using what is known as a "loss function," and then gradually reduce this error or loss by adjusting the values in the U and V matrices. This process will be described in the following text.

Before we address how to find the values for U and V, we should take a moment to develop an intuition for what these latent factors represent and the kind of information the U and V matrices contain. Consider the Last.fm dataset containing user listen counts for a wide range of musical artists. We will take each single listen to be a form of implicit feedback. To match the code we develop later, we sometimes refer to listens as "purchases." By simulating a sequence of these listens, we can gradually build a user-artist matrix. Next, we can compute the U and V matrices with 50 factors. But how do we make sense of what these new U and V matrices contain?

We will focus on the V matrix since it represents musical artists, which make sense to us. Using **multidimensional scaling**, we can find a 2D coordinate for each artist in V such that the distances (similarities) between artists is represented proportionally as the distance between points on a 2D scatterplot.

In other words, two artists represented as points on a 2D scatterplot will be close together if their 50-dimensional vectors are similar, and the points will be far if the vectors are dissimilar. If we see artists grouped together in the scatterplot, we can say the cluster represents a genre of artists.

Figure 2 shows a scatterplot of artist similarity after applying multidimensional scaling of the 50-dimension factor vectors. We see that the distances between artists reflect their musical similarities or dissimilarities. Recall that these factor vectors resulted from matrix factorization of the user-artist listen matrix. In other words, the artists are clustered according to listening habits of users on Last.fm, that is, collaborative filtering, rather than any kind of similarity in the artists' biographies, genre labels, song titles, and so on, which would be content-based filtering. It is clear collaborative filtering can provide insight into how artists (and users, though we do not show user similarity here) relate to each other. It is also clear how collaborative filtering can yield a kind of artist recommendation service, for example, *users who listen to X also listen to Y*:

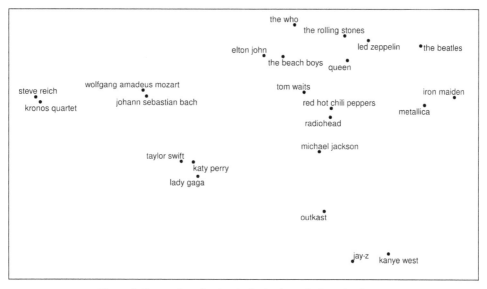

Figure 2: Scatterplot of artist similarity from the Last.fm dataset

Now that we have an intuition for what the user-factor and item-factor matrices, U and V, respectively, are representing, we are ready to see how the matrices are created. Since the purpose of U and V is to reproduce the original matrix P, our goal is to find U and V that minimize the error in reproducing the values of P:

$$\min_{u',v'} \sum_{i,j} \left(p_{ij} - \sum_{0 \le f \le F} u_{if} * v_{fj} \right)^2 + \lambda \left(\|u_i\|^2 + \|v_j\|^2 \right)$$

In this case, u' and v' represent the vectors (rows) of U and V, whose values we wish to find, and $\lambda(\|u_i\|^2 + \|v_j\|^2)$ is a regularizing parameter (where λ is a free parameter around 0.01) ensuring that we keep the values of U and V as small as possible to avoid overfitting. The notations $\|u_i\|$ and $\|v_j\|$ find the magnitude (distance to the origin) of a vector in U and V, so large values (large magnitudes) are penalized.

We cannot easily find both the optimal U and V simultaneously. In machine learning terminology, the optimization function stated in the preceding text is not convex, meaning there is not one single low point for the minimization, rather there are several local minima. If possible, we always prefer a convex function, so that we can use common techniques such as gradient descent to iteratively update values and find the single minimum state. However, if we hold the U matrix constant, or alternatively the V matrix, and then optimize for the other, we have a convex function. We can alternate which matrix is fixed, back-and-forth, thereby optimizing for both "simultaneously."

This technique is called **alternating least squares** (ALS) because we alternate between optimizing for minimum squared error (whose equation is shown in the preceding text) for the U and V matrices. Once formulated this way, a bit of calculus applied to the error function and gradient descent give us an update formula for each vector of U or V:

$$u_i \leftarrow u_i + \gamma\left(e_{ij}v_j - \lambda u_i\right)$$

$$v_j \leftarrow v_j + \gamma\left(e_{ij}u_i - \lambda v_j\right)$$

In this example, $e_{ij} = p_{ij} - \sum u_{if} * v_{fj}$ is the error for the matrix value at i,j. Note that the initial values of U and V before the algorithm begins may be set randomly to values between about -0.1 and 0.1. With ALS, since either U or V is fixed at each iteration, all rows in U or V can be updated in parallel in a single iteration. The `implicit` library makes good use of this fact by either creating lots of threads for these updates or using the massive parallelization available on a modern GPU. Refer to a paper by Koren and others in IEEE's *Computer* journal (*Koren, Yehuda, Robert Bell, and Chris Volinsky, Matrix factorization techniques for recommender systems, Computer Vol. 42, no. 8, pp. 42-49, 2009,* https://www.computer.org/csdl/mags/co/2009/08/mco2009080030-abs.html) for a good overview of ALS and Ben Frederickson's implementation notes for his `implicit` library (https://www.benfrederickson.com/matrix-factorization/).

Once the U and V matrices have been found, we can find similar items for a particular query item by finding the item vector whose dot-product (cosine similarity) with the query item's vector is maximal.

Likewise, for recommending items to a particular user, we take that user's vector and find the item vector with the maximal dot-product between the two. So, matrix factorization makes recommendation straightforward: to find similar items, take the item vector and find the most similar other item vectors. To recommend items for a particular user, take the user's vector and find the most similar item vectors. Both user and item vectors have the same 50 values since they are both represented in terms of the latent factors. Thus, they are directly comparable. Again, we can think of these latent factors as genres, so a user vector tells us how much a user prefers each genre, and an item vector tells us how closely an item matches each genre. Two user-item or item-item vectors are similar if they have the same combination of genres.

We usually want to find the top 3 or top 10 similar vectors. This is a nearest neighbor search because we want to find the closest (maximal) values among a set of vectors. A naive nearest neighbor algorithm requires comparing the query vector with every other vector, but a library such as `faiss` can build an index ahead of time and make this search significantly faster. Luckily, the `implicit` library includes `faiss` support, as well as other efficient nearest neighbor search libraries. The `implicit` library also provides a standard nearest neighbor search if none of the previously mentioned libraries, such as `faiss`, are installed.

Deployment strategy

We will build a simple recommendation system that may be easily integrated into an existing platform. Our recommendation system will be deployed as an isolated HTTP API with its own internal memory of purchases (or clicks, or listens, and so on), which is periodically saved to disk. For simplicity, we will not use a database in our code. Our API will offer recommendations for a particular user and recommendations for similar items. It will also keep track of its accuracy, explained further in the *Continuous evaluation* section.

The bulk of the features of our recommendation system are provided by Ben Frederickson's `implicit` library (`https://github.com/benfred/implicit`), named as such because it computes recommendations from implicit feedback. The library supports the ALS algorithm for computing the matrix factorization described previously. It can use an internal nearest neighbor search or `faiss` (`https://github.com/facebookresearch/faiss`) if installed, and other similar libraries.

The `implicit` library and ALS algorithm generally are designed for batch model updates. By "batch," we mean that the algorithm requires that all the user-item information is known ahead of time and the factored matrices will be built from scratch.

Batch model training usually takes a significant amount of processing time (at least, it cannot be done in real-time, that is, some low number of milliseconds), so it must be done ahead of time or in a separate processing thread as real-time recommendation generation. The alternative to batch training is online model training, where the model may be extended in real-time. The reason that recommendation systems usually cannot support online training is that matrix factorization requires that the entire user-item matrix is known ahead of time. After the matrix is factored into user and item factor matrices, it is non-trivial to add a new column and row to the U or V matrices or to update any of the values based on a user's purchase. All other values in the matrices would require updating as well, resulting in a full factorization process again. However, some researchers have found clever ways to perform online matrix factorization (*Google news personalization: scalable online collaborative filtering, Das, Abhinandan S., Mayur Datar, Ashutosh Garg,* and *Shyam Rajaram,* in *Proceedings of the 16th international conference on World Wide Web, pp. 271-280, ACM, 2007,* https:// dl.acm.org/citation.cfm?id=1242610). Alternative approaches that do not use matrix factorization have also been developed, such as the recommendation system used by Google News (*Google news personalization: scalable online collaborative filtering, Das, Abhinandan S., Mayur Datar, Ashutosh Garg,* and *Shyam Rajaram,* in *Proceedings of the 16th international conference on World Wide Web, pp. 271-280, ACM, 2007,* https:// dl.acm.org/citation.cfm?id=1242610), which must handle new users and new items (published news articles) on a continuous basis.

In order to simulate online model updates, our system will periodically batch-retrain its recommendation model. Luckily, the `implicit` library is fast. Model training takes a few seconds at most with on the order of 10^6 users and items. Most of the time is spent collecting a Python list of purchases into a `NumPy` matrix that is required by the `implicit` library.

We also use the popular `Flask` library (http://flask.pocoo.org) to provide an HTTP API. Our API supports the following requests:

- `/purchased` (POST) – parameters: User id, username, product id, product name; we only request the username and product name for logging purposes; they are not necessary for generating recommendations with collaborative filtering.
- `/recommend` (GET) – parameters: User id, product id; the product id is the product being viewed by the user.
- `/update-model` (POST) – no parameters; this request retrains the model.
- `/user-purchases` (GET) – parameters: User id; this request is for debugging purposes to see all purchases (or clicks, or likes, and so on) from this user.
- `/stats` (GET) – no parameters; this request is for continuous evaluation, described in the following section.

Although our API refers to purchases, it may be used to keep track of any kind of implicit feedback, such as clicks, likes, listens, and so on.

We use several global variables to keep track of various data structures. We use a thread lock to update these data structures across various requests since the `Flask` HTTP server supports multiple simultaneous connections:

```
model = None
model_lock = threading.Lock()
purchases = {}
purchases_pickle = Path('purchases.pkl')
userids = []
userids_reverse = {}
usernames = {}
productids = []
productids_reverse = []
productnames = {}
purchases_matrix = None
purchases_matrix_T = None
stats = {'purchase_count': 0, 'user_rec': 0}
```

The `model` variable holds the trained model (an object of the `FaissAlternatingLeastSquares` class from the `implicit` library), and `model_lock` protects write access to the model and many of these other global variables. The `purchases_matrix` and `purchases_matrix_T` variables hold the original matrix of purchases and its transpose. The `purchases` dictionary holds the history of user purchases; its keys are `userids`, and its values are further dictionaries, with `productid` keys and user-product purchase count values (integers). This dictionary is saved to disk whenever the model is updated, using the `pickle` library and the file referred to by `purchases_pickle`. In order to generate recommendations for a particular user and to find similar items for a particular product, we need a mapping from `userid` to matrix row and `productid` to matrix column. We also need a reverse mapping. Additionally, for logging purposes, we would like to see the username and product names, so we have a mapping from `userids` to usernames and `productids` to product names. The variables `userids`, `userids_reverse`, `usernames`, `productids`, `productids_reverse`, and `productnames` variables hold this information. Finally, the `stats` dictionary holds data used in our evaluation to keep track of the recommendation system's accuracy.

The `/purchased` request is straightforward. Ignoring the continuous evaluation code, which will be discussed later, we simply need to update our records of the users' purchases:

```
@app.route('/purchased', methods=['POST'])
def purchased():
```

```
global purchases, usernames, productnames
userid = request.form['userid'].strip()
username = request.form['username'].strip()
productid = request.form['productid'].strip()
productname = request.form['productname'].strip()
with model_lock:
  usernames[userid] = username
  productnames[productid] = productname
  if userid not in purchases:
    purchases[userid] = {}
  if productid not in purchases[userid]:
    purchases[userid][productid] = 0
  purchases[userid][productid] += 1
return 'OK\n'
```

Next, we have a simple /update-model request that calls our fit_model function:

```
@app.route('/update-model', methods=['POST'])
def update_model():
  fit_model()
  return 'OK\n'
```

Now for the interesting code. The fit_model function will update several global variables, and starts by saving the purchase history to a file:

```
def fit_model():
  global model, userids, userids_reverse, productids,\
productids_reverse, purchases_matrix, purchases_matrix_T
  with model_lock:
    app.logger.info("Fitting model...")
    start = time.time()
    with open(purchases_pickle, 'wb') as f:
      pickle.dump((purchases, usernames, productnames), f)
```

Next we create a new model object. If faiss is not installed (only implicit is installed), we can use this line of code:

```
model = AlternatingLeastSquares(factors=64, dtype=np.float32)
```

If faiss is installed, the nearest neighbor search will be much faster. We can then use this line of code instead:

```
model = FaissAlternatingLeastSquares(factors=64, dtype=np.float32)
```

The factors argument gives the size of the factored matrices. More factors result in a larger model, and it is non-obvious whether or not a larger model will be more accurate.

Next, we need to build a user-item matrix. We will iterate through the record of user purchases (built from calls to /purchased) to build three lists with an equal number of elements: the purchase counts, the user ids, and the product ids. We construct the matrix with these three lists because the matrix will be sparse (lots of missing values, that is, 0 values) since most users do not purchase most items. We can save considerable space in memory by only keeping track of non-zero values:

```
data = {'userid': [], 'productid': [], 'purchase_count': []}
for userid in purchases:
  for productid in purchases[userid]:
    data['userid'].append(userid)
    data['productid'].append(productid)
    data['purchase_count'].append(purchases[userid][productid])
```

These lists have `userids` and `productids`. We need to convert these to integer ids for the `faiss` library. We can use the `DataFrame` class of `pandas` to generate "categories," that is, integer codes for the `userids` and `productids`. At the same time, we save the reverse mappings:

```
df = pd.DataFrame(data)
df['userid'] = df['userid'].astype("category")
df['productid'] = df['productid'].astype("category")
userids = list(df['userid'].cat.categories)
userids_reverse = dict(zip(userids, list(range(len(userids)))))
productids = list(df['productid'].cat.categories)
productids_reverse = \
dict(zip(productids, list(range(len(productids)))))
```

Now we can create our user-items matrix using the `coo_matrix` constructor of `SciPy`. This function creates a sparse matrix using the lists of purchase counts, user ids, and product ids (after translating the `userids` and `productids` to integers). Note that we are actually generating an item-users matrix rather than a user-item matrix, due to peculiarities in the `implicit` library:

```
purchases_matrix = coo_matrix(
(df['purchase_count'].astype(np.float32),
(df['productid'].cat.codes.copy(),
df['userid'].cat.codes.copy())))
```

Now we use the BM25 weighting function of `implicit` library to recalculate the values in the matrix:

```
purchases_matrix = bm25_weight(purchases_matrix, K1=1.2, B=0.5)
```

We can also generate the transpose of the item-users matrix to get a user-item matrix for finding recommended items for a particular user. The requirements for the matrix structure (users as rows and items as columns, or items as rows and users as columns) are set by the `implicit` library – there is no specific theoretical reason the matrix must be one way or the other, as long as all corresponding functions agree in how they use it:

```
purchases_matrix_T = purchases_matrix.T.tocsr()
```

Finally, we can fit the model with alternating least squares:

```
model.fit(purchases_matrix)
```

The `/recommend` request generates user-specific recommendations and similar item recommendations. First, we check that we know about this user and item. It is possible that the user or item is not yet known, pending a model update:

```
@app.route('/recommend', methods=['GET'])
def recommend():
  userid = request.args['userid'].strip()
  productid = request.args['productid'].strip()
  if model is None or userid not in usernames or \
productid not in productnames:
    abort(500)
  else:
    result = {}
```

If we know about the user and item, we can generate a result with two keys: `user-specific` and `product-specific`. For user-specific recommendations, we call the `recommend` function of `implicit`. The return value is a list of product indexes, which we translate to product ids and names, and confidence scores (cosine similarities):

```
result['user-specific'] = []
for prodidx, score in model.recommend(
userids_reverse[userid], purchases_matrix_T, N=10):
  result['user-specific'].append(
(productnames[productids[prodidx]],
productids[prodidx], float(score)))
```

For item-specific recommendations, we call `similar_items` function of `implicit`, and we skip over the product referred to in the request so that we do not recommend the same product a user is viewing:

```
result['product-specific'] = []
for prodidx, score in model.similar_items(
```

```
productids_reverse[productid], 10):
  if productids[prodidx] != productid:
    result['product-specific'].append(
(productnames[productids[prodidx]], productids[prodidx],
float(score))))
```

Finally, we return a JSON format of the result:

```
return json.dumps(result)
```

The HTTP API can be started with `Flask`:

```
export FLASK_APP=http_api.py
export FLASK_ENV=development
flask run --port=5001
```

After training on the Last.fm dataset for a while (details are given in the following text), we can query for similar artists. The following table shows the top-3 nearest neighbor of some example artists. As with the scatterplot in *Figure 2*, these similarities are computed solely on users' listening patterns:

Query Artist	Similar Artists	Similarity
The Beatles	The Rolling Stones	0.971
	The Who	0.964
	The Beach Boys	0.960
Metallica	Iron Maiden	0.965
	System of a Down	0.958
	Pantera	0.957
Kanye West	Lupe Fiasco	0.966
	Jay-Z	0.963
	Outkast	0.940
Autechre	Aphex Twin	0.958
	AFX	0.954
	Squarepusher	0.945
Kronos Quartet	Philip Glass	0.905
	Erik Satie	0.904
	Steve Reich	0.884

After training on the Amazon dataset for a while (details in the following text), we can query for product recommendations for particular customers. A person who previously bought the book *Not for Parents: How to be a World Explorer (Lonely Planet Not for Parents)* was recommended these two books, among other items (such as soaps and pasta):

- Score: 0.74 - *Lonely Planet Pocket New York (Travel Guide)*
- Score: 0.72 - *Lonely Planet Discover New York City (Travel Guide)*

Interestingly, these recommendations appear to come solely from the customer previously buying the *Not for Parents* book. A quick examination of the dataset shows that other customers who bought that book also bought other *Lonely Planet* books. Note that in a twist of fate, the customer in question actually ended up buying *Lonely Planet Discover Las Vegas (Travel Guide)*, which was not recommended (since no one else had bought it before in the portion of the dataset the system had seen so far).

In another case, the system recommended *Wiley AP English Literature and Composition*, presumably based on this customer's purchase of *Wiley AP English Language and Composition*.

In one of the oddest cases, the system recommended the following items to a customer, with corresponding similarity scores:

- Score: 0.87 - *Barilla Whole Grain Thin Spaghetti Pasta, 13.25 Ounce Boxes (Pack of 4)*
- Score: 0.83 - *Knorr Pasta Sides, Thai Sweet Chili, 4.5 Ounce (Pack of 12)*
- Score: 0.80 - *Dove Men + Care Body and Face Bar, Extra Fresh, 4 Ounce, 8 Count*
- Score: 0.79 - *Knorr Roasters Roasting Bag and Seasoning Blend for Chicken, Garlic Parmesan, and Italian Herb, 1.02 Ounce Packages (Pack of 12)*
- Score: 0.76 - *Barilla Penne Plus, 14.5 Ounce Boxes (Pack of 8)*
- Score: 0.75 - *ANCO C-16-UB Contour Wiper Blade – 16", (Pack of 1)*

Discounting the pasta, the wiper blades and soap stand out as odd recommendations. Yet when the recommendation was generated, the customer, in fact, bought these exact wiper blades. Examining the dataset shows that these wiper blades are somewhat common, and curiously one of the customers who bought some of the *Lonely Planet* guides also bought these wiper blades.

These examples show that the recommendation system is able to pick up on user and item similarities that are non-obvious at face value. It is also able to identify similar items based on user purchase (or listening) histories. How well the system works in practice is the focus of our next section.

Continuous evaluation

A recommendation system may be evaluated in two ways: offline and online. In the offline evaluation, also known as batch evaluation, the total history of user purchases is segregated into to random subsets, a large training subset (typically 80%) and a small testing subset (typically 20%). The matrix factorization procedure is then used on the 80% training subset to build a recommendation model.

Next, with this trained model, each record in the testing subset is evaluated against the model. If the model predicts that the user would purchase the item with sufficient confidence, and indeed the user purchased the item in the testing subset, then we record a "true positive." If the model predicts a purchase but the user did not purchase the item, we record a "false positive." If the model fails to predict a purchase, it is a "false negative," and if it predicts the user will not purchase the item and indeed they do not, we have a "true negative." With these true/false positive/negative counts, we can calculate precision and recall.

Precision is *TP/(TP+FP)*, in other words, the ratio of purchases predicted by the model that were actual purchases. The recall is *TP/(TP+FN)*, the ratio of actual purchases that the model predicted. Naturally, we want both measures to be high (near 1.0). Normally, precision and recall are a tradeoff: just by increasing the likelihood the system will predict a purchase (that is, lowering its required confidence level), we can earn a higher recall at the cost of precision. By being more discriminatory, we can lower recall while raising precision. Whether high precision or high recall is preferred depends on the application and business use case. For example, a higher precision but a lower recall would ensure that nearly all recommendations that are shown are actually purchased by the user. This could give the impression that the recommendation works really well, while it is possible the user would have purchased even more items if they were recommended.

On the other hand, a higher recall but lower precision could result in showing the user more recommendations, some or many of which they do not purchase. At different points in this sliding scale, the recommendation system is either showing the user too few or too many recommendations. Each application needs to find its ideal trade off, usually from trial and error and an online evaluation, described in the following text.

Another offline approach often used with explicit feedback, such as numeric ratings from product reviews, is **root mean square error (RMSE)**, computed as:

$$E = \sqrt{\left(\frac{1}{N}\right)\sum(\hat{r}_i - r_i)^2}$$

In this case, N is the number of ratings in the testing subset, $\hat{r}_i$ is the predicted rating, and r_i is the actual rating. With this metric, lower is better. This metric is similar to the optimization criteria from the matrix factorization technique described previously. The goal there was to minimize the squared error by finding the optimal U and V matrices for approximating the original user-item matrix P.

Since we are interested in implicit ratings (1.0 or 0.0) rather than explicit numeric ratings, precision and recall are more appropriate measures than RMSE. Next, we will look at a way to calculate precision and recall in order to determine the best BM25 parameters for a dataset.

Calculating precision and recall for BM25 weighting

As a kind of offline evaluation, we next look at precision and recall for the MovieLens dataset (https://grouplens.org/datasets/movielens/20m/) across a range of BM25 parameters. This dataset has about 20 million ratings, scored 1-5, of thousands of movies by 138,000 users. We will turn these ratings into implicit data by considering any rating of 3.0 or higher to be positive implicit feedback and ratings below 3.0 to be non-existent feedback. If we do this, we will be left with about 10 million implicit values. The `implicit` library has this dataset built-in:

```
from implicit.datasets.movielens import get_movielens
_, ratings = get_movielens('20m')
```

We ignore the first returned value, the movie titles, of `get_movielens()` because we have no use for the titles.

Our goal is to study the impact of different BM25 parameters on precision and recall. We will iterate through several combinations of BM25 parameters and a confidence parameter. The confidence parameter will determine whether a predicted score is sufficiently high to predict that a particular user positively rated a particular movie. A low confidence parameter should produce more false positives, everything else being equal, than a high confidence parameter. We will save our output to a CSV file. We start by printing the column headers, then we iterate through each parameter combination. We also repeat each combination multiple times to get an average:

```
print("B,K1,Confidence,TP,FP,FN,Precision,Recall")
confidences = [0.0, 0.2, 0.4, 0.6, 0.8]
for iteration in range(5):
  seed = int(time.time())
  for conf in confidences:
    np.random.seed(seed)
    experiment(0.0, 0.0, conf)
```

```
for conf in confidences:
  np.random.seed(seed)
  experiment("NA", "NA", conf)
for B in [0.25, 0.50, 0.75, 1.0]:
  for K1 in [1.0, 3.0]:
    for conf in confidences:
      np.random.seed(seed)
      experiment(B, K1, conf)
```

Since $B=0$ is equivalent to $K1=0$ in BM25, we do not need to iterate over other values of B or $K1$ when either equals 0. Also, we will try cases with BM25 weighting turned off, indicated by $B=K1=NA$.

We will randomly hide (remove) some of the ratings and then attempt to predict them again. We do not want various parameter combinations to hide *different* random ratings. Rather, we want to ensure each parameter combination is tested on the same situation, so they are comparable. Only when we re-evaluate all the parameters in another iteration do we wish to choose a different random subset of ratings to hide. Hence, we establish a random seed at the beginning of each iteration and then use the same seed before running each experiment.

Our `experiment` function receives the parameters dictating the experiment. This function needs to load the data, randomly hide some of it, train a recommendation model, and then predict the implicit feedback of a subset of users for a subset of movies. Then, it needs to calculate precision and recall and print that information in CSV format.

While developing this function, we will make use of several NumPy features. Because we have relatively large datasets, we want to avoid, at all costs, any Python loops that manipulate the data. NumPy uses **Basic Linear Algebra Subprograms** (**BLAS**) to efficiently compute dot-products and matrix multiplications, possibly with parallelization (as with OpenBLAS). We should utilize NumPy array functions as much as possible to take advantage of these speedups.

We begin by loading the dataset and converting numeric ratings into implicit ratings:

```
def experiment(B, K1, conf, variant='20m', min_rating=3.0):
  # read in the input data file
  _, ratings = get_movielens(variant)
  ratings = ratings.tocsr()

  # remove things < min_rating, and convert to implicit dataset
  # by considering ratings as a binary preference only
  ratings.data[ratings.data < min_rating] = 0
  ratings.eliminate_zeros()
```

```
ratings.data = np.ones(len(ratings.data))
```

The 3.0+ ratings are very sparse. Only 0.05% of values in the matrix are non-zero after converting to implicit ratings. Thus, we make extensive use of SciPy's sparse matrix support. There are various kinds of sparse matrix data structures: **compressed sparse row matrix (CSR)**, and **row-based linked-list sparse matrix (LIL)**, among others. The CSR format allows us to directly access the data in the matrix as a linear array of values. We set all values to 1.0 to construct our implicit scores.

Next, we need to hide some ratings. To do this, we will start by creating a copy of the rating matrix before modifying it. Since we will be removing ratings, we'll convert the matrix to LIL format for efficient row removal:

```
training = ratings.tolil()
```

Next, we randomly choose a number of movies and a number of users. These are the row/column positions that we will set to 0 in order to hide some data that we will use later for evaluation. Note, due to the sparsity of the data, most of these row/column values will already be zeros:

```
movieids = np.random.randint(
low=0, high=np.shape(ratings)[0], size=100000)
userids = np.random.randint(
low=0, high=np.shape(ratings)[1], size=100000)
```

Now we set those ratings to 0:

```
training[movieids, userids] = 0
```

Next, we set up the ALS model and turn off some features we will not be using:

```
model = FaissAlternatingLeastSquares(factors=128, iterations=30)
model.approximate_recommend = False
model.approximate_similar_items = False
model.show_progress = False
```

If we have *B* and *K1* parameters (that is, they are not NA), we apply BM25 weighting:

```
if B != "NA":
    training = bm25_weight(training, B=B, K1=K1)
```

Now we train the model:

```
model.fit(training)
```

Once the model is trained, we want to generate predictions for those ratings we removed. We do not wish to use the model's recommendation functions since we have no need to perform a nearest neighbor search. Rather, we just want to know the predictions for those missing values.

Recall that the ALS method uses matrix factorization to produce an items-factors matrix and a users-factors matrix (in our case, a movies-factors matrix and users-factors matrix). The factors are latent factors that somewhat represent genres. Our model constructor established that we will have 128 factors. The factor matrices can be obtained from the model:

```
model.item_factors # a matrix with dimensions: (# of movies, 128)
model.user_factors # a matrix with dimensions: (# of users, 128)
```

Suppose we want to find the predicted value for movie i and user j. Then `model.item_factors[i]` will give us a 1D array with 128 values, and `model.user_factors[j]` will give us another 1D array with 128 values. We can apply a dot-product to these two vectors to get the predicted rating:

```
np.dot(model.item_factors[i], model.user_factors[j])
```

However, we want to check on lots of user/movie combinations, 100,000 in fact. We must avoid running `np.dot()` in a `for()` loop in Python because doing so would be horrendously slow. Luckily, NumPy has an (oddly named) function called `einsum` for summation using the "Einstein summation convention," also known as "Einstein notation." This notation allows us to collect lots of item factors and user factors together and then apply the dot product to each. Without this notation, NumPy would think we are performing matrix multiplication since the two inputs would be matrices. Instead, we want to collect 100,000 individual item factors, producing a 2D array size (100000,128), and 100,000 individual user factors, producing another 2D array of the same size. If we were to perform matrix multiplication, we would have to transpose the second one (yielding size (128,100000)),resulting in a matrix size of (100000,100000), which would require 38 GB in memory. With such a matrix, we would only use the 100,000 diagonal values, so all that work and memory for multiplying the matrices is a waste. Using Einstein notation, we can indicate that two 2D matrices are inputs, but we want the dot products to be applied row-wise: `ij,ij->i`. The first two values, `ij`, indicate both input formats, and the value after the arrow indicates how they should be grouped when computing the dot-products. We write `i` to indicate they should be grouped by their first dimensions. If we wrote `j`, the dot products would be computed by column rather than row, and if we wrote `ij`, then each value with dot-product itself (that is, return its own value). In NumPy, we write:

```
moviescores = np.einsum('ij,ij->i', model.item_factors[movieids],
model.user_factors[userids])
```

The result is 100,000 predicted scores, each corresponding to ratings we hid when we loaded the dataset.

Next, we apply the confidence threshold to get boolean predicted values:

```
preds = (moviescores >= conf)
```

We also need to grab the original (true) values. We use the `ravel` function to return a 1D array of the same size as the `preds` boolean array:

```
true_ratings = np.ravel(ratings[movieids,userids])
```

Now we can calculate TP, FP, and FN. For TP, we check that the predicted rating was a True and the true rating was a 1.0. This is accomplished by summing the values from the true ratings at the positions where the model predicted there would be a 1.0 rating. In other words, we use the boolean `preds` array as the positions to pull out of the `true_ratings` array. Since the true ratings are 1.0 or 0.0, a simple summation suffices to count the 1.0s:

```
tp = true_ratings[preds].sum()
```

For FP, we want to know how many predicted 1.0 ratings were false, that is, they were 0.0s in the true ratings. This is straightforward, as we simply count how many ratings were predicted to be 1.0 and subtract the TP. This leaves behind all the "positive" (1.0) predictions that are not true:

```
fp = preds.sum() - tp
```

Finally, for FN, we count the number of true 1.0 ratings and subtract all the ones we correctly predicted (TP). This leaves behind the count of 1.0 ratings we should have predicted but did not:

```
fn = true_ratings.sum() - tp
```

All that is left now is to calculate precision and recall and print the statistics:

```
if tp+fp == 0:
  prec = float('nan')
else:
  prec = float(tp)/float(tp+fp)
if tp+fn == 0:
  recall = float('nan')
else:
  recall = float(tp)/float(tp+fn)
if B != "NA":
  print("%.2f,%.2f,%.2f,%d,%d,%d,%.2f,%.2f" % \
(B, K1, conf, tp, fp, fn, prec, recall))
else:
```

```
    print("NA,NA,%.2f,%d,%d,%d,%.2f,%.2f" % \
  (conf, tp, fp, fn, prec, recall))
```

The results of the experiment are shown in *Figure 3*. In this plot, we see the tradeoff between precision and recall. The best place to be is in the upper-right, where precision and recall are both high. The confidence parameter determines the relationship between precision and recall for given *B* and *K1* parameters. A larger confidence parameter sets a higher threshold for predicting a 1.0 rating, so higher confidence yields less recall but greater precision. For each *B* and *K1* parameter combination, we vary the confidence value to create a line. Normally, we would use a confidence value in the range of 0.25 to 0.75, but it is instructive to see the effect of a wider range of values. The confidence values are marked on the right side of the solid line curve.

We see that different values for *B* and *K1* yield different performance. In fact, with *B=K1=0* and confidence about 0.50, we get the best performance. Recall that with these *B* and *K1* values, BM25 effectively yields the IDF value. This tells us that the most accurate way to predict implicit ratings in this dataset is to consider only the number of ratings for the user. Thus, if this user positively rates a lot of movies, he or she will likely positively rate this one as well. It is curious however that BM25 weighting does not provide much value for this dataset, though using the IDF values is better than using the original 1.0/0.0 scores (that is, no BM25 weighting, indicated by the "NA" line in the plot):

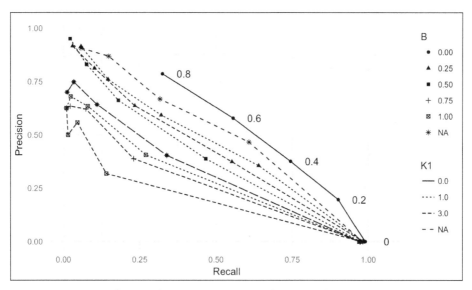

Figure 3: Precision-Recall curves for various parameters of BM25 weighting on the MovieLens dataset

Online evaluation of our recommendation system

Our main interest in this chapter is an online evaluation. Recall that offline evaluation asks how well the recommendation system is able to predict that a user will *ever* purchase a particular item. An online evaluation methodology, on the other hand, measures how well the system is able to predict the user's *next* purchase. This metric is similar to the click-through rate for advertisements and other kinds of links. Every time a purchase is registered, our system will ask which user-specific recommendations were shown to the user (or could have been shown) and keep track of how often the user purchased one of the recommended items. We will compute the ratio of purchases that were recommended versus all purchases.

We will update our /purchased API request to calculate whether the product being purchased was among the top-10 items recommended for this user. Before doing so, however, we also check a few conditions. First, we will check whether the trained model exists (that is, a call to /update-model has occurred). Secondly, we will see if we know about this user *and* this product. If this test fails, the system could not have possibly recommended the product to the user because it either did not know about this user (so the user has no corresponding vector in *U*) or does not know about this product (so there is no corresponding vector in *V*). We should not penalize the system for failing to recommend to users or recommend products that it knows nothing about. We also check whether this user has purchased at least 10 items to ensure we have enough information about the user to make recommendations, and we check that the recommendations are at least somewhat confident. We should not penalize the system for making bad recommendations if it was never confident about those recommendations in the first place:

```
# check if we know this user and product already
# and we could have recommended this product
if model is not None and userid in userids_reverse and \
productid in productids_reverse:
  # check if we have enough history for this user
  # to bother with recommendations
  user_purchase_count = 0
  for productid in purchases[userid]:
    user_purchase_count += purchases[userid][productid]
  if user_purchase_count >= 10:
    # keep track if we ever compute a confident recommendation
    confident = False
    # check if this product was recommended as
    # a user-specific recommendation
    for prodidx, score in model.recommend(
userids_reverse[userid], purchases_matrix_T, N=10):
```

```
    if score >= 0.5:
      confident = True
      # check if we matched the product
      if productids[prodidx] == productid:
        stats['user_rec'] += 1
        break
  if confident:
    # record the fact we were confident and
    # should have matched the product
    stats['purchase_count'] += 1
```

We demonstrate the system's performance on two datasets: Last.fm listens and Amazon.com purchases. In fact, the Amazon dataset contains reviews not purchases, but we will consider each review to be evidence of purchase.

The Last.fm dataset (`https://www.dtic.upf.edu/~ocelma/ MusicRecommendationDataset/lastfm-360K.html`) contains the count of listens for each user and each artist. For an online evaluation, we need to simulate listens over time. Since the dataset contains no information about when each user listened to each artist, we will randomize the sequence of listens. Thus, we take each user-listen count and generate the same number of single listens. If user X listened to *Radiohead* 100 times in total, as found in the dataset, we generate 100 separate single-listens of *Radiohead* for user X. Then we shuffle all these listens across all users and feed them, one at a time, to the API through the `/purchased` request. With every 10,000 listens, we update the model and record statistics about the number of listens and correct recommendations. The left side of *Figure 4*, shows the percent age of times a user was recommended to listen to artist Y and the user actually listened to artist Y when the recommendation was generated. We can see that the accuracy of recommendations declined after an initial model building phase. This is a sign of overfitting and might be fixed by adjusting the BM25 weighting parameters (*K1* and *B*) for this dataset or changing the number of latent factors.

The Amazon dataset (`http://jmcauley.ucsd.edu/data/amazon/`) contains product reviews with timestamps. We will ignore the actual review score (even low scores) and consider each review as an indication of a purchase. We sequence the reviews by their timestamps and feed them into the `/purchased` API one at a time. For every 10,000 purchases, we update the model and compute statistics. The right side of *Figure 4*, shows the ratio of purchases that were also recommended to the user at the time of purchase. We see that the model gradually learned to recommend items and achieved 8% accuracy.

Note that in both graphs, the x-axis shows the number of purchases (or listens) for which a confident recommendation was generated. This number is far less than the number of purchases since we do not recommend products if we know nothing about the user or the product being purchased yet, or we have no confident recommendation. Thus, significantly more data was processed than the numbers of the x-axis indicate. Also, these percentages (between 3% and 8%) seem low when comparing to offline recommendation system accuracies in terms of RMSE or similar metrics. This is because our online evaluation is measuring whether a user purchases an item that is presently being recommended to them, such as **click-through rate (CTR)** on advertisements. Offline evaluations check whether a user *ever* purchased an item that was recommended. As a CTR metric, 3-8% is quite high (*Mailchimp, Average Email Campaign Stats of MailChimp Customers by Industry, March 2018,* `https://mailchimp.com/resources/research/email-marketing-benchmarks/`):

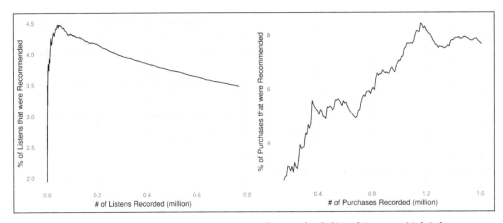

Figure 4: Accuracy of the recommendation system for Last.fm (left) and Amazon (right) datasets

These online evaluation statistics may be generated over time, as purchases occur. Thus, they can be used to provide live, continuous evaluation of the system. In *Chapter 3, A Blueprint for Making Sense of Feedback,* we developed a live-updating plot of the internet's sentiment about particular topics. We could use the same technology here to show a live-updating plot of the recommendation system's accuracy. Using insights developed in *Chapter 6, A Blueprint for Discovering Trends and Recognizing Anomalies,* we can then detect anomalies, or sudden changes in accuracy, and throw alerts to figure out what changed in the recommendation system or the data provided to it.

Summary

This chapter developed a recommendation system with a wide range of use cases. We looked at content-based filtering to find similar items based on the items' titles and descriptions, and more extensively at collaborative filtering, which considers users' interests in the items rather than the items' content. Since we focused on implicit feedback, our collaborative filtering recommendation system does not need user ratings or other numeric scores to represent user preferences. Only passive data collection suffices to generate enough knowledge to make recommendations. Such passive data may include purchases, listens, clicks, and so on.

After collecting data for some users, along with their purchase/listen/click patterns, we used matrix factorization to represent how users and items relate and to reduce the size of the data. The `implicit` and `faiss` libraries are used to make an effective recommendation system, and the `Flask` library is used to create a simple HTTP API that is general purpose and easily integrated into an existing platform. Finally, we reviewed the performance of the recommendation system with Last.fm and Amazon datasets. Importantly, we developed an online evaluation that allows us to monitor the recommendation system's performance over time to detect changes and ensure it continues to operate with sufficient accuracy.

5
A Blueprint for Detecting Your Logo in Social Media

For much of the history of AI research and applications, working with images was particularly difficult. In the early days, machines could barely hold images in their small memories, let alone process them. Computer vision as a subfield of AI and ML made significant strides throughout the 1990s and 2000s with the proliferation of cheap hardware, webcams and new and improved processing-intensive algorithms such as **feature detection** and **optical flow**, **dimensionality reduction**, and 3D reconstruction from stereo images. Through this entire time, extracting good features from images required a bit of cleverness and luck. A face recognition algorithm, for example, could not do its job if the image features provided to the algorithm were insufficiently distinctive. Computer vision techniques for feature extraction included convolutions (such as blurring, dilation, edge detection, and so on); principal component analysis to reduce the dimensions of a set of images; corner, circle, and line detection; and so on. Once features were extracted, a second algorithm would examine these features and learn to recognize different faces, recognize objects, track vehicles, and other use cases. If we look specifically at the use case of classifying images, for example, labeling a photo as "cat," "dog," "boat," and so on, neural networks were often used due to their success at classifying other kinds of data such as audio and text. The input features for the neural network included an image's color distribution, edge direction histograms, and spatial moments (that is, the image's orientation or locations of bright regions). Notably, these features are generated from the image's pixels but do not include the pixels themselves. Running a neural network on a list of pixel color values, without any feature extraction pre-processing, yielded poor results.

The new approach, **deep learning** (**DL**), figures out the best features on its own, saving us significant time and saving us from engaging in a lot of guesswork. This chapter will demonstrate how to use DL to recognize logos in photos. We will grab these photos from Twitter, and we'll be looking for soft drinks and beer.

Along the way, we will examine how neural networks and DL work and demonstrate the use of state-of-the-art open source software.

In this chapter, together we will cover and explore:

- How neural networks and DL are used for image processing
- How to use an application of DL for detecting and recognizing brand logos in images
- The `Keras` library, part of `TensorFlow`, and **YOLO** for the purpose of image classification

The rise of machine learning

The first thing we must do is to examine the recent and dramatic increase in the adoption of **ML**, specifically with respect to image processing. In 2016, *The Economist* wrote a story titled, *From not working to neural networking* about the yearly **ImageNet Large Scale Visual Recognition Challenge (ILSVRC)**, which started in 2010 and finalized in 2017 (*From not working to neural networking*, The Economist, June 25, 2016, `https://www.economist.com/special-report/2016/06/25/from-not-working-to-neural-networking`). This competition challenged researchers to develop techniques for labeling millions of photos of 1,000 everyday objects. Humans would, on average, label these photos correctly about 95% of the time. Image classification algorithms, such as those we alluded to previously, performed at best with 72% accuracy in the first year of the competition. In 2011, the algorithms were improved to achieve 74% accuracy.

In 2012, *Krizhevsky*, *Sutskever*, and *Hinton* from the University of Toronto cleverly combined several existing ideas known as **convolutional neural networks (CNN)** and **max pooling**, added **rectified linear units (ReLUs)** and GPU processing for significant speedups, and built a neural network composed of several "layers." These extra network layers led to the rise of the term "deep learning," resulting in an accuracy jump to 85% (*ImageNet classification with deep convolutional neural networks, Krizhevsky, Alex, Ilya Sutskever*, and *Geoffrey E. Hinton*, in *Advances in neural information processing systems, pp. 1097-1105, 2012,* `http://papers.nips.cc/paper/4824-imagenet-classification-with-deep-convolutional-neural-networks.pdf`). In the five following years, this fundamental design has been refined to achieve 97% accuracy, which was beating the human performance. The rise of DL and the rejuvenation of interest in ML began here. Their paper about this new DL approach, titled *ImageNet classification with deep convolutional neural networks*, has been cited nearly 29,000 times, at a dramatically increasing rate over the years:

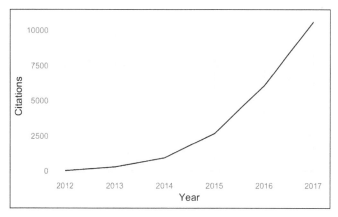

Figure 1: Count of citations per year of the paper, *ImageNet classification with deep convolutional neural networks*, according to Google Scholar

The key contribution of their work was showing how you could achieve dramatically improved performance while simultaneously completely avoiding the need for feature extraction. The deep neural network does it all: the input is the image without any pre-processing, the output is the predicted classification. Less work, and greater accuracy! Even better, this approach was quickly shown to work well in a number of other domains besides image classification. Today, we use DL for speech recognition, NLP, and so much more.

A recent *Nature* paper, titled *Deep learning (Deep learning, LeCun, Yann, Yoshua Bengio, and Geoffrey Hinton, Nature 521(7553), pp. 436-444, 2015)*, summarizes its benefits:

> *Deep learning is making major advances in solving problems that have resisted the best attempts of the artificial intelligence community for many years. It has turned out to be very good at discovering intricate structures in high-dimensional data and is therefore applicable to many domains of science, business, and government. In addition to beating records in image recognition and speech recognition, it has beaten other machine-learning techniques at predicting the activity of potential drug molecules, analyzing particle accelerator data, reconstructing brain circuits, and predicting the effects of mutations in non-coding DNA on gene expression and disease. Perhaps more surprisingly, deep learning has produced extremely promising results for various tasks in natural language understanding, particularly topic classification, sentiment analysis, question answering, and language translation.*

> *We think that deep learning will have many more successes in the near future because it requires very little engineering by hand, so it can easily take advantage of increases in the amount of available computation and data. New learning algorithms and architectures that are currently being developed for deep neural networks will only accelerate this progress.*

*Deep learning, LeCun, Yann, Yoshua Bengio, and Geoffrey Hinton, Nature
521(7553), pp. 436-444, 2015*

The general public's interest in ML and DL can be demonstrated by plotting Google
search trends. It's clear that a revolution has been underway since about 2012:

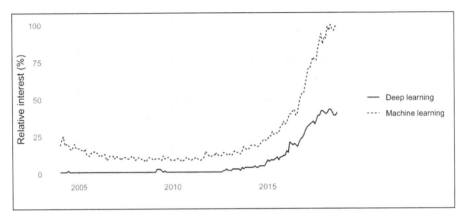

Figure 2: Google search frequency for "deep learning" and "machine learning."
The y-axis shows relative interest rather than a raw count, so the largest value raw count will be marked 100%.

This revolution is not just an outcome of that 2012 paper. Rather, it's more of
a result of a combination of factors that have caused ML to achieve a staggering
series of successes across many domains in just the last few years.

First, large datasets (such as ImageNet's millions of images) have been acquired
from the web and other sources. DL and most other ML techniques require lots
of example data to achieve good performance. Second, algorithms have been
updated to make use of GPUs to fundamentally change the expectations of ML
training algorithms. Before GPUs, one could not reasonably train a neural network
on millions of images; that would take weeks or months of computing time. With
GPUs and new optimized algorithms, the same task can be done in hours. The
proliferation of consumer-grade GPUs was initially the result of computer gaming,
but their usefulness has now extended into ML and bitcoin mining. In fact, bitcoin
mining has been such a popular use of GPUs that the demand dramatically impacted
prices of GPUs for a period of time (*Bitcoin mining leads to an unexpected GPU gold
rush, Lucas Mearian, ComputerWorld, April 2, 2018,* `https://www.computerworld.`
`com/article/3267744/computer-hardware/bitcoin-mining-leads-to-an-`
`unexpected-gpu-gold-rush.html`), in some cases causing prices to double.

Third, the field of ML has developed a culture of sharing of code and techniques.
State-of-the-art, industrial-strength libraries such as `TensorFlow` (`https://www.`
`tensorflow.org/`), PyTorch (`https://pytorch.org/`), and scikit-learn (`http://`
`scikit-learn.org/stable/`) are open source and simple to install.

Researchers and hobbyists often implement algorithms described in newly published papers using these tools, thus allowing software engineers, who may be outside the research field, to quickly make use of the latest developments.

Further evidence of the rapid increase in publications, conference attendance, venture capital funding, college course enrolment, and other metrics that bear witness to the growing interest in ML and DL can be found in AI Index's 2017 annual report (`http://www.aiindex.org/2017-report.pdf`). For example:

- Published papers in AI have more than tripled from 2005 to 2015
- The number of startup companies developing AI systems in the US in 2017 was fourteen times the number in 2000
- `TensorFlow`, the software we will be using in this chapter, had 20,000 GitHub stars (similar to Facebook likes) in 2016, and this number grew to more than 80,000 by 2017

Goal and business case

Social media is an obvious source of insights about the public's interactions with one's brands and products. No marketing department in a modern organization fails to have one or more social media accounts in order to publicize their marketing efforts but also to collect feedback in the form of likes, mentions, retweets, and so on. Some social media services such as Twitter provide APIs for keyword searches to identify relevant comments by users all around the world. However, these keyword searches are limited to text – it's not possible to find tweets that, say, include a photo of a particular brand.

However, using DL, we can make our own image filter, and thereby detect a previously untapped source of feedback from social media. We will focus on Twitter and use somewhat generic keyword searches to find tweets with photos. Each photo will then be sent through a custom classifier to identify if any logos of interest are found in the photos. If found, these photos, and the tweet content and user information, is saved to a file for later processing and trend analysis.

The same technique would be applicable to other social media platforms that include images, such as Reddit. Interestingly, the largest photo sharing service, Instagram, is deprecating their public API at the end of 2018 due to privacy concerns. This means that it will no longer be possible to obtain publicly shared photos on Instagram. Instead, API access will be limited to retrieving information about a business Instagram account, such as mentions, likes, and so on.

We will look at two techniques for recognizing logos in photos:

1. The first is a deep neural network built using `Keras`, a library included in `TensorFlow`, to detect whether an image has a logo anywhere

2. A second approach, using YOLO, will allow us to detect multiple logos and their actual positions in the photo

We then build a small Java tool that monitors Twitter for photos and sends them to YOLO for detection and recognition. If one of a small set of logos is found, we save relevant information about the tweet and the detected logos to a CSV file.

Neural networks and deep learning

Neural networks, also known as artificial neural networks, are an ML paradigm inspired by animal neurons. A neural network consists of many nodes, playing the role of neurons, connected via edges, playing the role of synaptic connections. Typically, the neurons are arranged in layers, with each layer fully connected to the next. The first and last layers are input and output layers, respectively. Inputs may be continuous (but often normalized to [-1, 1]) or binary, while outputs are typically binary or probabilities. The network is trained by repeatedly examining the training set. Each repetition on the full training set is called an "epoch." During each epoch, the weights on each edge are slightly adjusted in order to reduce the prediction error for the next epoch. We must decide when to stop training, that is, how many epochs to execute. The resulting learned "model" consists of the network topology as well as the various weights.

Each neuron has a set of input values (from the previous layer of neurons or the input data) and a single output value. The output is determined by adding the input values with their weights, and then running an "activation function." We also add a "bias" weight to influence the activation function even if we have no input values. Thus, we can describe how a single neuron behaves with the following equation:

$$y = f\left(b + \sum w_i x_i\right)$$

where f is the activation function (discussed shortly), b is the bias value, w_i are the individual weights, and x_i are the individual inputs from the prior layer or the original input data.

The network is composed of neurons connected to each other, usually segregated into layers as shown in *Figure 3*. The input data serves as the x_i values for the first layer of neurons. In a "dense" or "fully connected" layer, every different input value is fed to every neuron in the next layer.

Likewise, every neuron in this layer gives its output to every neuron in the next layer. Ultimately, we reach the output layer of neurons, where the y value of each neuron is used to identify the answer. With two output neurons, as shown in the figure, we might take the largest y value to be the answer; for example, the top neuron could represent "cat" and the bottom could represent "dog" in a cat versus dog photo classification task:

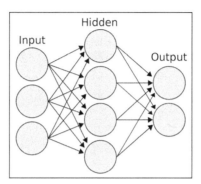

Figure 3: A diagram of a simple fully connected neural network (source: Wikipedia)

Clearly, the weights and the bias term influence the network's output. In fact, these weights, the network structure, and the activation function are the *only* aspects of neural networks that influence the output. As we will see, the network can automatically learn the weights. But the network structure and the activation function must be decided by the designer.

The neural network learning process examines the input data repeatedly over multiple epochs, and gradually adjusts the weights (and the bias term) of every neuron in order to achieve higher accuracy. For each input, the desired output is known. The input is fed through the network, and the resulting output values are collected. If the output values correctly match the desired output, no changes are needed. If they do not match, some weights must be adjusted. They are adjusted very little each time to ensure they do not wildly oscillate during training. This is why tens or hundreds of epochs are required.

The activation functions play a critical role in the performance of the network. Interestingly, if the activation functions are just the identity function, the whole network performs as if it was just a single layer, and virtually nothing of practical use can be learned. Eventually, researchers devised more sophisticated, non-linear activation functions that ensure the network can eventually learn to match any kinds of inputs and outputs, theoretically speaking. How well it does depends on a number of factors, including the activation function, network design, and quality of the input data. A common activation function in the early days of neural networks research was "sigmoid," also known as the logistic function:

$$f(x) = \frac{e^x}{e^x + 1}$$

While this function may be non-intuitive, it has a few special properties. First, its derivative is $f'(x) = f(x)(1 - f(x))$, which is very convenient. The derivative is used to determine which weights need to be modified, and by how much, in each epoch. Also, its plot looks a bit like a binary decision, which is useful for a neuron because the neuron can be said to "fire" (1.0 output) or "not fire" (0.0 output) based on its inputs. The plot for sigmoid is shown in the following figure:

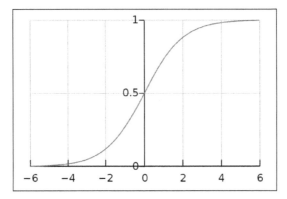

Figure 4: Sigmoid plot (https://en.wikipedia.org/wiki/Logistic_function)

Another common activation function is hyperbolic tangent (also known as tanh), which has a similarly convenient derivative. Its plot is shown in *Figure 5*. Notice that unlike sigmoid, which tends towards 0.0 for low values, tanh tends towards -1.0. Thus, neurons with tanh activation function can actually *inhibit* the next layer of neurons by giving them negative values:

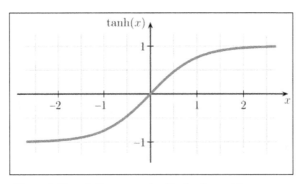

Figure 5: Hyperbolic tangent (tanh) plot (https://commons.
wikimedia.org/wiki/Trigonometric_function_plots)

Neural networks enjoyed a wide variety of successful uses throughout the 90s and early 2000s. Assuming one could extract the right features, they could be used to predict the topic of a news story, convert scanned documents into text, predict the likelihood of loan defaults, and so on. However, images proved difficult because pixels could not just be fed into the network without pre-processing and feature extraction. What is important about images is that *regions* of pixels, not individual pixels, determine the content of an image. So, we needed a way to process images in two dimensions – this was traditionally the role of feature extraction (for example, corner detection). We also needed deep neural networks with multiple layers in order to increase their ability to recognize subtle differences in the data. But deep networks were hard to train because the weight updates in some layers became so small (known as the "vanishing gradient" problem). Additionally, deep networks took a long time to train because there were millions of weights.

Eventually, all of these problems were solved, yielding what we now know as "deep learning."

Deep learning

While DL may be considered a buzzword much like "big data," it nevertheless refers to a profoundly transformative evolution of neural network architectures and training algorithms. The central idea is to take a multilayer neural network, which typically has one hidden layer, and add several more layers. We then need an appropriate training algorithm that can handle the vanishing gradient problem and efficiently update hundreds of thousands of weights at each layer. New activation functions and special operations, such as dropout and pooling are some of the techniques that make training many-layered neural networks possible.

By adding more layers, we allow the network to learn the subtle properties of the data. We can even abandon careful feature extraction in many cases, and just let the various hidden layers learn their own complex representations. CNNs are a prime example of this: some of the earliest layers apply various image manipulations known as "convolutions" (for example, increased contrast, edge detection, and so on) in order to learn which features (perhaps diagonal high-contrast edges?) are best for the given data.

We will look at each of these new developments in turn. First, we show how convolutions work; then we talk about pooling, dropout, and a new activation function.

Convolutions

A convolution transforms an image by taking a matrix, known as the **kernel**, and processing the image through this filter. Consider a 3x3 kernel. Every pixel in the original image is processed through the kernel. The center of the kernel is moved onto each pixel, and the kernel's values are treated as weights on this pixel and its neighbors. In the case of a 3x3 kernel, each pixel's neighbors are the pixel above, below, left, right, to the upper-left, to the upper-right, to the lower-left, and to the lower-right of the pixel. The values in the kernel are multiplied by the corresponding pixel value, and are then added up to a weighted sum. The center pixel's value is then replaced with this weighted sum.

Figure 6 shows some random kernels, and the impact different kernels can have on a (grayscale) image. Notice that some kernels effectively brighten the image, some make it blurry, some detect edges by turning edges white and non-edges black, and so on:

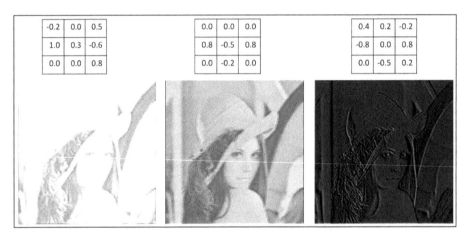

Figure 6: Some examples of random convolution kernels and their effect on an image

A kernel does not need to touch every pixel. If we adjust its **stride**, we can simultaneously reduce the size of the image. The kernels shown in the preceding image have stride (1,1), meaning the kernel moves left-to-right by one pixel at a time, and top-to-bottom one pixel at a time. So, every pixel is computed, and the image size is the same as before. If we change the stride to (2,2), then every other pixel is computed, resulting in an image with half the width and half the height as the original. The following figure shows various strides on a zoomed-in portion of the image:

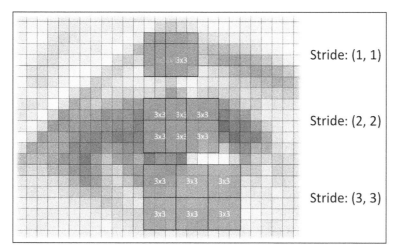

Figure 7: Visualization of how strides determine how a kernel moves across an image

Besides adjusting the stride, we can also reduce an image's dimensions with **pooling**. Pooling looks at a small region of pixels and picks out the max or computes the average value (giving us max pooling or average pooling, respectively). Depending on the stride, which is typically the same size as the region, so there is no overlap, we can reduce the image's dimensions. *Figure 8* shows an example of a (2,2) region with (2,2) stride.

Convolutions and pooling accomplish two important tasks. First, convolutions give us image features such as edges or vague regions of color (if the convolution produces a blur), among other possibilities. These image features are somewhat simplistic compared to the more exotic features used in prior image processing work such as edge direction, color histograms, and so on. Second, pooling allows us to reduce the size of the image without losing the important features produced by convolutions. For example, if a convolution produces edges, max pooling reduces the size of the image while keeping the dominant edges and eliminating the tiny edges.

We note that convolutions require a kernel of weights, while pooling has no parameters (stride is determined by the software engineer). It's not clear which convolutions are most appropriate for a certain image processing task such as logo detection, and we don't want to fall back into the laborious task of manual feature engineering. Instead, we create a special kind of layer in a neural network and treat the convolution's kernel weights like the neuron weights in a more traditional network. The convolutions are not neurons per se, but their weights can still be adjusted each epoch.

If we do this, we can have the system learn which convolutions, that is, which features, are best for the task.

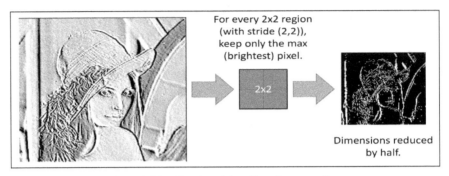

Figure 8: Visualization of the effect of max pooling

Furthermore, rather than try to find that single convolution that's best, we can combine lots of convolutions and weigh them all differently based on how much they contribute to the task. In other words, this "convolutional layer" will have lots of convolutions, each with a different kernel. In fact, we'll sequence these layers one-after-another to build convolutions on top of convolutions, thus arriving at more complex image features.

If we mix pooling in between some of these convolutional layers, we can reduce the image dimensions as we go. Reducing dimensionality is important for two reasons. First, with a smaller image, convolutions may be computed faster. Second, dimensionality reduction decreases the likelihood of "overfitting," or learning the training set too specifically and performing poorly on new examples not found in the training set. Without reducing dimensions as we go, we could end up with a neural network that is able to virtually perfectly identify logos in our training images but completely fail to identify logos in new images we find on the web. For all we know, the network may be able to memorize that any photo with green grass has a Pepsi logo just because one example in the training set had both green grass and this logo. With dimensionality reduction, the network is forced to learn how to detect logos with limited information, such that minor details such as the grass may be reduced or eliminated across the various convolutional and pooling layers.

Figure 9 shows an example of a CNN. Specifically, just a few convolutions are shown (three at each layer), and the pooling layers between the convolutions are identified in the labels under the images. The image dimensions for each layer are also shown:

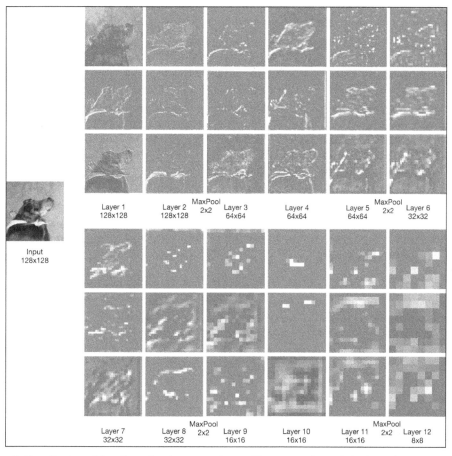

Figure 9: Visualization of the effect of various convolutional layers in a CNN. Only three of 32 convolutions are shown at each layer. The original input image comes from the Kaggle "Dogs vs. Cats" competition dataset (https://www.kaggle.com/c/dogs-vs-cats).

The images of the dog are produced by convolutions on a fully trained network that did a good job of distinguishing photos of cats from photos of dogs. At layer 12, the 8x8 images that result from all the convolutions are, apparently, actually quite useful for distinguishing cats from dogs. From the examples in the figure, it's anyone's guess exactly how that could be the case. Neural networks generally, and DL networks particularly, are usually considered "non-interpretable" ML models because even when we can see the data that the network used to come to its conclusion (such as shown in the figure), we have no idea what it all means. Thus, we have no idea how to fix it if the network performs poorly. Building and training highly accurate neural networks are more art than science and only experience yields expertise.

Network architecture

Convolutional and pooling layers operate on two-dimensional data, that is, images. Actually, convolutions and pooling are also available for one-dimensional data such as audio, but for our purposes, we will use only their 2D forms. The original photo can be fed directly into the first convolutional layer. At the other side, a smaller image, say 8x8 pixels, comes out of each convolution (usually a convolutional layer has many, say 32, convolutions). We could continue in this way until we have a single pixel (as in *Fully convolutional networks for semantic segmentation, Long, Jonathan, Evan Shelhamer,* and *Trevor Darrell,* in *Proceedings of the IEEE conference on computer vision and pattern recognition, pp. 3431-3440, 2015,* https://www.cv-foundation. org/openaccess/content_cvpr_2015/papers/Long_Fully_Convolutional_ Networks_2015_CVPR_paper.pdf). But classification tasks such as ours usually need a fully connected traditional neural network on the output side of the deep network. In this way, the convolutional layers effectively find the features to feed into the traditional network.

We convert the 2D data to the 1D data required by the fully connected network by flattening the 2D data. Flattening involves just taking each pixel value in order and treating them as a 1D array of values. The order of the flattening operation does not matter, as long as it stays consistent.

Successful CNNs for image classification typically involve multiple convolutional and pooling layers, followed by a large fully connected network. Some advanced architectures even split the image into regions and run convolutions on the regions before joining back together. For example, the following figure shows an architecture diagram of the Inception network, which achieved a 94% accuracy on the ImageNet challenge:

Figure 10: Abstract representation of the Inception network (https://github.com/tensorflow/models/tree/master/research/inception)

This network has many advanced features, some of which we do not have space to cover in this chapter. But notice that the diagram shows many stacked convolutions, followed by average or max pooling. There is a fully connected layer on the far-right. Interestingly, there is another fully connected layer in the middle/bottom. This means the network is predicting the image classifications twice. This middle output is used to help adjust the convolutions earlier in the network. The designers found that without this extra output, the size of the network caused extremely small updates to the earlier convolutions (a case of the vanishing gradient problem).

Modern neural network engineering has a heavy focus on network architecture. Network architectures are continuously invented and revised to achieve better performance. Neural networks have been used in many different scenarios, not just image processing, and the network architectures change accordingly. The Asimov Institute's "Neural Network Zoo" (`http://www.asimovinstitute.org/neural-network-zoo/`) web post shows a good overview of the common architectural patterns.

Activation functions

The choice of activation function impacts the speed of learning (in processing time per epoch) and generality (that is, to prevent overfitting). One of the most important advancements in Krizhevsky and others' 2012 paper, *ImageNet classification with deep convolutional neural networks*, was the use of ReLU for deep neural networks. This function is 0 below some threshold and the identity function above. In other words, $f(x) = \max(0, x)$. Such a simple function has some important characteristics that make it better than sigmoid and tanh in most DL applications. First, it can be computed very quickly, especially by GPUs. Second, it eliminates data that has low importance. For example, if we use ReLU after a convolutional layer (which is often done in practice), only the brightest pixels survive, and the rest turn to black. These black pixels have no influence on later convolutions or other activity in the network. In this way, ReLU acts as a filter, keeping only high-value information. Third, ReLUs do not "saturate" like sigmoid and tanh. Recall that both sigmoid and tanh have an upper limit of 1.0, and the curves get gradually closer to this limit. ReLU, on the other hand, gives back the original value (assuming it is above the threshold), so large values stay large. This reduces the chance of the vanishing gradient problem, which occurs when there is too little information to update weights early in the network.

The following figure shows the plot of ReLU, plus its continuous-valued and differentiable cousin, known as **softplus**:

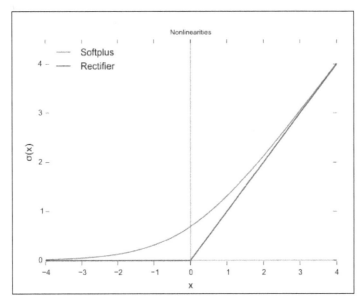

Figure 11: ReLU and softplus plots (https://en.wikipedia.org/wiki/Rectifier_(neural_networks))

Finally, our last interesting feature of DL is the dropout layer. In order to reduce the chance of overfitting, we can add a virtual layer that causes the network to update only a random subset of weights each epoch (the subset changes each epoch). Using a dropout layer with parameter 0.50 causes only 50% of the weights on the prior layer prior to update.

This quick tour of neural networks and DL shows that the "deep learning revolution," if we may call it that, is the result of a convergence of many ideas and technologies, as well as a dramatic increase in the abundance of publicly available data and ease of research with open source libraries. DL is not a single technology or algorithm. It is a rich array of techniques for solving many different kinds of problems.

TensorFlow and Keras

In order to detect which photos on social media have logos and recognize which logos they are, we will develop a series of increasingly sophisticated DL neural networks. Ultimately, we will demonstrate two approaches: one using the Keras library in the TensorFlow platform, and one using YOLO in the Darknet platform. We will write some Python code for the Keras example, and we will use existing open source code for YOLO.

First, we create a straightforward deep network with several convolutional and pooling layers, followed by a fully connected (dense) network. We will use images from the FlickrLogos dataset (*Scalable Logo Recognition in Real-World Images, Stefan Romberg, Lluis Garcia Pueyo, Rainer Lienhart, Roelof van Zwol, ACM International Conference on Multimedia Retrieval 2011 (ICMR11), Trento, April 2011,* http://www.multimedia-computing.de/flickrlogos/), specifically the version with 32 different kinds of logos. Later, with YOLO, we will use the version with 47 logos. This dataset contains 320 training images (10 examples per logo), and 3,960 testing images (30 per logo plus 3,000 images without logos). This is quite a small number of training photos per logo. Also, note that we do not have any no-logo images for training.

The images are stored in directories named after their respective logos. For example, images with an Adidas logo are in the FlickrLogos-v2/train/classes/jpg/adidas folder. Keras includes a convenient image loading functionality via its ImageDataGenerator and DirectoryIterator classes. Just by organizing the images into these folders, we can avoid all the work of loading images and informing Keras of the class of each image.

We start by importing our libraries and setting up the directory iterator. We indicate the image size we want for our first convolutional layer. Images will be resized as necessary when loaded. We also indicate the number of channels (red, green, blue). These channels are separated before the convolutions operate on the images, so each convolution is only applied to one channel at a time:

```
import re
import numpy as np
from tensorflow.python.keras.models import Sequential, load_model
from tensorflow.python.keras.layers import Input, Dropout, \
Flatten, Conv2D, MaxPooling2D, Dense, Activation
from tensorflow.python.keras.preprocessing.image import \
DirectoryIterator, ImageDataGenerator

# all images will be converted to this size
ROWS = 256
COLS = 256
CHANNELS = 3

TRAIN_DIR = '.../FlickrLogos-v2/train/classes/jpg/'

img_generator = ImageDataGenerator() # do not modify images

train_dir_iterator = DirectoryIterator(TRAIN_DIR, img_generator,
target_size=(ROWS, COLS), color_mode='rgb', seed=1)
```

Next, we specify the network's architecture. We specify that we will use a sequential model (that is, not a recurrent model with loops in it), and then proceed to add our layers in order. In the convolutional layers, the first argument (for example, 32) indicates how many different convolutions should be learned (per each of the three channels); the second argument gives the kernel size; the third argument gives the stride; and the fourth argument indicates that we want padding on the image for when the convolutions are applied to the edges. This padding, known as "same," is used to ensure the output image (after being convolved) is the same size as the input (assuming the stride is (1,1)):

```
model = Sequential()
model.add(Conv2D(32, (3,3), strides=(1,1), padding='same',
input_shape=(ROWS, COLS, CHANNELS)))
model.add(Activation('relu'))
model.add(Conv2D(32, (3,3), strides=(1,1), padding='same'))
model.add(Activation('relu'))
model.add(MaxPooling2D(pool_size=(2,2)))
model.add(Conv2D(64, (3,3), strides=(1,1), padding='same'))
model.add(Activation('relu'))
model.add(Conv2D(64, (3,3), strides=(1,1), padding='same'))
model.add(Activation('relu'))
model.add(MaxPooling2D(pool_size=(2,2)))
model.add(Conv2D(128, (3,3), strides=(1,1), padding='same'))
model.add(Activation('relu'))
model.add(Conv2D(128, (3,3), strides=(1,1), padding='same'))
model.add(Activation('relu'))
model.add(MaxPooling2D(pool_size=(2,2)))
model.add(Flatten())
model.add(Dense(64))
model.add(Activation('relu'))
model.add(Dropout(0.5))
model.add(Dense(32)) # i.e., one output neuron per class
model.add(Activation('sigmoid'))
```

Next, we compile the model and specify that we have binary decisions (yes/no for each of the possible logos) and that we want to use stochastic gradient descent. Different choices for these parameters are beyond the scope of this chapter. We also indicate we want to see accuracy scores as the network learns:

```
model.compile(loss='binary_crossentropy', optimizer='sgd',
metrics=['accuracy'])
```

We can ask for a summary of the network, which shows the layers and the number of weights that are involved in each layer, plus a total number of weights across the whole network:

```
model.summary()
```

This network has about 8.6 million weights (also known as trainable parameters).

Lastly, we run the `fit_generator` function and feed in our training images. We also specify the number of epochs we want, that is, the number of times to look at all the training images:

```
model.fit_generator(train_dir_iterator, epochs=20)
```

But nothing is this easy. Our first network performs very poorly, achieving about 3% precision in recognizing logos. With so few examples per logo (just 10), how could we have expected this to work?

In our second attempt, we will use another feature of the image pre-processing library of `Keras`. Instead of using a default `ImageDataGenerator`, we can specify that we want the training images to be modified in various ways, thus producing new training images from the existing ones. We can zoom in/out, rotate, and shear. We'll also rescale the pixel values to values between 0.0 and 1.0 rather than 0 and 255:

```
img_generator = ImageDataGenerator(rescale=1./255,
rotation_range=45, zoom_range=0.5, shear_range=30)
```

Figure 12 shows an example of a single image undergoing random zooming, rotation, and shearing:

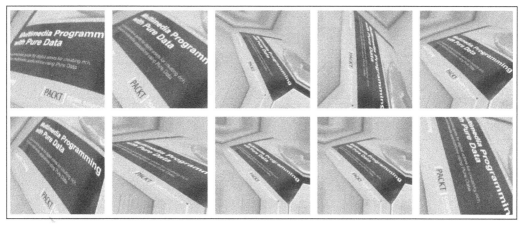

Figure 12: Example of image transformations produced by Keras' ImageDataGenerator; photo from https://www.flickr.com/photos/hellocatfood/9364615943

With this expanded training set, we get a few percent better precision. Still not nearly good enough.

The problem is two-fold: our network is quite shallow, and we do not have nearly enough training examples. Combined, these two problems result in the network being unable to develop useful convolutions, thus unable to develop useful features, to feed into the fully connected network.

We will not be able to obtain more training examples, and it would do us no good to simply increase the complexity and depth of the network without having more training examples to train it.

However, we can make use of a technique known as **transfer learning**. Suppose we take one of those highly accurate deep networks developed for the ImageNet challenge and trained on millions of photos of everyday objects. Since our task is to detect *logos* on everyday objects, we can reuse the convolutions learned by these massive networks and just stick a different fully connected network on it. We then train the fully connected network using these convolutions, without updating them. For a little extra boost, we can follow this by training again, this time updating the convolutions and the fully connected network simultaneously. In essence, we'll follow this analogy: grab an existing camera and learn to see through it as best we can; then, adjust the camera a little bit to see even better.

`Keras` has support for several ImageNet models, shown in the following table (`https://keras.io/applications/`). Since the **Xception** model is one of the most accurate but not extremely large, we will use it as a base model:

Model	Size	Top-1 Accuracy	Top-5 Accuracy	Parameters	Depth
Xception (`https://keras.io/ applications/#xception`)	88 MB	0.79	0.945	22,910,480	126
VGG16 (`https://keras.io/ applications/#vgg16`)	528 MB	0.715	0.901	138,357,544	23
VGG19 (`https://keras.io/ applications/#vgg19`)	549 MB	0.727	0.91	143,667,240	26
ResNet50 (`https://keras.io/ applications/#resnet50`)	99 MB	0.759	0.929	25,636,712	168
InceptionV3 (`https://keras. io/applications/ #inceptionv3`)	92 MB	0.788	0.944	23,851,784	159
InceptionResNetV2 (`https:// keras.io/applications/ #inceptionresnetv2`)	215 MB	0.804	0.953	55,873,736	572
MobileNet (`https:// keras.io/ applications/#mobilenet`)	17 MB	0.665	0.871	4,253,864	88
DenseNet121 (`https://keras.io/ applications/#densenet`)	33 MB	0.745	0.918	8,062,504	121

DenseNet169 (https://keras.io/ applications/#densenet)	57 MB	0.759	0.928	14,307,880	169
DenseNet201 (https://keras.io/ applications/#densenet)	80 MB	0.77	0.933	20,242,984	201

First, we import the Xception model and remove the top (its fully connected layers), keeping only its convolutional and pooling layers:

```
from tensorflow.python.keras.applications.xception import Xception

# create the base pre-trained model
base_model = Xception(weights='imagenet', include_top=False,
pooling='avg')
```

Then we create new fully connected layers:

```
# add some fully-connected layers
dense_layer = Dense(1024, activation='relu')(base_model.output)
out_layer = Dense(32)(dense_layer)
out_layer_activation = Activation('sigmoid')(out_layer)
```

We put the fully connected layers on top to complete the network:

```
# this is the model we will train
model = Model(inputs=base_model.input,
outputs=out_layer_activation)
```

Next, we indicate that we don't want the convolutions to change during training:

```
# first: train only the dense top layers
# (which were randomly initialized)
# i.e. freeze all convolutional Xception layers
for layer in base_model.layers:
  layer.trainable = False
```

We then compile the model, print a summary, and train it:

```
model.compile(loss='categorical_crossentropy', optimizer='sgd',
metrics=['accuracy'])

model.summary()

model.fit_generator(train_dir_iterator, epochs=EPOCHS)
```

Now we're ready to update the convolutions and the fully connected layers simultaneously for that extra little boost in accuracy:

```
# unfreeze all layers for more training
for layer in model.layers:
  layer.trainable = True

model.compile(loss='categorical_crossentropy', optimizer='sgd',
metrics=['accuracy'])

model.fit_generator(train_dir_iterator, epochs=EPOCHS)
```

We use `ImageDataGenerator` to split the training data into 80% training examples and 20% validation examples. These validation images allow us to see how well we're doing during training. They simulate what it is like to look at the testing data, that is, photos we have not seen during training.

We can plot the accuracy of logo detection per epoch. Across 400 epochs (200 without updating the convolutions, then another 200 updating the convolutions), we get the plot in *Figure 13*. Training took a couple hours on an NVIDIA Titan X Pascal, though less powerful GPUs may be used. In some cases, a batch size of 16 or 32 must be specified to indicate how many images to process at once so that the GPU's memory limit is not exceeded. One may also train using no GPU (that is, just the CPU) but this takes considerably longer (like, 10-20x longer).

Interestingly, accuracy on the validation set gets a huge boost when we train the second time and update the convolutions. Eventually, the accuracy of the training set is maximized (nearly 100%) since the network has effectively memorized the training set. This is not necessarily evidence of overfitting, however, since accuracy on the validation set remains relatively constant after a certain point. If we were overfitting, we would see accuracy in the validation set begin to drop:

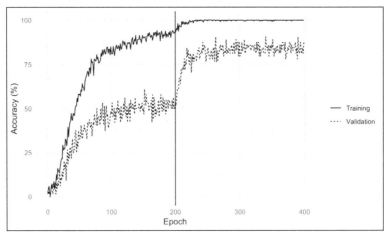

Figure 13: Accuracy over many epochs of our Xception-based model

With this advanced network, we achieve far better accuracy in logo recognition. We have one last issue to solve. Since our training images all had logos, our network is not trained on "no-logo" images. Thus, it will assume every image has a logo, and it is just a matter of figuring out which one. However, the actual situation is that some photos have logos and some do not, so we need to first detect whether there is a logo, and second recognize which logo it is.

We will use a simple detection scheme: if the network is not sufficiently confident about any particular logo (depending on a threshold that we choose), we will say there is no logo. Now that we are able to detect images with logos, we can measure how accurately it recognizes the logo in those images. Our detection threshold influences this accuracy since a high confidence threshold will result in fewer recognized logos, reducing recall. However, a high threshold increases precision since, among those logos it is confident about, it is less likely to be wrong. This tradeoff is often plotted in a precision/recall graph, as shown in *Figure 14*. Here, we show the impact of different numbers of epochs and different confidence thresholds (the numbers above the lines). The best position to be in is the top-right. Note that the precision scale (y-axis) goes to 1.0 since we are able to achieve high precision, but the recall scale (x-axis) only goes to about 0.40 since we are never able to achieve high recall without disastrous loss of precision. Also note that with more epochs, the output values of the network are smaller (the weights have been adjusted many times, creating a very subtle distinction between different outputs, that is, different logos), so we adjust the confidence threshold lower:

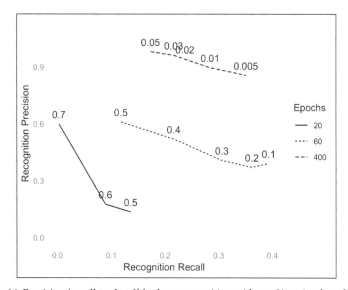

Figure 14: Precision/recall trade-off for logo recognition with our Xception-based model and different numbers of epochs and threshold values

Although our recognition recall value is low (about 40%, meaning we fail to detect logos in 60% of the photos that have logos), our precision is very high (about 90%, meaning we almost always get the right logo when we detect that there is a logo at all).

It is interesting to see how the network mis-identifies logos. We can visualize this with a **confusion matrix**, which shows the true logo on the left axis and the predicted logo on the bottom axis. In the matrix, a dark blue box indicates the network produces lots of cases of that row/column combination. *Figure 15* shows the matrix for our network after 100 epochs. We see that it mostly gets everything right: the diagonal is the darkest blue, in most cases. However, where it gets the logos confused is instructive.

For example, Paulaner and Erdinger are sometimes confused. This makes sense because both logos are circular (one circle inside another) with white text around the edge. Heineken and Becks logos are also sometimes confused. They both have a dark strip in the middle of their logo with white text, and a surrounding oval or rectangular border. NVIDIA and UPS are sometimes confused, though it is not at all obvious why.

Most interestingly, DHL, FedEx, and UPS are sometimes confused. These logos do not appear to have any visual similarities. But we have no reason to believe the neural network, even with all its sophistication and somewhat miraculous accuracy, actually knows anything about logos. Nothing in these algorithms forces it to learn about the logo in each image rather than learn about the image itself. We can imagine that most or all of the photos with DHL, FedEx, or UPS logos have some sort of package, truck, and/or plane in the image as well. Perhaps the network learned that planes go with DHL, packages with FedEx, and trucks with UPS? If this is the case, it will declare (inaccurately) that a photo with a UPS logo on a package is a photo with a FedEx logo, *not because it confuses the logos, but because it confuses the rest of the image.* This gives evidence that the network *has no idea what a logo is.* It knows packages, trucks, beer glasses, and so on. Or maybe not. The only way we would be able to tell what it learned is to process images with logos removed and see what it says. We can also visualize some of the convolutions for different images, as we did in *Figure 9,* though with so many convolutions in the Xception network, this technique will probably provide little insight.

Explaining how a deep neural network does its job, explaining why it arrives at its conclusions, is ongoing active research and currently a big drawback of DL. However, DL is so successful in so many domains that the explainability of it takes a back seat to the performance. MIT's *Technology Review* addressed this issue in an article written by *Will Knight* titled, *The Dark Secret at the Heart of AI,* and subtitled, *No one really knows how the most advanced algorithms do what they do. That could be a problem* (https://www.technologyreview.com/s/604087/the-dark-secret-at-the-heart-of-ai/).

This issue matters little for logo detection, but the stakes are completely different when DL is used in an autonomous vehicle or medical imaging and diagnosis. In these use cases, if the AI gets it wrong and someone is hurt, it is important that we can determine why and find a solution.

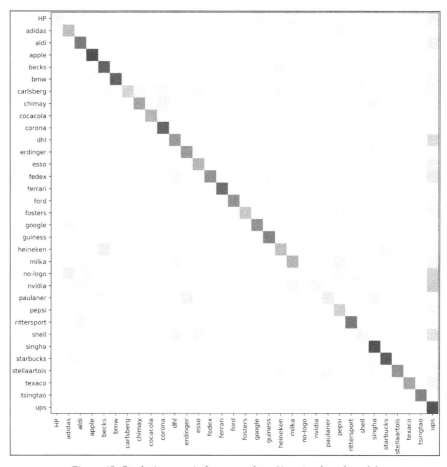

Figure 15: Confusion matrix for a run of our Xception-based model

YOLO and Darknet

A more advanced image classification competition, what we might call the spiritual successor of the ImageNet challenge, is known as **COCO: Common Objects in Context** (http://cocodataset.org/). The goal with COCO is to find multiple objects within an image and identify their location and category. For example, a single photo may have two people and two horses. The COCO dataset has 1.5 million labeled objects spanning 80 different categories and 330,000 images.

Several deep neural network architectures have been developed to solve the COCO challenge, achieving varying levels of accuracy. Measuring accuracy on this task is a little more involved considering one has to account for multiple objects in the same image and also give credit for identifying the correct location in the image for each object. The details of these measurements are beyond the scope of this chapter, though Jonathan Hui provides a good explanation (`https://medium.com/@jonathan_hui/map-mean-average-precision-for-object-detection-45c121a31173`).

Another important factor in the COCO challenge is efficiency. Recognizing people and objects in video is a critically important feature of self-driving cars, among other use cases. Doing this at the speed of the video (for example, 30 frames per second) is required.

One of the fastest network architectures and implementations for the COCO task is known as **YOLO: You Only Look Once**, developed by Joseph Redmon and Ali Farhadi (`https://pjreddie.com/darknet/yolo/`). YOLOv3 has 53 convolutional layers before a fully connected layer. These convolutional layers allow the network to divide up the image into regions and predict whether or not an object, and which object, is present in each region. In most cases, YOLOv3 performs nearly as well as significantly more complicated networks but is hundreds to thousands of times faster, achieving 30 frames per second on a single NVIDIA Titan X GPU.

Although we do not need to detect the region of a logo in the photos we acquire from Twitter; we will take advantage of YOLO's ability to find multiple logos in the same photo. The `FlickrLogos` dataset was updated from its 32 logos to 47 logos and added region information for each example image. This is helpful because YOLO will require this region information during training. We use Akarsh Zingade's guide for converting the `FlickrLogos` data to YOLO training format (*Logo detection using YOLOv2, Akarsh Zingade*, `https://medium.com/@akarshzingade/logo-detection-using-yolov2-8cda5a68740e`):

```
python convert_annotations_for_yolov2.py \
--input_directory train \
--obj_names_path . \
--text_filename train \
--output_directory train_yolo

python convert_annotations_for_yolov2.py \
--input_directory test \
--obj_names_path . \
--text_filename test \
--output_directory test_yolo
```

Next, we install `Darknet` (`https://github.com/pjreddie/darknet`), the platform in which YOLO is implemented. `Darknet` is a DL library like `TensorFlow`. Different kinds of network architectures may be coded in `Darknet`, just as YOLO may also be coded in `TensorFlow`. In any case, it is easiest to just install `Darknet` since YOLO is already implemented.

Compiling `Darknet` is straightforward. However, before doing so, we make one minor change to the source code. This change helps us later when we build a Twitter logo detector. In the `examples/detector.c file`, we add a newline (\n) character to the `printf` statement in the first line of the first else block in the `test_detector` function definition:

```
printf("Enter Image Path:\n");
```

Once `Darknet` is compiled, we can then train YOLO on the `FlickrLogos-47` dataset. We use transfer learning as before by starting with the `darknet53.conv.74` weights, which was trained on the COCO dataset:

```
./darknet detector train flickrlogo47.data \
yolov3_logo_detection.cfg darknet53.conv.74
```

This training process took 17 hours on an NVIDIA Titan X. The resulting model (that is, the final weights) are found in a `backup` folder, and the file is called `yolov3_logo_detection_final.weights`.

To detect the logos in a single image, we can run this command:

```
./darknet detector test flickrlogo47.data \
yolov3_logo_detection.cfg \
backup/yolov3_logo_detection_final.weights \
test_image.png
```

Akarsh Zingade reports that an earlier version of YOLO (known as v2) achieved about 48% precision and 58% recall on the `FlickrLogos-47` dataset. It is not immediately clear whether this level of accuracy is sufficient for practical use of a logo detector and recognizer, but in any case, the methods we will develop do not depend on this exact network. As network architectures improve, the logo detector presumably will also improve.

One way to improve the network is to provide more training examples. Since YOLO detects the region of a logo as well as the logo label, our training data needs region and label information. This can be time-consuming to produce since each logo will need x,y boundaries in each image. A tool such as **YOLO_mark** (`https://github.com/AlexeyAB/Yolo_mark`) can help by providing a "GUI for marking bounded boxes of objects in images for training neural network Yolo v3 and v2."

Figure 16 shows some examples of logo detection and region information (shown as bounding boxes). All but one of these examples show correct predictions, though the UPS logo is confused for the Fosters logo. Note, one benefit of YOLO over our `Keras` code is that we do not need to set a threshold for logo detection – if YOLO cannot find any logo, it just predicts nothing for the image:

Figure 16: Example logo detections by YOLOv3. Images from, in order (left to right, top to bottom): 1) Photo by "the real Tiggy," https://www.flickr.com/photos/21238273@N03/24336870601, Licensed Attribution 2.0 Generic (CC BY 2.0) Deployment strategy; 2) Photo by "Pexels," https://pixabay.com/en/apple-computer-girl-iphone-laptop-1853337/, Licensed CC0 Creative Commons; 3) https://pxhere.com/en/photo/1240717, Licensed CC0 Creative Commons; 4) Photo by "Orin Zebest," https://www.flickr.com/photos/orinrobertjohn/1054035018, Licensed Attribution 2.0 Generic (CC BY 2.0); 5) Photo by "MoneyBlogNewz", https://www.flickr.com/photos/moneyblognewz/5301705526, Licensed Attribution 2.0 Generic (CC BY 2.0)

With YOLO trained and capable of detecting and recognizing logos, we are now ready to write some code that watches Twitter for tweets with photos. Of course, we will want to focus on certain topics rather than examine every photo that is posted around the world. We will use the Twitter API in a very similar way to our implementation in *Chapter 3, A Blueprint for Making Sense of Feedback.* That is to say, we will search the global Twitter feed with a set of keywords, and for each result, we will check whether there is a photo in the tweet. If so, we download the photo and send it to YOLO. If YOLO detects any one of a subset of logos that we are interested in, we save the tweet and photo to a log file.

For this demonstration, we will look for a soft drink and beer logos. Our search terms will be "Pepsi," "coke," "soda," "drink," and "beer." We will look for 26 different logos, mostly beer logos since the `FlickrLogos-47` dataset includes several such logos.

Our Java code that connects to the Twitter API will also talk to a running YOLO process. Previously, we showed how to run YOLO with a single image. This is a slow procedure because the network must be loaded from its saved state every time YOLO is run. If we simply do not provide an image filename, YOLO will start up and wait for input. We then give it an image filename, and it quickly tells us whether it found any logos (and its confidence). In order to communicate with YOLO this way, we use Java's support for running and communicating with external processes.

The following figure shows a high-level perspective of our architecture:

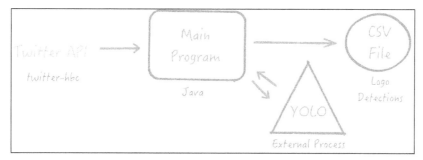

Figure 17: Architectural overview of our logo detector application

The Twitter feed monitor and the logo detector will run in separate threads. This way, we can acquire tweets and process images simultaneously. This is helpful in case there are suddenly a lot of tweets that we don't want to miss and/or in case YOLO is suddenly tasked with handling a lot of images. As tweets with photos are discovered, they are added to a queue. This queue is monitored by the logo detector code. Whenever the logo detector is ready to process an image, and a tweet with a photo is available, it grabs this tweet from the queue, downloads the image, and sends it to YOLO.

Our Twitter code is mostly the same from *Chapter 3, A Blueprint for Making Sense of Feedback,* but updated slightly so that it can detect tweets with images and save these tweets into the shared queue:

```
while (!client.isDone())
{
  String msg = msgQueue.take();
  Map<String, Object> msgobj = gson.fromJson(msg, Map.class);
  Map<String, Object> entities =
(Map<String, Object>)msgobj.get("entities");

  // check for an image in the tweet
  List<Map<String, Object>> media =
(List<Map<String, Object>>)entities.get("media");
  if(media != null)
  {
    for(Map<String, Object> entity : media)
    {
      String type = (String)entity.get("type");
      if(type.equals("photo"))
      {
        // we found an image, add the tweet to the queue
        imageQueue.add(msgobj);
      }
    }
  }
}
```

In the `ImageProcessor` class, which runs on its own thread, we first start the YOLO application and connect its input/output streams to a buffered reader and writer. This way, we can simulate typing image filenames into YOLO and catch all of its print outputs:

```
// get YOLO command from config.properties
ProcessBuilder builder = new ProcessBuilder(
props.getProperty("yolo_cmd"));
builder.redirectErrorStream(true);

Process process = builder.start();
OutputStream stdin = process.getOutputStream();
InputStream stdout = process.getInputStream();
BufferedReader reader = new BufferedReader(
new InputStreamReader(stdout));
BufferedWriter writer = new BufferedWriter(
new OutputStreamWriter(stdin));
```

Next, we wait for YOLO to start up before proceeding. We know YOLO is ready when it prints `Enter Image Path`:

```
String line = reader.readLine();
System.out.println(line);
while(!line.equals("Enter Image Path:"))
{
  line = reader.readLine();
  System.out.println(line);
}
```

The small change we made to the preceding `Darknet` source code enables us to use the `readLine` method to detect this message. Without that change, we would have to read YOLO's output character by character, a significantly more involved task.

Now we are ready to watch for tweets to appear in the shared queue:

```
while(true)
{
  Map<String, Object> msgobj = imageQueue.take();
...
```

After grabbing a tweet from the queue, we'll find all the photos linked in the tweet, and process each separately:

```
Map<String, Object> entities =
(Map<String, Object>)msgobj.get("entities");
List<Map<String, Object>> media =
(List<Map<String, Object>>)entities.get("media");
for(Map<String, Object> entity : media)
{
  String type = (String)entity.get("type");
  if(type.equals("photo"))
  {
...
```

We now need to download the image to a temporary location:

```
String url = (String)entity.get("media_url");
// download photo
File destFile = File.createTempFile("logo-", ".jpg");
FileUtils.copyURLToFile(new URL(url), destFile);
System.out.println("Downloaded " + url + " to " + destFile);
```

And we give this temporary filename to YOLO so that it can find the logos:

```
writer.write(destFile + "\n");
writer.flush();
```

Next, we watch for YOLO's output and extract the data about any logos it detected, plus its confidence. Notice that we check whether the detected logo is among the 26 we care about:

```
// save all detections in a map, key = logo, value = confidence
Map<String, Double> detections = new HashMap<String, Double>();
line = reader.readLine();
System.out.println(line);
while(!line.equals("Enter Image Path:"))
{
  line = reader.readLine();
  System.out.println(line);
  Matcher m = detectionPattern.matcher(line);
  // find out which logo was detected and if its
  // one of the logos we care about
  if(m.matches() && logos.contains(m.group(1)))
  {
    detections.put(
m.group(1), Double.parseDouble(m.group(2))/100.0);
  }
}
```

Finally, we print the tweet information and logo information to a CSV file. One row in the CSV file corresponds to one logo, so a single tweet may have multiple rows for multiple logos:

```
for(String k : detections.keySet())
{
  System.out.println(detections);
  csvPrinter.printRecord(
(String)((Map<String, Object>)msgobj.get("user"))
.get("screen_name"), (String)msgobj.get("id_str"),
(String)msgobj.get("created_at"), (String)msgobj.get("text"),
url, k, detections.get(k));
  csvPrinter.flush();
}
```

Over a period of a few hours, our application found about 600 logos. A cursory examination shows that it is not a highly precise detector. For example, photos with a beer in a glass are labeled as a random beer company logo, though usually not with high confidence. We can increase precision by requiring high confidence in the detections. But our results show that there is a more serious problem. Every image in the training data for YOLO or our Keras code included one or more logos (among a set of 32 or 47 logos, depending on the dataset) or no logos at all. However, real photos from Twitter may include no logos or logos from a virtually unbounded set of possibilities.

Just imagine how many different beer brands may be found throughout the world, while our application only knows of about 20. This causes YOLO to detect, say, a Heineken logo on a glass of beer when in fact the logo on the glass is something it has never seen before. Just like our confusion matrix in *Figure 15*, YOLO is picking up on the glass and the surrounding environment just as much as it is picking up on details of the logo itself. It is difficult to impossible to prevent this from happening in DL since we have no control over the features it is learning to distinguish images in the training set. Our only hope for better accuracy is to increase the diversity of the training set, both in terms of a number of logos represented and variation in the photos themselves (some outside, some in bars, logos on glasses, logos on cans, and so on). Furthermore, if only a single kind of logo is to be detected, the network should be trained with lots of negative examples (photos without this logo) that also include other, similar logos. The only way the network can learn to distinguish subtle differences between logos, and not focus on background information, is to provide it positive and negative training examples that only differ in these subtle ways. At best, the network will only learn how to detect what it is given. At worst, it can't even do that!

Continuous evaluation

The logo detector developed in this chapter does not continuously update its network weights after being deployed. Once it is trained to recognize a set of logos, it should continue to do so with the same accuracy. There is a chance that, after being deployed, the kinds of photos people take gradually changes over time. For example, the increased popularity of Instagram filters and related image manipulations might begin to confuse the logo detector.

In any case, it is still important to continuously evaluate whether the detector is working as expected. This is a somewhat challenging exercise because it requires that humans are in the loop. Every photo with a detected logo can be saved to a database for later examination. Our logo detector code does this. Every so often, a team of people can be asked to critique the tool's predictions to produce a continuously updated measure of precision.

Measuring recall is more challenging. Among the universe of photos shared on social media, it will never be possible for a human to find and examine them all. So, we will not be able to accurately judge recall. Instead, we can ask users to pay attention to social media for any photos that include their brand's logos, and when they see one, check if the system both found and downloaded the image and correctly identified the logo in the image. A record of successes and failures can be maintained to approximate recall.

If the system must detect new logos or there is a need to retrain the system on more examples, then an abundance of images must be labeled for training. We already mentioned YOLO_mark (`https://github.com/AlexeyAB/Yolo_mark`) for marking images for YOLO training. Other tools include the open source Labelbox (`https://github.com/Labelbox/Labelbox`) and the proprietary Prodigy (`https://prodi.gy/`).

Summary

In this chapter, we've demonstrated how to design and implement a CNN to detect and recognize logos in photos. These photos were obtained from social media using the Twitter API and some search keywords. As photos are found, and logos were detected, records of the detections were saved to a CSV file for later processing or viewing.

Along the way, we looked at the origin of the term deep learning and discussed the various components that led to a revolution in ML in the last few years. We showed how a convergence of technologies and sociological factors helped this revolution. We've also seen multiple demonstrations of how far we have come in such a short amount of time – with very little code, a set of training examples (made available to researchers for free), and a GPU, we can create our deep neural network with ease.

In the next chapter, we'll show how to use statistics and other techniques to discover trends and recognize anomalies such as a dramatic increase or decrease in the number of photos on social media with your logo.

6
A Blueprint for Discovering Trends and Recognizing Anomalies

Effective companies make use of numerous data sources. These can range from customer activity to supplier prices, data processing throughput, system logs, and so on, depending on the nature of the business. By just having the data, even graphing it using a plotly graph, like the one we developed in *Chapter 3, A Blueprint for Making Sense of Feedback*, might not be proactive enough. Usually, it's not the case that somebody is watching every data stream or graph constantly. Thus, it is equally important that the data can be summarized, and the right people be notified when interesting events occur. These events could be anything from changes in the overall trend of the data to anomalous activity. In fact, the two analyses, trends, and anomalies are sometimes found with the same techniques, as we will discover in this chapter.

Trends and anomalies may also serve as a user-facing feature of a company's services. There are numerous such examples on the internet. For instance, consider Google Analytics' (`https://analytics.google.com/analytics/web/`) website traffic tools. These tools are designed to find trends and anomalies in website traffic, among other data analysis operations. On the front dashboard, one is presented with a plot of daily/weekly/monthly website traffic counts (*Figure 1*, left). Interestingly, though the plot is labeled, **How are your active users trending over time?** Analytics does not actually compute a trend, as we will do in this chapter, but instead gives you a plot so that you can visually identify the trends. More interestingly, analytics sometimes notifies the user on the dashboard of anomalous activity. A small plot shows the forecasted value and actual value; if the actual value (say, of website hits) significantly differs from the forecasted value, the data point is considered anomalous and warrants a notification for the user. A quick search on Google gives us an explanation of this anomaly detector (`https://support.google.com/analytics/answer/7507748`):

First, Intelligence selects a period of historical data to train its forecasting model. For detection of daily anomalies, the training period is 90 days. For detection of weekly anomalies, the training period is 32 weeks.

Then, Intelligence applies a Bayesian state space-time series model to the historical data to forecast the value of the most recent observed data point in the time series.

Finally, Intelligence flags the data point as an anomaly using a statistical significance test with p-value thresholds based on the amount of data in the reporting view.

Anomaly detection, Google

In this chapter, we will develop a **Bayesian state space time-series model**, also known as a **dynamic linear model** (**DLM**), for forecasting website traffic. We will also be looking at techniques for identifying anomalies based on a data point's significant deviation from expectation.

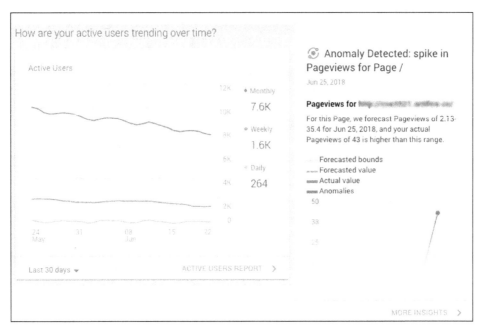

Figure 1: Google Analytics trend and anomaly report

Twitter is another case of a company that highlights trends to provide value to its users. By examining hashtags and proper nouns mentioned in tweets, Twitter is able to group tweets into categories and then analyze which categories are rising the most rapidly in terms of a number of tweets in a short time period. Their home page (for visitors who are not logged in) highlights these trending categories (*Figure 2*). Without any user information, they show worldwide trending categories, but the feature also works on a more local level. In this chapter, we will look at a technique that we can use for determining the rate of increase in a data stream. Identifying trending categories is then a matter of highlighting the categories with the greatest rate of change. However, it's clear from *Figure 2* that Twitter is not focusing on the diversity of trending categories since several of the trends related to the same global phenomenon (World Cup 2018):

Figure 2: Twitter home page

Both these examples highlight the value that trends and anomalies can provide to users. But, at the same time, organizations can also find value in these techniques by looking at internal data streams. For example, it's crucial that the IT department of an organization detects anomalous network activity, possibly indicative of hacking attempts or botnet activity, data processing delays, unexpected website traffic changes, and other customer engagement trends such as activity on a product support forum. A variety of algorithms are available to analyze data streams, depending on what exactly the nature of the data is and the kinds of trends and/or anomalies we wish to detect.

In this chapter, we will be covering:

- Discovering linear trends with static models and moving-average models
- Discovering seasonal trends, that is, patterns of behavior that can change depending on the day of the week or month of the year
- Recognizing anomalies by noticing significant deviations from normal activity, both with static and moving average trend models
- Recognizing anomalies with a **robust principle component analysis (RPCA)**
- Recognizing anomalies with clustering rather than trend analysis

Overview of techniques

Identifying trends and anomalies involve similar techniques. In both cases, we must fit a model to the data. This model describes what is "normal" about the data. In order to discover trends, we'll fit a trend model for the data. A trend model fits a linear, quadratic, exponential, or another kind of trend to the data. If the data does not actually represent such a trend, the model will fit poorly. Thus, we must also ask how well a chosen model fits the data, and if it does not match the data sufficiently well, we should try another model. It's important to make this point because, for example, a linear trend model can be applied to any dataset, even those without linear trends (for example, a boom-and-bust cycle like bitcoin - USD prices between mid-2017 and mid-2018). The model will fit very poorly, yet we could still use it to predict future events – we will just likely be wrong about those future events.

In order to recognize anomalies, we take a model of what is normal about the data and identify those data points that are too far from normal. This normal model may be a trend model, and then we can identify points that do not match the trend. Or the normal model may be something simpler like just an average value (not a trend, which occurs over time). Any data point that is significantly different from this average is deemed an anomaly.

This chapter covers a variety of trend and anomaly detectors. Which approach is best suited for a particular data stream and a particular question depends on a variety of factors, represented in the following decision trees:

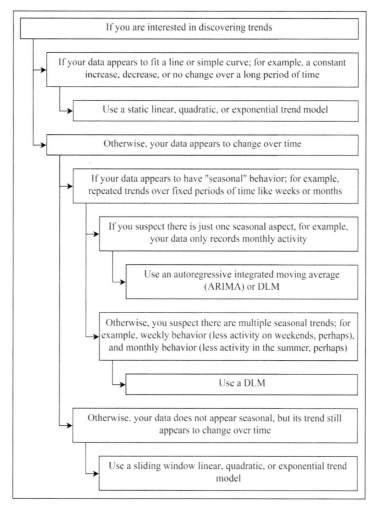

Figure 3: Decision tree for finalizing an approach for discovering trends

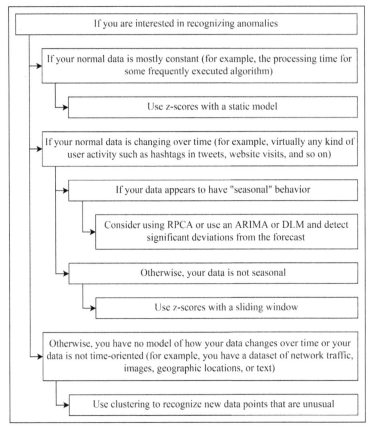

Figure 4: Decision tree for finalizing an approach for recognizing anomalies

The remainder of this chapter examines each of these techniques in turn and then concludes with some advice about deployment and evaluation.

Discovering linear trends

Perhaps the simplest trend is the linear trend. Naturally, we would only attempt to find such a trend on serial data, such as data ordered by time. For this example, we will use the daily frequency of email messages on the R-help mailing list (https://stat.ethz.ch/mailman/listinfo/r-help), an email list for users seeking help with the R programming language. The mailing list archive includes every message and the time it was sent. We wish to find a daily linear trend of message frequency, as opposed to hourly, minutely, monthly, yearly, and so on. We must decide the unit of frequency before applying trend or anomaly analysis, as the count of messages per day may be strongly linear while the count per hour may be non-linear and highly seasonal (that is, some hours are consistently higher than others), thus dramatically changing the technique that should be applied for the analysis.

Before loading the dataset, we must import `pandas` for loading the CSV file, `sklearn` (scikit-learn (`http://scikit-learn.org/stable/`)) for the trend fitting algorithms and a metric for the goodness of fit known as a mean squared error, and `matplotlib` for plotting the results:

```
import numpy as np
from sklearn import linear_model
from sklearn.metrics import mean_squared_error
import pandas as pd
import matplotlib
matplotlib.use('Agg') # for saving figures
import matplotlib.pyplot as plt
```

Next, we'll load the dataset. Conveniently, `pandas` is able to read directly from a zipped CSV file. Since the data has a `date` field, we indicate the position of this field and use it as the index of the dataset, thus creating a serial (time-oriented) dataset:

```
msgs = pd.read_csv(
'r-help.csv.zip', usecols=[0,3], parse_dates=[1], index_col=[1])
```

The dataset includes every email message, so we next group the messages by the day they were sent and count how many were sent each day. We also introduce a new column, `date_delta`, which will record the day as the number of days since the beginning of the dataset, rather than a calendar date. This helps us when we apply the linear trend model since the model is not designed to work on calendar dates:

```
msgs_daily_cnts = msgs.resample('D').count()
msgs_daily_cnts['date_delta'] = \
(msgs_daily_cnts.index - msgs_daily_cnts.index.min()) / \
np.timedelta64(1,'D')
msgs_daily_cnts.sort_values(by=['date_delta'])
msgs_daily_cnts = msgs_daily_cnts[:5000]
```

Notice the last line in the preceding code block. We'll only take the first 5,000 days counts. After this first example, we will use the whole dataset, and compare the results.

The next step is to isolate the last 1,000 values to test our model. This allows us to build the model on the early data (the training set) and test on the later data (the testing set) to more accurately gauge the accuracy of the model on data it has never seen before:

```
train = msgs_daily_cnts[:-1000]
train_X = train['date_delta'].values.reshape((-1,1))
train_y = train['Message-ID']
```

```
test = msgs_daily_cnts[-1000:]
test_X = test['date_delta'].values.reshape((-1,1))
test_y = test['Message-ID']
```

Next, we use a **linear regression** algorithm to fit a line to the data. We print the coefficients (of which there will be just one since we only have one input value, the number of days since the beginning of the data), which indicates the slope of the line:

```
reg = linear_model.LinearRegression()
reg.fit(train_X, train_y)
print('Coefficients: \n', reg.coef_)
```

The last step for us to do is to forecast (predict) some new values with the testing data's inputs and then plot all the data plus the trend line. We'll also compute the mean squared error of the predicted values. This metric adds up all of the errors and divides by the number of points: $\sum (p-x)^2/n$, where p is the predicted value, x is the true value, and n is the number of points. We will consistently use this error metric to get a sense of how well the forecast matches the testing data:

```
predicted_cnts = reg.predict(test_X)

# The mean squared error
print("Mean squared error: %.2f" % mean_squared_error(test_y,
predicted_cnts))

plt.scatter(train_X, train_y, color='gray', s=1)
plt.scatter(test_X, test_y, color='black', s=1)
plt.plot(test_X, predicted_cnts, color='blue', linewidth=3)
```

The result is shown in *Figure 5*. The coefficient, that is, the slope of the line, was 0.025, indicating each day has about 0.025 more messages sent than the day before. The mean squared error was 1623.79. On its own, this error value is not highly informative, but it will be useful to compare this value with future examples with this same dataset.

Suppose now that we do not look at just the first 5,000 days of the mailing list, but rather examine all 7,259 days (04-01-1997 to 02-13-2017). Again, we will reserve the last 1,000 days as the testing set to forecast against and measure our error. About 10 years ago, the frequency of messages to the mailing list declined. A linear model that fits the entire dataset will probably not account for this decline since the majority of the data had an increasing trend. We see this is indeed the case, in *Figure 6*. The coefficient slightly decreased to 0.018, indicating that the decrease in message rate caused the linear trend to adjust downward, but the trend is still positive and significantly overshoots the testing data. The mean squared error is now 10,057.39.

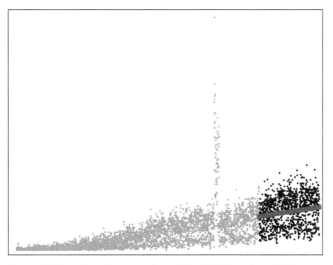

Figure 5: Linear trend on a portion of the R-Help mailing list dataset

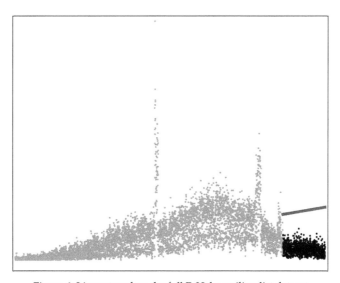

Figure 6: Linear trend on the full R-Help mailing list dataset

These two examples show that some phenomena change over time and one single linear trend will not accurately account for such changes. Next, we'll look at a simple variation of our code that fits multiple linear trends over various time frames.

Discovering dynamic linear trends with a sliding window

In order to more accurately model changes in trends, we can fit multiple lines to the same dataset. This is done by using a **sliding window** which examines a different window or chunk of data at a time. For this example, we will use a window of 1,000 days, and each window will slide by 500 days at a time. The rest of the code is the same, just updated to operate on the chunk of data rather than the full dataset:

```
for chunk in range(1000, len(msgs_daily_cnts.index)-1000, 500):
    train = msgs_daily_cnts[chunk-1000:chunk]
    train_X = train['date_delta'].values.reshape((-1,1))
    train_y = train['Message-ID']

    test = msgs_daily_cnts[chunk:chunk+1000]
    test_X = test['date_delta'].values.reshape((-1,1))
    test_y = test['Message-ID']

    reg = linear_model.LinearRegression()
    reg.fit(train_X, train_y)
    print('Coefficients: \n', reg.coef_)

    predicted_cnts = reg.predict(test_X)
```

The result is shown in *Figure 7*. We test the models by predicting the next 1,000 days for each line. The mean squared errors range from 245.63 (left side of the figure) to 3,800.30 (middle of the figure) back to 1,995.32 (right side):

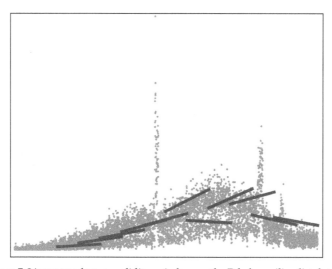

Figure 7: Linear trends over a sliding window on the R-help mailing list dataset

A sliding window approach is equal to Google Analytics' technique, quoted at the beginning of this chapter, of training on only recent data in order to find trends and detect anomalies. In the R-help mailing list case, trends from 1997 do not have much to say about mailing list activity in 2017.

Discovering seasonal trends

Often, data follows seasonal or cyclical trends. This is true not only for natural phenomena such as tides, weather, and wildlife populations, but also for human activities such as website hits and purchasing habits. Some trends are hourly, such as the times of day when people send an email (that is, mostly working hours), and others are monthly, such as the months when people buy the most ice cream, and then there's everything in between (per minute, per day of the week, per year, and so on). With seasonal data, if we just fit a linear trend to the data, we will miss most of the ups and downs that reflect the seasonal aspects. Instead, what we'll see is only the general long-term trend. Yet, sometimes we want to be able to forecast the next month's sales or the next week's website traffic. In order to do this, we will need a more refined model.

We will look at two approaches: **autoregressive integrated moving average (ARIMA)** and DLMs. In each case, we'll use a dataset of website traffic to one of my old college course websites about AI. This website is no longer used for my current courses, so any traffic to it arrives from Google searches, not from students in any specific course associated with the website. Thus, we should expect to see seasonal trends representing the general interest in college-level material about AI, that is, seasonal trends that correlate to the common fall/spring academic year, with low points in the summers. Likewise, we might see that weekdays produce a different level of activity than weekends. The following figure shows a few years of daily users to this website:

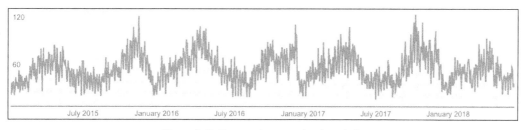

Figure 8: Daily users to an academic website

At a glance, we can see this daily traffic has several components. First, there is a certain average level of activity, a kind of constant trend around 40-50 users per day. The actual number of users per day is higher or lower than this constant value according to the month and day of the week.

It's not evident from the plot that there is any yearly cycle (for example, odd-even years), nor does it appear that activity is increasing or decreasing over the long term. Thus, our trend model will only need to account for a constant activity level plus seasonal effects of day of week and month of year.

ARIMA

A popular technique for modeling seasonal data is ARIMA. The acronym identifies the important features of this approach. First, the autoregressive aspect predicts the next value of the data as a weighted sum of the previous values. A parameter known as p adjusts how many prior data points are used. Autoregression improves accuracy if the data appear to have the property that once the values start rising, they keep rising, and once they start falling, they keep falling. For example, consider the popularity effects in which a popular video is watched by more people the more other people watch and share it. Note that autoregression is equivalent to our sliding window linear trends shown previously, except in ARIMA the window slides by one point at a time.

The moving average component (skipping the integrated component for the moment) predicts the next value in the data as a weighted sum of the recent errors, where errors are those dramatic changes in the data that seem to be caused by external factors not found in the data. For example, if a website is linked from a popular news site, say our college course website is linked from *Fox News*, then the number of visitors for that day will suddenly jump, and probably for several future days as well (though gradually decline back to normal). This jump is an error because the number of users is suddenly different than usual, and its effect can be propagated to a certain number of future points. How many points are influenced by each error value is determined by a parameter. Note, as with the autoregressive portion of ARIMA, the weighted sum in the moving average portion can have negative weights in the sum, meaning a big increase in prior data points can cause a big decrease in the forecast. We do not see this kind of trend in website traffic, but in something like population models, a large increase in a population can then cause resources to be consumed too rapidly, thereby causing a dramatic decrease in population.

Now we have two parameters, p and q, for the autoregressive lag (how many prior points to consider) and the moving average lag. The model known as **ARMA** uses these two parameters without the third parameter representing the "I" in ARIMA. Thus, ARIMA adds one final complication to the model: an integrated differencing "I" component, which replaces the data with the difference of each data point minus its prior. Thus, the model is actually describing how the data increases or decreases according to various factors (the autoregressive and moving average components), which we can describe as velocity.

This is useful for data that increases or decreases over time, such as temperature or stock prices, in which each value is slightly higher or lower than the prior value. This integrated component is not as useful for data that "starts over" each period (ignoring seasonal trends), such as the amount of electricity used by a household in a day or the number of users visiting a website in a day or month. The parameter *d* determines how many differences to compute. When *d=0*, the integrated component is not used (the data are not changed); when *d=1*, each value has its prior value subtracted from it; when *d=2*, this occurs again, thus creating data that represents accelerations of change rather than velocity; and so on.

ARIMA forecasts new values by adding up the contributions of the autoregressive and moving average components after applying the integrated differencing, if any.

ARIMA can capture some seasonality with the *p*, *d*, *q* parameters. For example, with the right values for these parameters, it can model daily ups and downs with a long-term increasing trend. However, longer-term seasonality requires additional parameters, *P*, *D*, and *Q*, plus yet another parameter *m*. The parameter *m* determines how many points are in a season (for example, seven days in a weekly season), and *P*, *D*, and *Q* work as before but on the seasonal data. For example, the *D* parameter says how many differences to take of the seasonal data, so *D=1* causes each data point to have its prior seasonal data point subtracted once. Its prior seasonal data point depends on the length of a season, *m*. So, if *m=7*, then each data point has the value from 7 days prior subtracted. Likewise, for the autoregressive and moving average seasonal aspects: they work the same as before, except rather than looking at the prior data points, they look at the prior seasonal data points (for example, each Tuesday data point looks at the prior Tuesdays if the season is weekly). These seasonal autoregressive and moving average aspects are multiplied with the non-seasonal autoregressive and moving average aspects to produce the final seasonal ARIMA model, parameterized by *p*, *d*, *q*, *P*, *D*, *Q*, and *m*.

The Python library `statsmodels` (http://www.statsmodels.org/stable/index. html) provides us with the algorithm for fitting an ARIMA model with certain parameters. The `Pyramid` library (https://github.com/tgsmith61591/pyramid) adds the `auto_arima` function (a Python implementation of R's `auto.arima` function) to find the best parameters for the ARIMA model.

We start by loading our data:

```
series = pd.read_csv('daily-users.csv', header=0, parse_dates=[0],
index_col=0, squeeze=True)
```

The next step we need to do is set up an ARIMA search procedure by specifying the season length (`m=7` for weekly seasons) and the starting and maximum values for *p* and *q*. Note that we only fit the model on a subset of the data, from the beginning to 12-31-2017. We will use the rest of the data for testing the model:

```
from statsmodels.tsa.arima_model import ARIMA
from pyramid.arima import auto_arima
stepwise_model = auto_arima(series.ix[:'2017-12-31'], start_p=1,
start_q=1, max_p=5, max_q=5, m=7, start_P=0, seasonal=True,
trace=True, error_action='ignore', suppress_warnings=True,
stepwise=True)
```

The search process finds that, *p=0, d=1, q=2, P=1, D=0,* and *Q=1* are best. With these results, we fit the model again and then use it to predict values in the testing data:

```
stepwise_model.fit(series.ix[:'2017-12-31'])

predictions =
stepwise_model.predict(n_periods=len(series.ix['2018-01-01':]))
```

We get a mean squared error of 563.10, a value that is only important later when we compare a different approach. *Figure 9* shows the predictions in black. We see it picked up on the seasonal aspect (some days have more visits than other) and a linear trend downward, indicated by the *d=1* parameter. It's clear this model failed to pick up on the monthly seasonal aspect of the data. In fact, we would need two seasonal components (weekly and monthly), which ARIMA does not support – we would have to introduce new columns in the data to represent the month that corresponds to each data point:

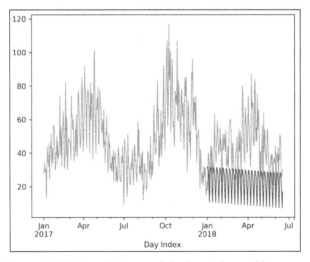

Figure 9: ARIMA predictions on daily data with a weekly season

If we convert the data to monthly data, ARIMA will do a better job since there is just one season to account for. We can do this conversion by summing the number of users per month:

```
series = series.groupby(pd.Grouper(freq='M')).sum()
```

Now we change our season length to 12: `m=12`, and run `auto_arima` again:

```
stepwise_model =
auto_arima(series.ix['2015-01-01':'2016-12-31'],
start_p=1, start_q=1, max_p=5, max_q=5, m=12, start_P=0,
seasonal=True, trace=True, error_action='ignore',
suppress_warnings=True, stepwise=True)
```

The following figure shows the result, which clearly matches better with a mean squared error of 118,285.30 (a higher number just because there are many more website users per month than there are per day):

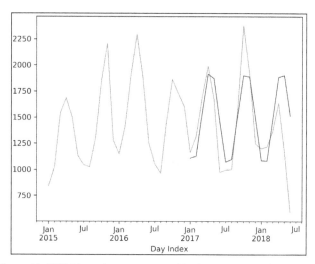

Figure 10: ARIMA predictions on monthly data with a monthly season

Next, we will be looking at a different, and sometimes more accurate, technique for modeling seasonal data.

Dynamic linear models

A DLM is a generalization of the ARIMA model. They are a kind of state-space model (also known as Bayesian state space-time series models) in which various dynamics of the model, for example, the linear trend, the weekly trend, and the monthly trend, can be represented as distinct components that contribute to the observed value (for example, the number of website visitors). The parameters of the different components, such as how much change there is in visitors from Sundays to Mondays, are all learned simultaneously so that the final model has the optimally weighted contributions from each component.

The Python library `pydlm` (`https://github.com/wwrechard/PyDLM`) allows us to declaratively specify our model's components. Rather than restrict ourselves to a single seasonal component, as in the simple uses of ARIMA, we can build several components into our model with different time scales. We also do not need to think about unintuitive parameters such as autoregression versus moving average as in ARIMA.

A `pydlm` model can include trends (constant, linear, quadratic, and more, specified by the `degree` parameter), seasonal information, and long-term seasonal information. First, we will build a model with a constant trend plus a weekly seasonal component. The constant trend allows the model to start at a particular value (about 50 with our data) and then deviate higher or lower from that value with the weekly seasonal influence (Sunday will be lower, Monday slightly higher):

```
from pydlm import dlm, trend, seasonality, longSeason

constant = trend(degree=0, name="constant")
seasonal_week = seasonality(period=7, name='seasonal_week')
model = dlm(series.ix['2015-01-01':'2017-12-31']) + \
constant + seasonal_week
```

Next, we fit the model (learn the parameters) and get the mean squared error to see how closely it learned to match the training data. Then we make some predictions from the test data:

```
model.fit()
predictions, _ = model.predictN(N=168)
```

Figure 11 shows the constant trend that was learned over the range of the data. After examining all the training data, the model finalized on a constant value of about 50 visitors per day. This constant value is then adjusted by a weekly cycle, which looks like a sine curve ranging from +7 to about -12. In other words, the impact of the day of the week can change the visitor count up 7 visitors from average or down 12 from average. Combining these two components, we get the predictions shown in *Figure 12*. There is no downward trend in these predictions since we indicated we wanted a constant trend. The ARIMA figure for the same weekly seasonality showed a downward trend; this was due to the *d=1* parameter, which effectively changed the original visitor counts to the velocity of visitors (up or down from previous day), thus allowing a linear trend to be learned in the process. The DLM approach supports the same if we change the `degree=0` parameter in the `trend()` function in the preceding code. In any event, the DLM predictions achieve a mean squared error of 229.86, less than half of the error we saw in the ARIMA example. This is mostly due to the fact the predictions hover around the mean of the data rather than the minimum. In either case, the predictions are not useful because the monthly seasonal aspect is not accounted for in either model:

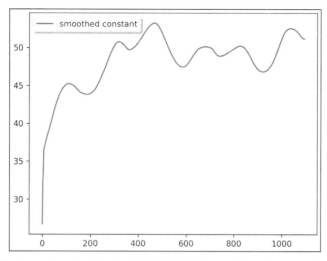

Figure 11: The learned constant trend with the DLM. The x-axis has the same units as the data, that is, number of daily website visitors.

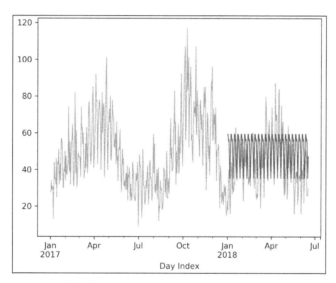

Figure 12: Predicted daily values from the DLM with weekly seasonality

To improve our model, we can add a `longseason` component in the DLM model. This would be difficult with ARIMA (we would have to introduce additional fields in the data), but is straightforward with `pydlm`:

```
constant = trend(degree=0, name="constant")
seasonal_week = seasonality(period=7, name='seasonal_week')
seasonal_month = longSeason(period=12, stay=31,
data=series['2015-01-01':'2017-12-31'], name='seasonal_month')
```

```
model = dlm(series.ix['2015-01-01':'2017-12-31']) + \
constant + seasonal_week + seasonal_month
model.tune()
model.fit()
```

This time we use `model.tune()` so that `pydlm` spends more time searching for the optimal weights of the different components.

Note that a long season differs from a regular season in `pydlm` as in a regular season, each row in the dataset changes its seasonal field. For example, with weekly seasonality, row 1 is day 1, row 2 is day 2, row 3 is day 3, and so on, until it wraps around again: row 8 is day 1, and so on. The `period` parameter indicates how long until the values wrap around. On the other hand, in a long season, the same value persists for different rows until the `stay` length has been reached. So, row 1 is month 1, row 2 is month 1, row 3 is month 1, and so on, until row 31 is month 2, and so on. Eventually, the months wrap around too, according to the `period` parameter: row 373 is month 1, and so on (12*31 = 372, not exactly matching the number of days in a year).

After fitting the model, we can plot the constant component and the monthly component. The weekly component may also be plotted, but because there are so many weeks in the data, it is difficult to understand; it looks like a sine curve just as before. The following figure shows the constant and monthly trends:

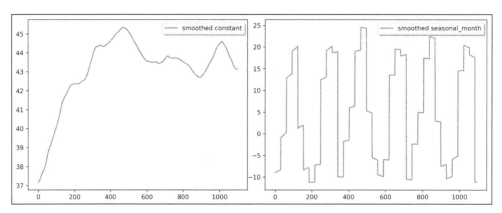

Figure 13: Constant and monthly trends with a DLM

Now, our daily predictions better match the test data, as shown in *Figure 14*. We can see the weekly seasonal influence (the fast ups and downs) as well as the monthly influence (the periodic jumps and drops of the weekly cycles). The mean squared error is 254.89, slightly higher than we saw before adding the monthly component. But it is clear from the figure that the monthly component is playing a major role and we should expect the predictions to be more accurate over time (across a wider span of months) than the model that did not include the monthly component:

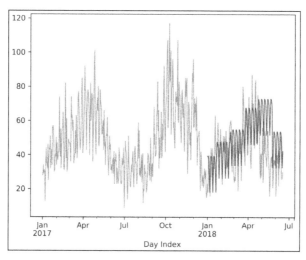

Figure 14: Predicted daily values from the DLM with weekly and monthly seasonality

Finally, we can aggregate the website usage data to monthly values and build a DLM model that just uses a constant and monthly seasonality, as we did with our second ARIMA example:

```
series = series.groupby(pd.Grouper(freq='M')).sum()

from pydlm import dlm, trend, seasonality, longSeason

constant = trend(degree=0, name="constant")
seasonal_month = seasonality(period=12, name='seasonal_month')
model = dlm(series.ix['2015-01-01':'2016-12-31']) + \
constant + seasonal_month

model.tune()
model.fit()
```

Note that we did not use the long season approach this time because now every row represents a count for the month, so the month should change on every row. The following figure shows the predictions. The model achieves a mean squared error of 146,976.77, slightly higher (worse) than ARIMA:

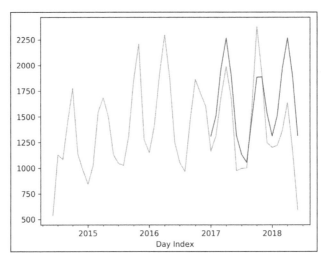

Figure 15: Predicted monthly values from the DLM with monthly seasonality

Recognizing anomalies

Anomalies are a different but related kind of information from trends. While trend analysis aims to discover what is normal about a data stream, recognizing anomalies is about finding out which events represented in the data stream are clearly abnormal. To recognize anomalies, one must already have an idea of what is normal. Additionally, recognizing anomalies requires deciding some threshold of how far from normal data may be before it is labeled anomalous.

We will look at four techniques for recognizing anomalies. First, we'll devise two ways to use **z-scores** to identify data points that are significantly different from the average data point. Then we will look at a variation of principal component analysis, a kind of matrix decomposition technique similar to singular value decomposition from *Chapter 4, A Blueprint for Recommending Products and Services*, that separates normal data from anomalous or extreme events from noise. Finally, we will use a cosine similarity technique from cluster analysis to recognize events that significantly deviate from the norm.

Recognizing anomalies allows us to identify, and possibly remove, data points that do not fit the overall trend. For example, we can identify sudden increases in activity or sudden drops in data processing efficiency.

We will use three datasets for our examples: a record of processing time for a certain text analysis operation, page view counts for Wikipedia's main English page (`https://tools.wmflabs.org/pageviews/?project=en.wikipedia.org&platform=all-access&agent=user&start=2015-07-01&end=2018-06-29&pages=Main_Page`), and a log of network traffic to a thermostat before and after **Gafgyt** (`https://krebsonsecurity.com/2016/09/krebsonsecurity-hit-with-record-ddos/`) and **Mirai** (`https://blog.cloudflare.com/inside-mirai-the-infamous-iot-botnet-a-retrospective-analysis/`) attacks occurred.

Z-scores with static models

Perhaps the simplest way to recognize an anomaly is to check whether a data point is quite a bit different from the average for a given data stream. Consider a processing time dataset, which measures how long a certain text processing task (identifying keywords in documents) takes for different documents. This is a classic "long tail" distribution in which most documents take a small amount of time (say, 50-100ms) but some documents take extraordinarily long times (1s or longer). Luckily, there are few cases of these long processing times. Also, there is quite a bit of variation in document processing times, so we will have a wide threshold for anomalous processing time. The following figure shows us a histogram of the processing times, demonstrating the long tail:

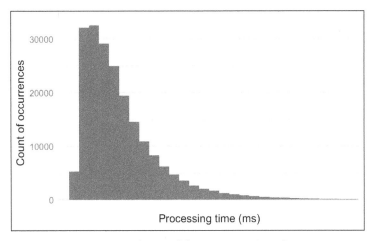

Figure 16: Distribution of the processing times dataset

We can use a simple calculation known as a z-score to calculate how normal or abnormal a certain value is relative to the average value and deviation of the values in the dataset. For each value x, its z-score is defined as $z = x - \mu/\sigma$, where μ is the mean of the values and σ is the standard deviation. The mean and standard deviation can easily be calculated in Python with the `mean()` and `std()` functions of NumPy, but we can also just use the statistics library function of SciPy called `zscore()`.

First, we load the dataset; then we compute the z-score for every value:

```
import pandas as pd
import scipy.stats

times = pd.read_csv('proctime.csv.zip', ...)

zscores = scipy.stats.zscore(times['proctime'])
```

Next, we can plot the data points with the `matplotlib` library, marking those below a z-score threshold as gray (normal) and those above a threshold as anomalous (black). Z-scores can be negative as well, indicating a significant difference *below* the average, but our processing times data do not exhibit this property (recall the histogram in `Figure 16`), so we do not bother to distinguish especially fast processing times:

```
plt.scatter(times.ix[zscores < 5.0].index.astype(np.int64),
times.ix[zscores < 5.0]['proctime'], color='gray')
plt.scatter(times.ix[zscores >= 5.0].index.astype(np.int64),
times.ix[zscores >= 5.0]['proctime'], color='red')
```

The result, in the following figure, shows that any processing time significantly longer than normal is identified in black. We could devise a system that logs these values and the document that caused the long processing times for further investigation:

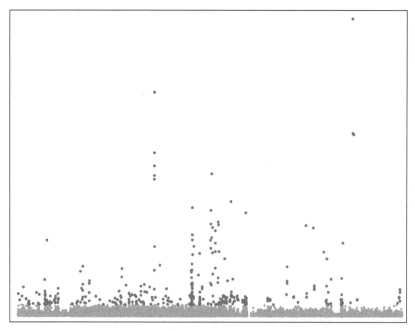

Figure 17: Anomalies in the processing times dataset

Next, we will switch to a dataset of page views on the Wikipedia English homepage. This data was downloaded from the Wikimedia Toolforge (`https://tools.wmflabs.org/pageviews/?project=en.wikipedia.org&platform=all-access&agent=user&start=2015-07-01&end=2018-06-29&pages=Main_Page`). The following figure shows a plot of the data. Notice that, for some unknown reason, page views spiked in July 2016. It would be interesting to find out of our anomaly detectors can identify this spike:

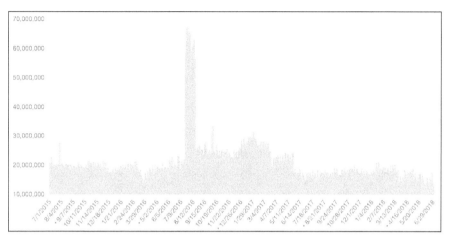

Figure 18: Wikipedia English homepage views

Applying the same z-score approach to the Wikipedia dataset is straightforward. However, it's instructive at this point to experiment with different z-score thresholds. In the processing times dataset, we only demonstrated a threshold of 5.0, which is quite large. *Figure 19* shows the impact of different z-score thresholds. In all cases, we check the absolute value of the z-score, so if a threshold is 0.5, we consider the data point anomalous if its z-score is <-0.5 or >0.5. For low thresholds, such as 0.5, anomalies are detected above and below the average range of daily page views. The spike in July is considered completely anomalous. At higher thresholds, such as 2.0 and 3.0, only the tip of the spike is considered anomalous.

At this point, we should ask ourselves, is this the kind of anomaly detection we want? Unlike the processing times dataset, the Wikipedia Pageview stats dataset is a dynamic system. Interest increases and decreases over time, while processing times should be relatively constant (unless the documents being processed dramatically change or the processing algorithm changes, both of which are unlikely to occur without the system engineers knowing about it). If interest in Wikipedia rises over time, eventually interest will rise so much that all those data points will be considered anomalous until, that is, the higher interest starts to dominate the dataset and becomes the new normal.

Thus, it is probably more appropriate to have a moving average or sliding window by which to evaluate the Wikipedia dataset. Anomalous page view counts depend on what happened recently, not what happened five years ago. If *recent* interest suddenly spikes or drops, we want to know about it. We will apply our z-score methodology to a sliding window in the next section.

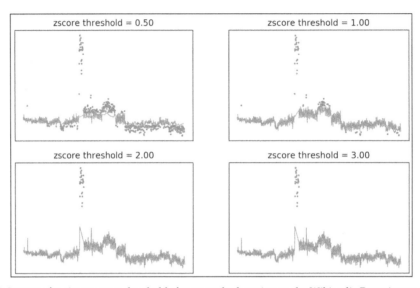

Figure 19: Impact of various z-score thresholds for anomaly detection on the Wikipedia Pageview stats dataset

Z-scores with sliding windows

In order to apply a z-score to a sliding window, we simply need to keep a chunk or window of data, calculate z-scores, and separate anomalies, and then slide the window forward. For this example, we will look one month backward, so we have a window size of 30 days (30 rows of data). We will calculate the z-score for the most recent day in the window, not all values; then we slide the window forward one day and check the z-score for that data (based on the prior 29 days), and so on (note that we will not be able to detect anomalies in the first 29 days of data):

```
chunksz = 30 # one month
chunk = pageviews.ix[:chunksz]['Views']
for i in range(1, len(pageviews)-chunksz):

    zscores = np.absolute(scipy.stats.zscore(chunk))

    # check if most recent value is anomalous
    if zscores[-1] > zscore_threshold:
        pageviews.at[pageviews.index[i+chunksz-2], 'Anomalous'] = True
```

```
# drop oldest value, add new value
chunk = pageviews.ix[i:i+chunksz]['Views']
```

Figure 20 shows the result of the sliding window and different z-score thresholds. Notice, particularly with thresholds 1.5 and 2.0, that the initial rise on the July 2016 spike is marked as anomalous, but the next days are not anomalous. Then the drop back to pre-July levels is again marked as anomalous. This is due to the fact that after the spike starts, the high values are now considered normal (they result in a higher average) so sustained page view counts at this new peak are not anomalous. This behavior is more like what Twitter and others demonstrate when they display "trending topics" and similar. Once a topic is no longer rising in popularity and just maintains its strong popularity for an extended period of time, it's no longer trending. It's just normal:

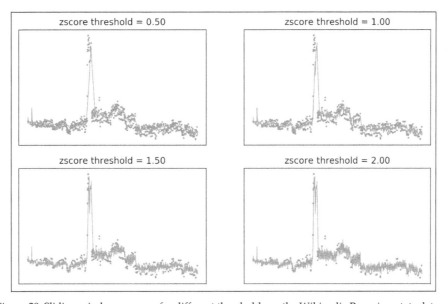

Figure 20: Sliding window z-scores for different thresholds on the Wikipedia Pageview stats dataset

RPCA

Now we will look at a completely different approach for identifying peaks in the Wikipedia Pageview stats dataset. A technique known as RPCA (*Robust principal component analysis?*, *Candès, Emmanuel J., Xiaodong Li, Yi Ma*, and *John Wright, Journal of the ACM (JACM) Vol. 58, No. 3, pp. 11-49, 2011*) uses principal component analysis (a technique similar to singular value decomposition shown in *Chapter 4, A Blueprint for Recommending Products and Services*) to decompose a matrix, M, into a low-rank matrix, L; a sparse matrix, S; and a matrix E containing small values.

These matrices add up to reconstruct M: $M=L+S+E$. Thus, all of the matrices are the same size (rows by columns). When we say L is low rank, we mean that most of its columns can be computed as multiples or combinations of other columns in L, and when we say S is sparse, we mean most of its values are zeros. The goal of the RPCA algorithm is to find optimal values for L, S, and E such that these constraints are met and that the sum to form the original matrix M.

At first glance, RPCA seems wholly unrelated to anomaly detection. However, consider the following scenario. Let M be a matrix of temperature observations with 365 rows and 10 columns. Each column has 365 values, and one temperature observation (say, the high temperature) for the day. In year 2, we move to column 2 and record 365 observations. And so on, across 10 years (10 columns). Now, if we apply RPCA, L will have low rank, meaning many of the columns will be some kind of multiple or combination of the others. This makes sense because the temperatures each year mostly repeat themselves, with some minor variations. Thus, the columns represent the seasonal component (yearly) of the data, and L exploits that fact. Any significant deviations, any outliers or anomalies, in the temperatures will be moved over to S. Most days do not have anomalies temperatures (record highs or lows), so S is mostly zeros. Finally, E has any minor variations day to day (that is, noise) that are pulled out of L so that L can remain low-rank. Temperatures are not perfectly cyclic, even after removing anomalies, so E has these minor errors.

For our purposes, we can read the anomalies out of S: anything non-zero is a recording of an anomaly. If it is useful, we can also look at L as a record of typical or smoothed values for the data and use those for forecasting.

The simplest way to use RPCA is through its R interface. First, the package must be installed:

```
library(devtools)
install_github(repo = "Surus", username = "Netflix",
subdir = "resources/R/RAD")
```

Next, after loading the dataset, we call the `AnomalyDetection.rpca` function, providing the daily values (x), the dates, and the frequency (we will choose 30 days):

```
anomalies <- AnomalyDetection.rpca(X=mainpage_dates["Views"],
dates=mainpage_dates["Date"], frequency=30)
```

The result is a data structure with the L, S, and E values for each data point. The library also provides a graphing function, which we use to produce *Figure 21*. The black line at the center is the original dataset, the black is L, the gray at the bottom is E, and the anomalies are dots, the non-zero values in S. The sizes of the black dots indicate the magnitude of the anomaly. We see that the RPCA approach identified many of the same anomalies as our prior approaches.

Interestingly, probably due to our 30-day frequency, almost all of the July 2016 peak is considered anomalous, and the decline back to normal is not considered anomalous. RPCA examines all the data at once and is able to detect long term trends (like a linear rise over the whole dataset time frame); but unlike our sliding window z-score approach, RPCA does not change its definition of normal on a continuous basis:

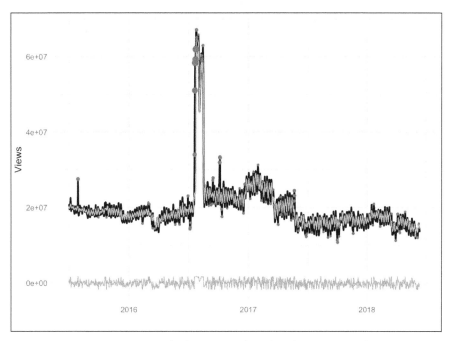

Figure 21: RPCA anomaly detection on the Wikipedia Page views dataset

Clustering

Our final technique for recognizing anomalies is among the simplest. As usual, we will develop a model of what is normal about the data, and like the z-score approach, we will not modify the data at all. We will use a distance calculation to measure how like or unlike a new data point is to the others, or to the average data point, and decide if it is too dissimilar and hence anomalous.

This approach is borrowed from the technique known as clustering, in which data are grouped according to how similar or dissimilar they are from each other. Similar things form clusters. Once we have a cluster, we can create a hypothetical average point to identify the center of the cluster. An algorithm like **k-means clustering** works this way.

For the sake of identifying anomalies, we do not necessarily need more than one cluster. We just need a similarity or distance function and a threshold for the maximum distance. A new data point can be far from the cluster center before we consider it anomalous. Several distance functions are available, including Euclidean distance (straight-line distance), Manhattan distance (length of a path from point A to point B that includes only 90-degree turns, no diagonals), and cosine similarity. We defined cosine similarity in *Chapter 4, A Blueprint for Recommending Products and Services*, when we looked at content-based recommendations. Cosine distance is just 1.0 – cosine similarity.

For a test dataset, we will use network traffic data and attempt to recognize Gafgyt and Mirai botnet attacks (*N-BaIoT: Network-based Detection of IoT Botnet Attacks Using Deep Autoencoders, Y. Meidan, M. Bohadana, Y. Mathov, Y. Mirsky, D. Breitenbacher, A. Shabtai, and Y. Elovici, IEEE Pervasive Computing, Special Issue - Securing the IoT, July/ Sep 2018*). First, we load the two datasets:

```
import numpy as np
import pandas as pd

benign_traffic = pd.read_csv('benign_traffic.csv.zip')
gafgyt_traffic = pd.read_csv('gafgyt_traffic.csv.zip', nrows=2000)
```

Each row in the dataset contains some simple statistics from different sliding windows of recent network traffic on an internet-connected thermostat device. The sliding windows are 100ms, 500ms, 1.5s, 10s, and 60s. The simple statistics include the average and variance of the packet size, the packet count, the time between packets, and so on. Ultimately, we have 115 attributes for each row of the dataset.

Next, we should visualize whether our distance metric (Euclidean, cosine, and so on) properly separates benign traffic from botnet traffic. We put the two datasets together and then find the distance (cosine distance in our case) between every two points. Then we use principal component analysis to reduce the large distance matrix to just two dimensions (x and y) that best describe the relationships (distances) between the points. The result is *Figure 22*. We see that, for the most part, benign traffic (gray) is separated from botnet traffic (black), though there is some overlap.

Now we will write code for the anomaly detector. First, we define an average data point to serve as the representative for benign traffic:

```
from sklearn.metrics.pairwise import cosine_distances
benign_avg = np.median(benign_traffic.values, axis=0,
keepdims=True)
```

Then we set a threshold for minimum distance to be considered an anomaly. We choose 0.99 (cosine distance ranges from 0 to 1). This threshold was found by checking the following:

- How similar are benign records to the average benign record? Answer: min = 0.0, max = 0.999, mean = 0.475, median = 0.436.

- How similar are botnet records to the average benign record? Answer: min = 0.992, max = 0.999, mean = 0.992, median = 0.992.

These results led us to conclude a very high threshold will work, though we will have some false positives (benign traffic labeled as botnet traffic) since there is some benign traffic that really stands out from the normal, benign traffic.

We set the threshold and then check how many true positives and false positives we have by computing all the distances to the average benign point and then applying the threshold:

```
threshold = 0.99

benign_avg_benign_dists = cosine_distances(
benign_avg, benign_traffic)
benign_avg_gafgyt_dists = cosine_distances(
benign_avg, gafgyt_traffic)

print("Benign >= threshold:")
print(np.shape(benign_avg_benign_dists[np.where(
benign_avg_benign_dists >= threshold)]))
print("Benign < threshold:")
print(np.shape(benign_avg_benign_dists[np.where(
benign_avg_benign_dists < threshold)]))

print("Gafgyt vs. benign >= threshold:")
print(np.shape(benign_avg_gafgyt_dists[np.where(
benign_avg_gafgyt_dists >= threshold)]))
print("Gafgyt vs. benign < threshold:")
print(np.shape(benign_avg_gafgyt_dists[np.where(
benign_avg_gafgyt_dists < threshold)]))
```

The results are as follows:

- Benign traffic > threshold (false positives): 1,291 records
- Benign traffic < threshold (true negatives): 11,820 records
- Gafgyt traffic > threshold (true positives): 2,000 records
- Gafgyt traffic < threshold (false negatives): 0 records

Thus, except for some positives, the approach seems to work. The false positives presumably correspond to those gray dots in the following figure showing that some benign traffic looks like (is cosine-similar to) botnet traffic:

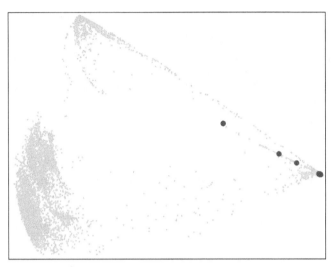

Figure 22: Benign (gray) and botnet (black) traffic according to cosine distance and reduced to two dimensions with principal component analysis

A more useful test of this approach would be to introduce new botnet traffic, in this case, Mirai traffic (https://blog.cloudflare.com/inside-mirai-the-infamous-iot-botnet-a-retrospective-analysis/), provided by the same dataset. Without changing the threshold, can this approach also identify Mirai traffic?:

```
# Final test, new attack data

mirai_traffic = pd.read_csv('mirai_udp.csv.zip', nrows=2000)

benign_avg_mirai_dists = cosine_distances(
benign_avg, mirai_traffic)

print("Mirai vs. benign >= threshold:")
print(np.shape(benign_avg_mirai_dists[np.where(
benign_avg_mirai_dists >= threshold)]))
print("Mirai vs. benign < threshold:")
print(np.shape(benign_avg_mirai_dists[np.where(
benign_avg_mirai_dists < threshold)]))
```

The results are as follows:

- Mirai traffic > threshold (true positives): 2,000 records
- Mirai traffic < threshold (false negatives): 0 records

So, for this data, the approach works, if we are comfortable with some false positives (benign traffic looking like botnet traffic). Note, however, that the researchers who published this dataset achieved about a 2.5% false positive rate compared to our 9.8% (*N-BaIoT: Network-based Detection of IoT Botnet Attacks Using Deep Autoencoders, Y. Meidan, M. Bohadana, Y. Mathov, Y. Mirsky, D. Breitenbacher, A. Shabtai,* and *Y. Elovici, IEEE Pervasive Computing, Special Issue - Securing the IoT, July/Sep 2018*). They used a more complex method known as a **deep autoencoder**.

Deployment strategy

There are many use cases for finding trends and anomalies, and many techniques for accomplishing these goals. This chapter has reviewed just a handful of popular approaches. We will not explore all of the various use cases with example code, but we will address two scenarios. First, recall the Google Analytics anomaly detector. It notified the user of anomalous (very high or very low) page views or visitors to a website by comparing the observed number of page views or visitors to the predicted number. The predicted number had a range (curiously, the range in the screenshot in *Figure 1* is 2.13 to 35.4 page views for the day, which is not an especially precise prediction), and the observed value (43 page views) exceeded this range. Recall also that the documentation for Google Analytics, quoted in the introduction to this chapter, states that they use a 90-day window with a Bayesian state space-time series model.

We developed such a model in a previous section, called a DLM. We used the DLM to detect trends, but we can also use the model to detect anomalies by comparing an observed value with the predicted value. The DLM model can give a prediction of the next value in the series, plus a confidence range. Technically, the model is sampled through simulations, and the prediction is a mean while the confidence is the variance. Using this mean and variance, we can compute a z-score and then convert that into a p-value. The p-value tells us whether the findings are significant or more likely just due to chance. When the p-value is low, that is, <0.10, we can consider the observation to be significant, that is, anomalous.

Here is the code to train a DLM on the past 90 days, make a prediction, and then ask the user for observations. For each observation, the model gives the p-value for that observation; any observation with p<0.10 we can consider anomalous:

```
import math
import pandas as pd
import scipy.stats

series = pd.read_csv('daily-users.csv', header=0, parse_dates=[0],
index_col=0, squeeze=True)
```

```
# Use just last 90 days
series = series.ix[-90:]

from pydlm import dlm, trend, seasonality

constant = trend(degree=0, name="constant")
seasonal_week = seasonality(period=7, name='seasonal_week')
model = dlm(series) + constant + seasonal_week
model.tune()
model.fit()

# Forecast one day
predictions, conf = model.predictN(N=1)
print("Prediction for next day: %.2f, confidence: %s" % \
(predictions[0], conf[0]))

while True:
  actual = float(input("Actual value? "))
  zscore = (actual - predictions[0]) / math.sqrt(conf[0])
  print("Z-score: %.2f" % zscore)
  pvalue = scipy.stats.norm.sf(abs(zscore))*2
  print("p-value: %.2f" % pvalue)
```

Here is an example run:

```
Prediction for next day: 53.24, confidence: 197.08857093375497
Actual value? 70
Z-score: 1.19
p-value: 0.23
Actual value? 80
Z-score: 1.91
p-value: 0.06
Actual value? 90
Z-score: 2.62
p-value: 0.01
Actual value? 30
Z-score: -1.66
p-value: 0.10
Actual value? 20
Z-score: -2.37
p-value: 0.02
```

We see the predicted visitor count for the next day is 53, and the variance of that prediction is 197. If we set a p-value threshold of 0.10, then (hypothetical) observed visitor counts of about 75+ or less than 30 would be considered anomalous.

In our second example of aspects related to deployment, we demonstrate how one must be careful to build a model on clean data. If using a model of any kind (DLM, ARIMA, z-scores, and so on), the model will come to represent what is normal about the training data. If that training data contains anomalous values, then it will be a poor trend estimator or anomaly detector. Consider our clustering approach, in which an average data point was constructed by taking the median of a set of observations. In the preceding example, these observations were known to be benign traffic, as opposed to botnet attack traffic. We then set a threshold of 0.99 to distinguish how far (in cosine distance) a new point was from this average to be considered too far, and thus traffic of a different sort (not benign, so therefore probably an attack).

If we are not completely certain the training data is not completely benign, our average benign data point might be influenced a bit by bad data in the training set. In the following code block, we simulate this by including different amounts of Gafgyt attack data in the benign dataset. We also lower the threshold to 0.90 to demonstrate a point. We will see that as the amount of bad data in the training data grows, it eventually reaches a point where all of the accuracy statistics (true positives, false positives, and so on) turn very bad. This is because the median benign data point has shifted so much due to this influence of bad data that the model is completely useless as an anomaly detector for network traffic:

```python
import numpy as np
import pandas as pd
from sklearn.metrics.pairwise import cosine_distances

benign_traffic_orig = pd.read_csv('benign_traffic.csv.zip',
nrows=2000)
gafgyt_traffic = pd.read_csv('gafgyt_traffic.csv.zip',
nrows=2000)

# inject different amounts of bad data
for n in [0, 500, 1000, 1500, 2000]:
  benign_traffic = pd.concat(
[benign_traffic_orig.copy(),gafgyt_traffic[:n]], axis=0)

  # Define the "average" benign traffic
  benign_avg = np.median(
benign_traffic.values, axis=0, keepdims=True)

  # Compute distances to this avg
  benign_avg_benign_dists = cosine_distances(
benign_avg, benign_traffic_orig)

  threshold = 0.90
```

```
    benign_avg_gafgyt_dists = cosine_distances(
benign_avg, gafgyt_traffic)

    fp = np.shape(benign_avg_benign_dists[np.where(
benign_avg_benign_dists >= threshold)])[0]
    tn = np.shape(benign_avg_benign_dists[np.where(
benign_avg_benign_dists < threshold)])[0]
    tp = np.shape(benign_avg_gafgyt_dists[np.where(
benign_avg_gafgyt_dists >= threshold)])[0]
    fn = np.shape(benign_avg_gafgyt_dists[np.where(
benign_avg_gafgyt_dists < threshold)])[0]
```

If we print the true positive, false positive, true negative, and false negative values for each iteration, we see the following:

```
Bad data: 0      tp = 2000    fp = 504     tn = 1496    fn = 0
Bad data: 500    tp = 2000    fp = 503     tn = 1497    fn = 0
Bad data: 1000   tp = 5       fp = 32      tn = 1968    fn = 1995
Bad data: 1500   tp = 3       fp = 1421    tn = 579     fn = 1997
Bad data: 2000   tp = 3       fp = 1428    tn = 572     fn = 1997
```

At 1,000 bad data points in the training set, the threshold value has become ill-fitted for the purpose of detecting anomalies.

Summary

This chapter demonstrated a variety of techniques for discovering trends and recognizing anomalies. These two outcomes, trends and anomalies, are related because they both rely on a model that describes the behavior or characteristics of the training data. For discovering trends, we fit a model and then query that model to find data streams that are dramatically increasing or decreasing in recent history. For anomaly detection, we can use the model to forecast the next observation and then check whether the true observation significantly differed from the forecast, or we can query the model to see how normal or abnormal a new observation is compared to the training data. How these techniques are deployed in practice depends on the technique used and the use case, but often one will train a model on recent data (say, the prior 90 days), while taking care to ensure the training data is not tarnished with anomalous data points that can undermine the model's ability to accurately detect trends and anomalies.

7
A Blueprint for Understanding Queries and Generating Responses

In all of the previous chapters of this book, we have developed AI solutions that operate behind the scenes, in a way that does not allow direct user interaction. For example, in *Chapter 3, A Blueprint for Making Sense of Feedback*, we showed how we could measure the overall sentiment of users based on their tweets and comments, but this user feedback was collected passively rather than directly asking users for their opinions. In *Chapter 5, A Blueprint for Detecting Your Logo in Social Media*, we developed a technique to detect a company's logo in random photos, but the people who took those photos did not have any direct interaction with our logo detector. Up to this point, we have explored several ways that AI and ML can help make sense of a big pile of data, be they images, tweets, website clicks, or song plays, for example. But the *interactive* prospects of AI have remained unaddressed.

Interactive systems take a wide variety of forms. For example, in the simplest case, the drop-down menus on a word processor application support direct user interaction with the machine. In a far more complex scenario, beyond the abilities of today's robot engineers, one can imagine a soccer team composed of a mix of humans and robots, in which the humans and robots must watch each other for subtle gestures to perform effectively as a team. The fields of **human-computer interaction (HCI)** and **human-robot interaction (HRI)** address the myriad and complex ways that humans and machines might be able to work together to achieve common goals.

This chapter addresses interactive AI systems that allow a user to directly ask the system for answers to various kinds of questions. Businesses have shown a big interest in these kinds of interactive systems. Often, they go by the name of chatbots, and are used as automated helpdesks and sales agents.

With the increasing popularity of Facebook Messenger for business-to-customer communication, and Slack for internal business communication, chatbots are seen as a way to extend marketing reach (in the case of Facebook Messenger) and optimize processes related to project management and information acquisition (in the case of Slack). Both Messenger (`https://developers.facebook.com/docs/messenger-platform/introduction`) and Slack (`https://api.slack.com/bot-users`) have rich documentation for developing chatbots on their respective platforms. For simplicity's sake, we will not use these platforms for our examples. However, they are popular choices for developing and deploying chatbots.

In this chapter, we will focus on the core features of a text-based interactive AI system: understanding and responding to a user's query. The query may take the form of speech or text – we will demonstrate the use of **Google Cloud Speech-to-Text** API (`https://cloud.google.com/speech-to-text/`) to convert speech to text. After receiving the query, the AI system must then make sense of it (*what's being asked?*), figure out a response (*what is the answer?*), and then communicate that response back to the user (*how do I say this?*). Each step in this process will make use of an AI technology most appropriate for that step.

In brief, we will use NLP, particularly the **Rasa NLU (natural language understanding)** Python library (`http://rasa.com/products/rasa-nlu/`), to figure out what the user is asking; we will then use logic programming, particularly the **Prolog** language, to find data that informs the response; and **natural language generation (NLG)**, particularly the `SimpleNLG` Java library (`https://github.com/simplenlg/simplenlg`), to generate a grammatically correct response. After we've done that, we'll be able to convert the response to speech using **Google Cloud Text-to-Speech** API (`https://cloud.google.com/text-to-speech/`) for applications that must be entirely hands-free.

In this chapter, we will cover:

- How to configure and train the Rasa NLU library to recognize user intents in text
- How to develop domain-specific logic using the Prolog programming language
- The process of generating grammatically correct responses using the `SimpleNLG` Java library
- Using Google's APIs to convert speech to text and text to speech

The problem, goal, and business case

Chatbots can, in theory, do just about anything that does not require a physical presence. They can help customers book flights, discover new recipes, solve banking issues, find the right TV to purchase, send flowers to a spouse, tutor a student, and tell a joke.

The natural language interface is so general purpose that it forms the basis of Turing's famous *Imitation Game* thought experiment. Turing's test, as it has come to be known, describes a way to gauge whether an AI is truly intelligent. In his test, a human and a machine communicate with a human judge through a text interface. The goal of the judge is to determine which of the two interlocutors is the machine.

A subtle but critical feature of Turing's test that many people fail to understand is that both the human behind the keyboard and the machine are trying to convince the judge that the *other* contestant is the computer. The test is not just whether a machine acts humanlike, but whether it can also defend against accusations that it is indeed a machine. Furthermore, the judge can ask any question from, *what's your favorite color*, and *what's the best chess move from a certain board position*, to *what does it mean to love*.

The textual interface hinders no subjects of discussion – it is maximally general. Text can do anything. Yet, that's part of the problem with chatbots. They have maximal promise. With the right chatbot, a company would no longer need bank tellers, call centers or extensive manuals. Yet most of us have experienced the *nuisance chatbot*, the pop-up window on a website that immediately attempts to engage you in a conversation. What makes these bots a nuisance is they fail to set the expectations and boundaries of the conversation and inevitably fail to understand the wide range of possible user queries. Instead, if the chatbot is activated by the user to solve a particular goal, such as booking a flight, then the conversation may proceed more smoothly by limiting the possible range of queries and responses. The following figure shows a sample interaction with Expedia's Facebook Messenger bot:

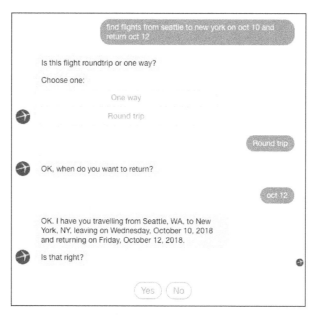

Figure 1: Expedia's chatbot

The interaction with the Expedia bot is not as smooth as it should be, but at least the bot is clearly focused on booking a flight. This clarity helps the user know how to interact with it. Unfortunately, as shown in the following figure, venturing outside the boundaries of booking a flight, but still within the boundaries of how a person might use the Expedia website confuses the bot:

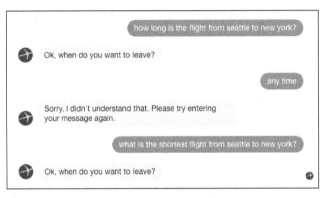

Figure 2: Expedia's chatbot

Whole Foods has also developed a natural language interface for their database of recipes. Due to the free-form text interface, a user might be forgiven for typing any relevant question that comes to mind, for example, asking how to make a vegan pumpkin pie (that is, without eggs), as shown in the following figure:

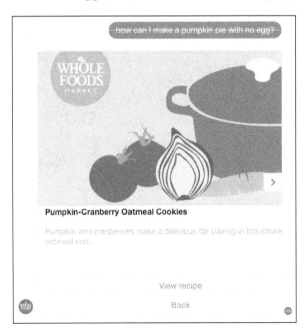

Figure 3: Whole Foods' chatbot

The preposition *with no egg* can be challenging to detect and utilize when searching the recipe database. The resulting recipe, **Pumpkin-Cranberry Oatmeal Cookies**, indeed includes eggs, let alone that the bot is picking up on a "cookie" dish and not a "pie." The simple query, *vegan pumpkin pie*, returns more appropriate results: dairy-free piecrust and vegan date-pecan pumpkin pie (which probably should have been the first result). However, the query, *do you have any recipes for vegan donuts?* gives a recipe for curry kale chips, while the simple query *vegan donut* returns vegan cocoa glaze. It appears that there are no recipes in Whole Foods' database for vegan donuts, which is perfectly reasonable. But the chatbot should know when to say, *Sorry, I don't have that one*.

Thus, the business case for chatbots is nuanced. If the bot answers to a narrow domain of questions, and the user is *informed* of this narrow domain, there is a possibility for success. Furthermore, the chatbot should aim for high confidence. In other words, if it is not highly confident about its understanding of the question, it should simply say, *I don't know*, or offer ways to rephrase the question. Finally, the AI should make a user's life easier or convert more visitors into customers. If the user is stuck in a nonsensical dialogue with a chatbot, they might soon just walk away.

Our approach

Our approach in this chapter takes these lessons into account in the following ways:

1. We'll focus on two narrow domains; the breeding rules of *Pokémon* (the video game originally published by Nintendo), and course advising for college students.

2. We'll set a high-confidence threshold for the AI component that attempts to understand the user's query; if this threshold is not met, we inform the user that we did not understand their question.

3. Once a user's query is understood, we'll use logical reasoning to construct the best answer to the query. This reasoning can be quite sophisticated as will be demonstrated by the course advising example.

4. We'll use NLG technology to produce reasonable responses that are designed to directly answer the user's query, rather than simply pointing them to a webpage or other documentation.

While many companies offer chatbot creation tools, these companies often claim that a chatbot can be created in just a few minutes without any programming. These claims make it clear that there is little sophistication between the query understanding and query response (that is, step 3 is missing). Usually, these no-programming frameworks allow bot creators to specify a different response to each possible question.

For example, if a user says "X," respond "Y" – that is, more like Whole Foods' search bot (minimal domain-specific logic) and less like Expedia's flight booking bot (more domain-specific logic, such as understanding locations, dates, round trips, and so on). We'll demonstrate the development of domain-specific logic using the Prolog language so that our chatbot is able to find meaningful responses to users' queries.

The Pokémon domain

The simpler of our two example domains cover some of the rules of Pokémon breeding. Data regarding the various species of Pokémon was obtained from the GitHub user *veekun* (`https://github.com/veekun/pokedex`). The rules for breeding were obtained from reading the *Bulbapedia* (`https://bulbapedia.bulbagarden.net/wiki/Main_Page`), a large resource of Pokémon facts.

We will implement just a few rules about Pokémon breeding, described in the following implementation section. We note that while these rules are based off the actual game rules of the VI/XY generation of the game, these rules are simplified and incomplete. They don't entirely factually represent the actual behavior of the various Pokémon games. However, even in this simplified form, they do a good job of demonstrating how to represent domain knowledge.

We will develop a simple chatbot that will be able to answer questions about Pokémon breeding. The domain logic will be represented in Prolog.

The course advising domain

In a more complex example, we will develop a chatbot that assists students in course selection and schedule planning. We will interface our chatbot with previously developed software known as TAROT. I developed TAROT to improve academic advising at the college or university level. Quoting the paper that *Ryan Anderson* and I wrote, titled *TAROT: A Course Advising System for the Future*, best explains its purpose:

> *We have developed a new software tool called TAROT to assist advisors and students. TAROT is designed to help with the complex constraints and rules inherent in planning multi-year course schedules. Although many academic departments design prototypical two- or four-year schedules to help guide entering students, not all students follow the same path or come from the same background. Once a student deviates from this pre-defined plan, e.g., they bring transfer credit, or add a second major, or study abroad, or need a course override, or must finish in 3.5 years, etc., then the pre-defined plan is useless.*

Now, the student and advisor must think through the intricacies of major requirements, course prerequisites, and offering times to find a plan for this student's particular circumstances. This cognitive burden introduces the possibility of mistakes and precludes any more advanced forecasting such as finding the best time to study abroad or finding every possible major elective that would satisfy graduation requirements.

Yet handling constraints and managing complex interactions is the raison d'être of planning engines from the field of artificial intelligence. TAROT is a planning engine designed specifically for course advising. Its use cases focus on developing a student's schedule across multiple semesters rather than scheduling courses for times/days in the week, rooms, etc. We implemented TAROT in Prolog and exploit this language's ability to perform backtracking search to find solutions that satisfy arbitrary constraints.

TAROT: A Course Advising System for the Future, J. Eckroth, R. Anderson, Journal of Computing Sciences in Colleges, 34(3), pp. 108-116, 2018

TAROT has already been developed with an HTTP API. This will mean our chatbot will interface with it through that protocol. TAROT is not yet open source; therefore, its code will not be shown in this chapter. We include an example chatbot that interfaces with TAROT in this chapter to demonstrate a more complex example, while the Pokémon example better serves as a demonstration of representing domain knowledge in the Prolog language.

Method – NLP + logic programming + NLG

Our method for building a natural language question-answering service is straightforward. Three primary components are involved, as shown in *Figure 4*. Our method will be as follows:

- The user first provides the query in text or voice. If voice is used, we can make a request to the Google Cloud Speech-to-Text API (`https://cloud.google.com/speech-to-text/`) to get the text version of the speech.

- Next, we need to figure out what the user is asking about. There are lots of ways to ask the same question, and we wish to support several different kinds of questions in both example domains. Also, a question may contain internal phrases, or entities, such as the name of a particular Pokémon, or the name of a college course. We will need to extract these entities while also figuring out what kind of question is being asked.

- Once we have the question and entities, we then compose a new kind of query. Since we are using Prolog to represent much of the domain knowledge, we have to use Prolog's conventions for computing answers. Prolog does not use functions, per se, but rather predicates that are executed by "queries." This will all be explained in more detail in the *Logic programming with Prolog and tuProlog* section. The result of the Prolog query is one or more solutions to the query, such as answers to a question.

- We next take one or more of these answers and generate a natural language response.

- Finally, this response is either shown directly to the user or sent through Google's Text-to-Speech API (`https://cloud.google.com/text-to-speech/`) to produce a voice response.

In the following figure, we have the three components: the first is the **question-understanding and entity extraction component**, which will use the Rasa NLU library (`http://rasa.com/products/rasa-nlu/`). We will also refer to this component as NLP. Next, we have the **domain knowledge** in Prolog. Finally, we have the **response generation component**, which uses the `SimpleNLG` (natural language generation) library (`https://github.com/simplenlg/simplenlg`):

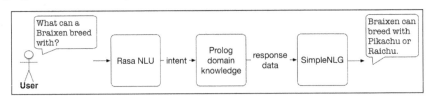

Figure 4: Processing pipeline

These components communicate with each other in varying ways. Rasa is a Python library that can run standalone as an HTTP server. Our Prolog code will either integrate directly with Java code using the `tuProlog` Java library in our Pokémon example, or our Prolog code will have its own HTTP server as in our course advising example. Finally, `SimpleNLG` is written in Java, so we will use it directly from the Java code. Thus, the simplest ways to implement our two examples are as follows.

This is the Pokémon example:

- Rasa runs as an HTTP server; the Java code connects with Rasa over HTTP, and uses `tuProlog` to interface with the Prolog code, and directly interfaces with the `SimpleNLG` library using normal Java methods

This is the course advising example:

- Rasa runs as an HTTP server; TAROT (Prolog code) runs as an HTTP server (`http://tarotdemo.artifice.cc:10333`); the Java code connects with Rasa and TAROT over HTTP and directly interfaces with `SimpleNLG`

In the next three sections, we'll provide some detail about how each of the three components of this system work.

NLP with Rasa

The purpose of Rasa is twofold: given a sentence or phrase, Rasa both:

- Detects the intent of the phrase, that is, the main content of the phrase
- Extracts entities from the phrase, that is, dates, times, names of people, names of cities, and so on

The intents and entities that Rasa attempts to detect and extract depends on the domain. Rasa uses ML, so it requires training data. These training examples consist of example phrases with their intent and any entities that should be extracted. Given these training examples, Rasa learns how to make sense of these domain-specific phrases.

For example, in our Pokémon domain, a user might ask a question like, *Which Pokémon can breed with a Braixen?* We would use Rasa to detect that the intent of this phrase, which is something like *can_breed_with* and the only relevant entity is *Braixen*. We will need to generate lots of phrases like this one in order to train Rasa, as well as any other kind of phrase that we want it to understand.

Rasa's training format uses **JavaScript Object Notation (JSON)** to list the example phrases and their intents and entities. Here is an example with two phrases:

```
{
  "rasa_nlu_data": {
    "common_examples": [
      {
        "text": "which pokemon breed with snorunt",
        "intent": "can_breed_with",
        "entities": [
          {
            "end": 32,
            "entity": "pokemon",
            "start": 25,
            "value": "snorunt"
          }
        ]
      },
      {
        "text": "find pokemon that can breed with skuntank",
        "intent": "can_breed_with",
```

```
        "entities": [
          {
            "end": 41,
            "entity": "pokemon",
            "start": 33,
            "value": "skuntank"
          }
        ]
      },
  ...
```

Each example goes into the `common_examples` section. Each example needs an intent and may include entities. If no entities need to be extracted (just the intent will be detected), the entities can be empty (`[]`). In these two examples, we can see the two ways that a user can ask what Pokémon a certain Pokémon can breed with. The actual Pokémon mentioned in the phrase is an entity that must be extracted, so we have to give the position in the phrase where the entity can be found.

Rasa itself is a Python library that can be installed with the usual Python package manager, pip: `pip install rasa_nlu`. We can then feed this JSON file into Rasa for training with the following command:

```
python -m rasa_nlu.train --config config.yml \
--data pokedex-training_rasa.json --path pokedex_rasa
```

The `pokedex_rasa` path indicates the directory where we want the trained model to be placed. The `config.yml` file provides some parameters to Rasa. These parameters are described in Rasa's documentation. Here is our `config.yml` file:

```
language: "en"
pipeline:
   - name: "nlp_spacy"
   - name: "tokenizer_spacy"
   - name: "intent_entity_featurizer_regex"
   - name: "intent_featurizer_spacy"
   - name: "ner_crf"
   - name: "ner_synonyms"
   - name: "intent_classifier_sklearn"
```

Once the trained model is ready, we can run Rasa as an HTTP server and send phrases to it via HTTP. Firstly, we must start Rasa:

```
python -m rasa_nlu.server --path pokedex_rasa
```

Next, we can send a phrase and see the result. We'll use the `curl` command for a quick example (the command should all be on one line):

```
curl 'localhost:5000/parse?q=what%20pokemon%20can%20
breed%20with%20pikachu' | python -m json.tool
```

The query (q= parameter) encodes the message *what pokemon can breed with pikachu*, and the result is as follows:

```
{
    "entities": [
        {
            "confidence": 0.9997784871228107,
            "end": 35,
            "entity": "pokemon",
            "extractor": "ner_crf",
            "start": 28,
            "value": "pikachu"
        }
    ],
    "intent": {
        "confidence": 0.9959038640688013,
        "name": "can_breed_with"
    },
    "intent_ranking": [
        {
            "confidence": 0.9959038640688013,
            "name": "can_breed_with"
        },
        {
            "confidence": 0.0030212196007807176,
            "name": "can_breed"
        },
        {
            "confidence": 0.001074916330417996,
            "name": "child_pok"
        }
    ],
    "model": "model_20180820-211906",
    "project": "default",
    "text": "what pokemon can breed with pikachu"
}
```

The result (also in JSON format) clearly shows that Rasa correctly identified the intent (*can_breed_with*) and the entity (*pikachu*). We can easily extract these pieces of information and send them to the Prolog code to figure out which Pokémon can breed with Pikachu.

The phrase *what pokemon can breed with pikachu* actually matches one of the training phrases in our training JSON file. So, let's try a different variant of the phrase, one that's not found in the training file, to see how Rasa performs. We will try the phrase, *what are the various pokemon that should be able to breed with pikachu*, yielding:

```
{
  "entities": [
    {
      "confidence": 0.608845509593439,
      "end": 43,
      "entity": "pokemon",
      "extractor": "ner_crf",
      "start": 41,
      "value": "be"
    },
    {
      "confidence": 0.99977848712259,
      "end": 70,
      "entity": "pokemon",
      "extractor": "ner_crf",
      "start": 63,
      "value": "pikachu"
    }
  ],
  "intent": {
    "confidence": 0.6212770831558388,
    "name": "can_breed_with"
  },
...
```

Firstly, we see that its confidence is much lower since this new test phrase has so many extra words beyond those found in the training data. We also see that it extracted *be* as an entity, which is incorrect, though at least it wasn't highly confident about this entity. However, it did correctly identify *pikachu* as an entity.

As with any ML technique, Rasa performs better when there is more diverse training data. But it becomes quite tedious to write all the JSON lines of training examples, particularly the entity character positions. Thus, we will make use of the **Chatito** tool by Rodrigo Pimentel (`https://github.com/rodrigopivi/Chatito`) to generate training examples from some simple patterns. In Chatito, variations of phrases that belong to the same intent are grouped under a % marker, and variations of entities are grouped under a @ marker. Additionally, we can use a ~ marker to indicate various ways to say the same thing. An example will make this clear:

```
%[can_breed_with]('training':'5000')
```

```
  ~[what] pokemon can breed with @[pokemon]
  ~[what] pokemon breed with @[pokemon]
  ~[what] can @[pokemon] breed with
  ~[what] can breed with @[pokemon]

%[can_breed]('training':'5000')
  can @[pokemon] and @[pokemon2] breed
  are @[pokemon] and @[pokemon2] able to breed
  are @[pokemon] and @[pokemon2] compatible

%[child_pok]('training':'5000')
  what is the child of @[pokemon] and @[pokemon2]
  what pokemon results from breeding @[pokemon] and @[pokemon2]
  if @[pokemon] and @[pokemon2] breed, what do we get

~[what]
  what
  which
  show me
  find

@[pokemon]
  ~[pokemon_variants]

@[pokemon2]
  ~[pokemon_variants]

~[pokemon_variants]
  abomasnow
  abra
  absol
  accelgor
  ...
```

This Chatito syntax in the preceding code block, indicates the following:

- We want 5,000 random non-repeating variations of the *can_breed_with* intent.
- A *can_breed_with* intent is defined by several different phrase patterns: *what pokemon can breed with [some pokemon name], what can [some pokemon name] breed with*, and so on.
- The word *what* in the pattern can be any of these words: *what, which, show me,* or *find*.

- The use of @[pokemon] and @[pokemon2] in the phrases indicates the word that appears there should be an entity (named pokemon and pokemon2 as appropriate). The valid words for these entities appear in the definitions of @[pokemon] and @[pokemon2], which themselves simply refer to the list of possible words in the ~[pokemon] list at the bottom. Note that ~[pokemon] is a list of variations (aliases) just like ~[what] was a list of variations.

The Chatito tool produces training examples by running through all the combinations specified in the file. For example, every different Pokémon name can be placed in the @[pokemon] position in the various phrases, producing potentially hundreds or thousands of different variations of each phrase. This is why we limit the number of training examples that Chatito should generate to 5,000 for each intent, just to ensure the resulting set of phrases is not outrageously large.

However, Rasa does not understand Chatito's syntax, so we'll have to use Chatito to convert this format to the Rasa format. Chatito is a Node.js program, so we use npx to run it:

```
npx chatito pokedex-training.chatito --format=rasa
```

Chatito then produces a JSON file in the Rasa format that we can then use for training Rasa.

Logic programming with Prolog and tuProlog

Prolog: Completely, 100% useless right up until it's exactly the right tool for a very hard, very specific job.

– TheTarquin on Reddit, September 28, 2016

```
https://www.reddit.com/r/compsci/comments/54tidh/what_in_your_
opinion_is_the_most_esoteric_and/d84x6xk/
```

Prolog is a programming language that allows us to program with logic statements. It is a full programming language, supporting loops, variables, and more. But Prolog programs consist primarily of **facts** and **rules** that state the relations between facts. The rules are activated by **queries**. By using variables in the queries, we can find out the values of the variables that make the queries true (according to the facts and rules involved), and thus we get a kind of computation.

Prolog programs have two parts: a database (of facts and rules), and an interactive query tool; the database must be saved in a text file, usually with extension .pl. We sometimes call the database the **theory**, because it describes the logic of a domain. When we execute a query against a theory, we are asking for the query's **solutions**.

There may be no solutions, one solution, or several. We can use variables in the query to indicate the kinds of information we want to include in the solution.

We've got a simple example. Let's suppose we want to represent the relations between members of a family, and then ask questions about these relationships. The theory contains the following lines:

```
parent(tom, liz).
parent(bob, ann).
parent(bob, pat).
parent(pat, jim).

male(tom).
male(bob).
male(jim).
female(pam).
female(liz).
female(pat).
female(ann).
```

With this theory, we can run some simple queries. In the following table, the query is shown on the left, and the solutions are on the right. Any Prolog system, such as tuProlog, will actually execute the query and produce the list of solutions. Since tuProlog is a Java interface, the set of solutions with be a collection of Java objects.

Variables in queries are represented as capital letters. Non-variables should be lowercase. When a query has a variable, Prolog searches for values for the variables that make the query true. A variable written _ means we do not care about the value:

Query	Solution(s)
female(X).	X = pam
	X = liz
	X = pat
	X = ann
parent(X, ann).	X = bob
parent(P, C).	P = tom, C = liz
	P = bob, C = ann
	P = bob, C = pat
	P = pat, C = jim
parent(P, _), female(P).	P = pat

The last query in the table shows a conjunction, meaning the variable P must both be a parent (with some child but we do not need to know the name, hence _) and be a female. Thus, this conjunction represents a query that finds any mothers in the theory (that is, database).

The predicates that are shown in the preceding text (parent, male, and female) are known as facts. In addition to facts, we can write rules. A rule is made up of conjunction, like our mother query. We can make a rule out of that query and add it to the end of our theory file:

```
mother(X) :- parent(X, _), female(X).
```

The :- syntax indicates we are defining a rule. On the left side, we write a name with some variables for arguments. On the right side, we write one or more queries with commas between them, forming a conjunction. Now we can directly query this rule:

Query	Solution(s)
mother(P).	P = pat

Here are some more examples of family relations, written as rules:

```
father(X) :- parent(X, _), male(X).
grandparent(X) :- parent(X, Y), parent(Y, _).
sisters(X, Y) :- parent(Z, X), parent(Z, Y), female(X), female(Y).
```

Here are the solutions to these queries:

Query	Solution(s)
father(X).	X = tom
	X = bob
	X = bob
grandparent(X).	X = bob
sisters(X, Y).	X = liz, Y = liz
	X = ann, Y = ann
	X = ann, Y = pat
	X = pat, Y = ann
	X = pat, Y = pat

The father(X) query shows that Prolog found two ways in which bob is a father (as a parent of ann and parent of pat). The last example, sisters(X, Y), shows that the sisters rule allows a female to be her own sister since she shares a parent with herself.

We can update the rule to ensure that the variable X is less than the variable Y (that is, alphabetically sorted), using the syntax @<, thus preventing liz from being her own sister, as well as preventing both X = ann, Y = pat, and X = pat, Y = ann duplication, since in the latter example, pat is not alphabetically before ann, so X = pat, Y = ann is not a solution. Here is the updated rule:

```
sisters(X, Y) :-
    parent(Z, X), parent(Z, Y), female(X), female(Y), X @< Y.
```

Now the only solution to that rule is X = ann, Y = pat.

Prolog unification and resolution

In order to effectively write code in Prolog, we must first understand how Prolog works. As we saw, we have two kinds of Prolog data: the theory (or database), consisting of facts and rules; and the queries, which can be thought of like questions, often with variables. Prolog will search for a way to make the query true by finding appropriate values for the variables, all while consulting the theory. If there are no values for the variables that make the query true, Prolog just reports false or no solution. So, for example, the query sisters(bob, X), using the theory about families in the preceding section, will simply return false.

There are two steps in how Prolog determines variable assignments in order to solve a query. The first is known as **unification**. This step figures out how to make two terms match, where a term is a simple query or fact such as sisters(X, Y) or female(pam).

Unification always applies to a pair of terms. Unification asks, *can we make these two terms match by finding particular values for the variables?* The following table shows a few examples of a pair of terms and the variable values required to make the two match, or the statement cannot unify if the two terms cannot unify. Note that the theory is not used for unification, so two terms can unify even if they're actually false (that is, female(bob) is false according to the theory we wrote in the preceding section, but it can unify with female(X)):

Term 1	Term 2	Can unify?
female(pam)	female(pam)	Yes, they are already the same.
female(X)	female(pam)	Yes, if X = pam.
female(pam)	female(Y)	Yes, if Y = pam.
female(bob)	female(Y)	Yes, if Y = bob (note, the theory is not used in unification).

`female(X)`	`female(Y)`	Yes, if X = Y (that is, X and Y can be any value as long as they are the same).
`parent(tom, X)`	`parent(Y, liz)`	Yes, if X = liz and Y = tom.
`parent(tom, X)`	`parent(X, liz)`	Cannot unify, because X would have to equal both tom and liz simultaneously.
`female(X)`	`parent(X, liz)`	Cannot unify because they're not even the same term (female vs. parent)
`sisters(X, Y)`	`sisters(Z)`	Cannot unify because the left term has two arguments and the right has one argument.

The second way Prolog finds solutions to a query is known as **resolution**. This technique actually refers to the theory about family relations we developed earlier on. When a query like `father(bob)` is run, Prolog searches the theory for any fact or rule that can unify. It finds a `father(X)` rule that can unify if it sets X = bob. Now Prolog asks, is the father rule true when X = bob?

To determine this, it looks at the first term in the rule, `parent(X, _)`. Since X has been decided to be bob, the question is really whether `parent(bob, _)` is true. The _ symbol means *a variable goes here, but don't worry about the name*, so Prolog creates a new variable name for that symbol, say _G10. So, the question is now, is `parent(bob, _G10)` true? Prolog looks in the theory for any facts or rules that unify with `parent(bob, _G10)`. It finds that if it sets the variable _G10 to equal ann, then it unifies with an existing fact.

So far, so good. The next part of the father rule is `male(X)`, where X has already been decided to be bob. So, Prolog searches the theory for a fact or rule that unifies with `male(bob)`. It finds one, so the father rule is satisfied, and `father(bob)` returns true.

Prolog searches for facts and rules top-down in the theory. So, facts and rules that you want to be found first should appear first. When you only want one answer to a query, for example, for the query `father(X)` you only want the first answer, X = tom, then you have to take care to organize the theory, so this answer is found first.

There is one small complication that's not described in the explanation of the resolution. Since various rules may use the same variable names like X and Y, the first thing Prolog does when a query is executed is to change all the variable names to new names like _G10 or _G203. This ensures it is not confused when repeat variable names are found during unification and resolution.

Sometimes, Prolog fails to find a satisfactory solution in its first attempts at unification and resolution. For example, the query mother(X) starts by using the mother rule and finding parent(X, _). The first parent fact in the theory is parent(tom, liz). So, X is set to tom. But the next part of the mother rule says female(X), which fails since X = tom and there is no fact in the theory that says female(tom). Thus, Prolog must backtrack and find a new value for X. This shows that Prolog is performing depth-first search, that is, deciding values for variables as soon as possible, and then possibly backing out of those decisions if they ultimately fail to succeed.

We can visualize Prolog's search for variable values in its attempt to find solutions for a query. The following figure shows a search that first failed, required backtracking, and then succeeded. The theory in this example is meaningless, just random facts f(a), f(b), and so on. But the order of the facts and rules in the theory dictate the order that Prolog tries the different possible values for the variables. We see it first renames the variables to _G34, and so on, and then sets _G34 = a, which ultimately fails. It later revises that to _G34 = b, which succeeds:

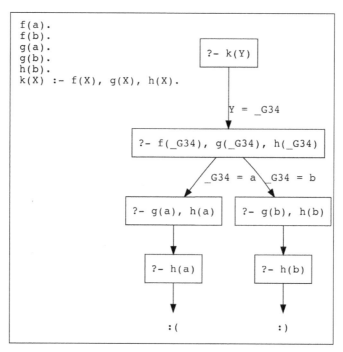

Figure 5: An example of Prolog's search procedure

In detail, the preceding figure shows the following steps, in order:

1. Create a temporary variable _G34 (randomly-named) to stand in for Y. This is an implementation detail, so that if some other rule uses Y (a completely different variable), then the variable names don't collide.

2. The goal is to find a solution for k(_G34). To do so, finding a solution for f(_G34), g(_G34), h(_G34) is required since this is the definition of the rule. This is the new goal.

3. To satisfy the first part of the new goal, f(_G34), the theory is searched. The fact f(a) is found. Thus, _G34 gets set to a (from unification).

4. Now, g(a), h(a) is the new goal. g(a) is satisfied just fine because exactly that term is found in the knowledge base.

5. Now, h(a) is the new goal. But, nothing in the theory unifies with h(a), so there is a problem.

6. Go to the last decision point. This was when _G34 was set to a. Try to set it to something else. f(b) is in theory as well, so go with _G34 = b.

7. The new goal is g(b), h(b) ... (which ultimately works).

In the following figure, we see another example of backtracking. In this case, the first choice works, yielding the happy face. But let's suppose we want *all solutions*, not just the first. Asking for all solutions causes Prolog to backtrack as many times as necessary to come up with all working variable values:

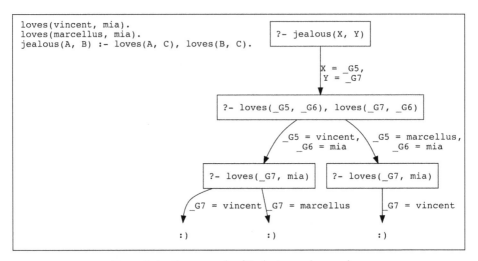

Figure 6: Another example of Prolog's search procedure

Using Prolog from Java with tuProlog

The tuProlog (http://apice.unibo.it/xwiki/bin/view/Tuprolog/WebHome)
Java library is an open source Prolog interpreter and graphical debugging
environment. With tuProlog, you can write normal Prolog code and execute it
from Java (which is what we will do), or you can have a deeper integration where
Java code creates Prolog facts and rules as Java objects, and the Prolog rules refer
to Java objects in their definitions. We will not need to do any complex integrations
between Prolog and Java, so we will write our Prolog code in a separate file and
simply execute it with a query from our Java code.

tuProlog has a graphical debugging environment that can be run by downloading
tuProlog from their website and running the 2p.jar file: java -jar 2p.jar. The
following figure shows this graphical environment plus a sample Prolog theory and
query. Notice that in the bottom status bar of the screenshot, tuProlog informs us
more solutions are available (**Other alternatives can be explored**). These additional
solutions can be obtained by clicking the **Next** button at the bottom of the window:

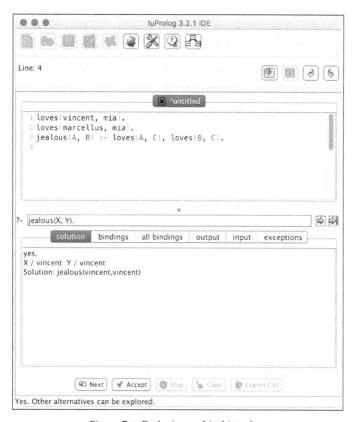

Figure 7: tuProlog's graphical interface

In order to execute Prolog queries against a specific theory from Java code, we need to include the Maven dependency for `tuProlog` in our `pom.xml`:

```
<dependency>
    <groupId>it.unibo.alice.tuprolog</groupId>
    <artifactId>tuprolog</artifactId>
    <version>3.2.1</version>
</dependency>
```

In our Java code, we first import the classes of `tuProlog`:

```
import alice.tuprolog.*;
```

We'll then create a Prolog engine object, load the theory file, execute a query, and iterate through the solutions (if any):

```
Prolog engine = new Prolog();
try {
  engine.setTheory(new Theory(new FileInputStream("theory.pl")));
  SolveInfo result = engine.solve("jealous(X, Y).");
  if(result.isHalted()) {
    System.out.println("Error.");
  } else if(!result.isSuccess()) {
    System.out.println("No solution.");
  } else if(!result.hasOpenAlternatives()) {
    System.out.println(result.getVarValue("X").toString() +
" / " + result.getVarValue("Y").toString());
  } else {
    while(result.hasOpenAlternatives()) {
      result = engine.solveNext();
      if(!result.isSuccess()) { break; }
      System.out.println(result.getVarValue("X").toString() +
" / " + result.getVarValue("Y").toString());
    }
  } catch(NoMoreSolutionException e) {
    System.out.println("No more solutions: " + e);
  } catch(NoSolutionException e) {
    System.out.println("No solution: " + e);
  } catch(MalformedGoalException e) {
    System.out.println("Error in goal: " + e);
  } catch(InvalidTheoryException e) {
    System.out.println("Bad theory.pl: " + e);
  }
```

Pokémon in Prolog

Now let's write some Prolog code for our Pokémon facts and rules. Firstly, we need a bunch of facts about each Pokémon's parent type (which we'll call "species"), egg group (which dictates who can breed), and a list of genderless Pokémon:

```
species_parent(abomasnow, snover).
species_parent(abra, none).
species_parent(absol, none).
species_parent(accelgor, shelmet).
species_parent(aegislash, doublade).
species_parent(aerodactyl, none).
species_parent(aggron, lairon).
species_parent(aipom, none).
...
species_egg_group(abomasnow, monster).
species_egg_group(abomasnow, plant).
species_egg_group(abra, humanshape).
species_egg_group(absol, ground).
species_egg_group(accelgor, bug).
species_egg_group(aegislash, mineral).
species_egg_group(aerodactyl, flying).
species_egg_group(aggron, monster).
species_egg_group(aipom, ground).
...
genderless(arceus).
genderless(articuno).
genderless(azelf).
genderless(baltoy).
genderless(beldum).
genderless(bronzong).
genderless(cryogonal).
...
```

For the next step, we'll encode the rules of Pokémon breeding. Again, these rules are simplified for the sake of this example and do not accurately represent how the games work.

In summary, two Pokémon can breed if:

- Both parents are adults in their species
- Neither parent is genderless
- Both parents have the same egg group, and that group is not the no eggs group

The Ditto species is an exception to all of those rules. A Ditto can breed with any other non-Ditto Pokémon, as long as the other is an adult in its evolution.

The child Pokémon is the baby version of the species of the mother, except in the case of breeding with Ditto, in which case the child is the baby version of the non-Ditto parent.

First, we need a rule that determines whether a Pokémon is in its adult form. Our `species_parent(pok1, pok2)` facts give all the different species evolutionary steps. For example, `species_parent(abomasnow, snover)` states that Abomasnow is the next step in evolution (the descendant) of Snover. If we look further, we find `species_parent(snover, none)`, by which we mean Snover has no earlier evolution, so Snover is the child form. (The names of the facts and the order of the arguments are all left up to us to decide, as programmers. Prolog places no constraints on these kinds of things, as long as we use correct syntax.) Thus, the logic for determining the child evolution of a Pokémon is to recursively search backward through the `species_parent` facts until we find a case where the parent is `none`, indicating a base evolution or child form. We will make a rule out of this:

```
species_base_evolution(Species, Species) :-
species_parent(Species, none).
species_base_evolution(Species, BaseSpecies) :-
species_parent(Species, ParentSpecies),
species_base_evolution(ParentSpecies, BaseSpecies).
```

The rule has two forms. First, the base case is true when the parent evolution is `none`. In the second case, we find the parent evolution and call the rule again with this new value. It is important for the base case (the non-recursive case) to appear first in the list of rules so that Prolog does not try the recursive case first and get stuck in a loop. Recall that Prolog resolution algorithm always tries facts and rules in the order they appear in the theory file.

Next, we'll define a rule that says whether a Pokémon is in its adult (non-child) form. This is as simple as ensuring the `species_base_evolution` for the Pokémon is not itself, which means it is in its adult form, that is, evolved at least one step away from the child form:

```
adult_evolution(Species) :-
species_base_evolution(Species, Base), Species \= Base.
```

We use \= (not equal) to check that the input species is not the same as the base species.

Now we can write the rules about breeding. First, we handle the cases for Ditto. Since it is the exception case, we put it first to ensure Prolog finds it first and does not attempt the general case if the exception case applies. Note that Dittos cannot breed with themselves, so if the male species is Ditto, the female cannot be, and vice versa.

We define the `can_breed` rule to take two inputs: the male species and the female species. In the Ditto special cases, we set the male or female species to `ditto` rather than using a variable:

```
can_breed(ditto, FemaleSpecies) :-
adult_evolution(FemaleSpecies), ditto \= FemaleSpecies.
can_breed(MaleSpecies, ditto) :-
adult_evolution(MaleSpecies), ditto \= MaleSpecies.
```

Now we'll write the general case. This case has several conditions, listed in the preceding bullet points.

First, we check that both the male and female Pokémon are adults.

Then we check that they're not genderless using `\+genderless(...)`. This Prolog syntax means "check that `genderless(...)` is false." The `\+` is supposed to look like the ⊬ symbol, while the `:-` rule definition symbol is supposed to look like ⊢, meaning *implies* or *follows* in mathematics.

Then the rule figures out the egg group of the female species, and next requires that the male's egg group matches (by using the same variable name for both the female and male egg group), and lastly checks that this egg group is not `no_eggs`. Note that we use the `%` symbol for code comments:

```
can_breed(MaleSpecies, FemaleSpecies) :-
  % both must be adults
  adult_evolution(MaleSpecies),
  adult_evolution(FemaleSpecies),
  % cannot be genderless species
  \+genderless(MaleSpecies),
  \+genderless(FemaleSpecies),
  % must match male/female egg group
  species_egg_group(FemaleSpecies, EggGroup),
  species_egg_group(MaleSpecies, EggGroup),
  % that egg group cannot be no_eggs
  EggGroup \= no_eggs.
```

We have one rule left in the Pokémon breeding rules. We've stated this as follows: *The child Pokémon is the baby version of the species of the mother, except in the case of breeding with Ditto, in which case the child is the baby version of the non-Ditto parent.*

Again, we have two special cases for Ditto (one in which the male is Ditto, one in which the female is Ditto), and then a general case:

```
child_pok(ditto, Female, ChildPok) :-
  can_breed(ditto, Female),
  species_base_evolution(Female, ChildPok).
```

```
child_pok(Male, ditto, ChildPok) :-
  can_breed(Male, ditto),
  species_base_evolution(Male, ChildPok).
child_pok(Male, Female, ChildPok) :-
  can_breed(Male, Female),
  Male \= ditto,
  Female \= ditto,
  species_base_evolution(Female, ChildPok).
```

With this complete Prolog theory, including the facts and rules, we can now run some queries:

Query	Solution(s)
`adult_evolution(pikachu).`	`true`
`adult_evolution(pichu).`	`false`

`adult_evolution(X).`	`X = abomasnow`
	`X = accelgor`
	`X = aegislash`
	(and so on)

`species_egg_group(froslass, Group).`	`Group = fairy` `Group = mineral`

`can_breed(froslass, F).`	`F = ditto`
	`F = aegislash`
	`F = aromatisse`
	(and so on)

These example queries demonstrate the range of questions we can ask about the Pokémon database and breeding rules. Our Rasa training phrases do not cover the whole range of possible questions, but likewise are sufficiently broad to demonstrate the capabilities.

Natural language generation with SimpleNLG

Once our Prolog code generates solutions, as shown in the preceding table, we'll need to generate a natural language response. By this we mean we should generate a sentence that, if spoken or read, appears to be written by a human with the correct subject-verb agreement, proper treatment of plurals and prepositions, and so on. This is known as NLG. Producing natural language can be very complicated, particularly when generating explanations of complex data. However, our use case will be relatively simple, and in fact, we will use a library known as `SimpleNLG` (`https://github.com/simplenlg/simplenlg`) to do the job.

`SimpleNLG` is a Java library with a broad range of classes and methods that support grammatical constructs such as prepositions, noun phrases, and so on. We start by importing the classes:

```
import simplenlg.framework.*;
import simplenlg.lexicon.*;
import simplenlg.realiser.english.*;
import simplenlg.phrasespec.*;
import simplenlg.features.*;
```

Next, we need to create a lexicon object, which contains rules about English, and a factory and realizer object. The factory allows us to create subjects, objects, prepositions, and more, and the realizer transforms these various objects into a phrase:

```
Lexicon lexicon = Lexicon.getDefaultLexicon();
NLGFactory nlgFactory = new NLGFactory(lexicon);
Realiser realiser = new Realiser(lexicon);
```

Consider the case in which we want to say something along the lines of, *Froslass can breed with Aegislash*. The values *froslass* and *aegislash* will be `String` variables, and we can build the rest of the sentence with `SimpleNLG`. The first step is to create an empty phrase specification:

```
SPhraseSpec p = nlgFactory.createClause();
```

The next step is to set the subject of the sentence, which in this case is Froslass. We'll use the Apache Commons' `StringUtils` library to capitalize the word:

```
p.setSubject(StringUtils.capitalize(male));
```

Next, we set the verb (*breed*):

```
p.setVerb("breed");
```

Our verb will have a modal *can*; alternatives are *will*, *should*, and so on. Without setting the modal, the sentence will read *Froslass breeds with Aegislash*:

```
p.setFeature(Feature.MODAL, "can");
```

At this point, the sentence might read, *Froslass can breed*. We want to tell the user which other Pokémon Froslass is able to breed with. Therefore we need to add the prepositional phrase, *with Aegislash*. This is accomplished by creating a propositional phrase object, setting its preposition (*with*) and adding the noun to it (*Aegislash*):

```
PPPhraseSpec prep_1 = nlgFactory.createPrepositionPhrase();
prep_1.setPreposition("with");
NPPhraseSpec object_1 = nlgFactory.createNounPhrase();
object_1.setNoun(StringUtils.capitalize(female));
```

```
prep_1.addComplement(object_1);
```

Finally, we associate this propositional phrase as the object of the sentence and then realize the sentence to a `String` object:

```
p.setObject(prep_1);
String output = realiser.realiseSentence(p);
```

The result is what we desired; `Froslass can breed with Aegislash.`

Now, you're probably wondering how we can justify the effort of 14 lines of code to create a `String` that can more easily be written as `String output = male + "` `can breed with " + female`. The benefit of a library like `SimpleNLG` is that small variations of this basic template of code can produce a wide range of sentences that are each appropriate in a slightly different context. Rather than create a special case for every variation (as would be required if we used the `male + " can breed with " + female` approach), we can adjust the grammatical properties of the `SimpleNLG` objects to achieve the desired effect. For example, we can remove the modal specifier (*can*) and change the verb's tense to past tense:

```
p.setVerb("breed");
//p.setFeature(Feature.MODAL, "can");
p.setTense(Tense.PAST);
```

Now the realizer produces *Froslass bred with Aegislash*. `SimpleNLG` knows how to convert *breed* to *bred* because it has access to more than 300,000 lexical features.

We can change the interrogative type to various kinds of questions:

```
p.setFeature(
Feature.INTERROGATIVE_TYPE, InterrogativeType.YES_NO);
// result: "Did Froslass breed with Aegislash?"

p.setFeature(
Feature.INTERROGATIVE_TYPE, InterrogativeType.WHY);
// result: "Why did Froslass breed with Aegislash?"

p.setFeature(
Feature.INTERROGATIVE_TYPE, InterrogativeType.WHO_SUBJECT);
// result: "Who breed with Aegislash?"
```

We can also create conjunction by combining two Pokémon names, and then adding any more we have in a loop:

```
CoordinatedPhraseElement coord_obj =
nlgFactory.createCoordinatedPhrase(object_1, object_2);
for(NPPhraseSpec obj : objects_to_add) {
```

```
        coord_obj.addCoordinate(object_3);
    }
    prep_1.addComplement(coord_obj);
```

Conjunctions produce something similar to *Froslass can breed with Raichu, Ditto, and Aromatisse*. We can change the conjunction to a disjunction by setting the conjunction feature to `or`:

```
    coord_obj.setFeature(Feature.CONJUNCTION, "or");
```

Now it is clear that `SimpleNLG` provides a framework for NLG. Considering the range of phrases, it is able to produce from the same components (the names of the Pokémon and the verb "breed"), This approach is simpler and likely less code than a large number of `if()` conditions required if the simple string concatenation approach is used (that is, `male + " can breed with " + female`).

Our completed Pokémon example is available in the code repository for this chapter. Here are some example queries and responses:

Query	Response
What can Pikachu breed with?	*Pikachu can breed with Ditto, Ambipom and 130 more.*
What can breed with Pikachu?	*Pikachu can breed with Ditto, Ambipom and 130 more.*
which pokemon can Pikachu breed with	*Pikachu can breed with Ditto, Ambipom and 130 more.*
What can Pikachu breed with? (Typo)	*Pikachu cannot breed with any others.*
are Ditto and Ditto compatible?	*Ditto cannot breed with Ditto.*
Can Pikachu and Ditto breed?	*Yup!*
What is the child of granbull and Pikachu?	*The child of Granbull and Pikachu is Pichu.*
if Lucario and Wailord breed, what do we get?	*The child of Lucario and Wailord is Wailmer.*
what is the child of foobar and Pikachu?	*Sorry, I cannot determine the child species of Foobar and Pikachu.*
what day is it?	*I do not understand that question. Try asking 'Can X and Y breed?' or 'What can X breed with?' or 'What is the child of X and Y?'*

This concludes our Pokémon example, as we have developed each stage of the processing pipeline. We have not demonstrated the use of Google's Speech-to-Text or Text-to-Speech APIs to allow spoken queries with the Pokémon example, but Google's own documentation (`https://cloud.google.com/text-to-speech/docs/reference/libraries#client-libraries-install-java`) should suffice for interested readers.

A second example – college course advising

For a more practical example, we implemented a textual interface for the TAROT course advising system (*TAROT: A Course Advising System for the Future, J. Eckroth, R. Anderson, Journal of Computing Sciences in Colleges, 34(3), pp. 108-116, 2018*). TAROT's domain logic is implemented in Prolog, like our Pokémon example. However, TAROT is not open source, so we included the Pokémon example to show a complete solution. Yet, the course advising example shows a few interesting variations that we detail in the following text.

TAROT itself runs an HTTP server (`http://tarotdemo.artifice.cc:10333`) that accepts a JSON list containing the Prolog rule to execute as well as its arguments. Some of those arguments will be variables (starting with a capital letter), thus causing the TAROT to compute their values. The HTTP server returns all the values for these variables that meet the rule's constraints. These returned values are formatted as a JSON list of key-value pairs, where the keys are the variable names, and the values are the variables' values.

For example, a `curl` command, which can be run from a macOS or Linux Terminal, that executes TAROT's `finishDegreeFromStudentId` rule. This rule uses a student's ID number (for example, 800000000), their desired major, the number of semesters they have remaining, the starting year and semester (Fall or Spring), and any courses they do not need (for example, the student received permission from the instructor to skip). The rule computes values for various arguments, including the courses the student has already taken (obtained by reading the student's information from a database), their multi-year schedule of courses as determined by TAROT, their current and minimum, and maximum future grade point average, and their course credit counts:

```
curl -X "POST" "http://tarotdemo.artifice.cc:10333/tarot"
-H 'Content-Type: application/json; charset=utf-8'
-d $'[
  "finishDegreeFromStudentId",
  "800000000",
  "Student",
  "ClassLevel",
  "Advisors",
  "Major",
  "[csci]",
  "4",
  "2018",
  "fall",
  "[csci141,fsem,jsem]",
  "Taken",
```

```
    "PlannedSemesters",
    "Gpa",
    "MinGpa",
    "MaxGpa",
    "CreditCount",
    "AllCreditCount",
    "PlannedCreditCount",
    "PlannedAllCreditCount"
  ]'
```

The data returned from the request includes all variable values, but the only value we will be interested in is the `PlannedSemesters` schedule. This value will be a string with a specific syntax that we will break apart with regular expressions in our Java code. The string contains a semester-by-semester schedule that shows all the classes the student should take to finish their degree.

Here is an example of the result of running the `finishDegreeFromStudentId` HTTP request (with newlines added for formatting):

```
[
  {
    "Advisors":"[(\"Smith\",\"Jane\")]",
    "AllCreditCount":"39.0",
    "ClassLevel":"senior",
    "CreditCount":"24.0",
    "Gpa":"3.333333333333333",
    "Major":"csci",
    "MaxGpa":"3.75",
    "MinGpa":"1.25",
    "PlannedAllCreditCount":"79.0",
    "PlannedCreditCount":"64.0",
    "PlannedSemesters":"[(2018,fall,[(csci311,_2148,4),
(csci321,_2304,4),(math142,_2460,4),(pcb141,_2616,4)]),
(2019,spring,[(csci301,_3516,4),(csci304,_3672,4),
(csci331,_3828,4),(pcb142,_3984,4)]),
(2019,fall,[(csci498,_4966,4),(free,x,x),(free,x,x),(free,x,x)]),
(2020,spring,[(csci499,_5342,4),(free,x,x),(free,x,x),(free,x,x)])
    ]",
    "Student":"\"Doe\",\"John\"",
    "Taken":"[(noyear,transfer,[(astr180,tr,3),(chem110,tr,4),
(csci111,tr,4)]),
(2016,fall,[(csci142,3.33,4),(csci211,3.67,4),(rels390,p,4)]),
(2017,spring,[(csci201,3.0,4),(csci221,3.67,4),(hlsc219,4.0,4),
(math141,2.33,4)])]"
  }
]
```

The _ syntax in the `PlannedSemesters` value indicates the grade is unknown because the course has not been taken. Additionally, a course written `(free,x,x)` means the course can be any general education requirement or a general elective.

For Rasa training, we wrote a Chatito script that supports multiple variations of three types of queries: *What courses do I need this next semester?*, *What courses do I need to finish my degree?*, and *What courses are the prerequisites for a specific course?*:

```
%[schedule_single_semester]('training':'1000')
  ~[what] ~[classes?] ~[can_i] ~[take] next ~[semester?]?
  ~[what] ~[classes?] ~[must_i] ~[take] next ~[semester?]?
  ~[what] ~[classes?] ~[can_i] ~[take] this ~[semester]?
  ~[what] ~[classes?] ~[must_i] ~[take] this ~[semester]?

%[schedule_finish_degree]('training':'500')
  ~[what] ~[classes] ~[are] ~[left]?
  ~[what] ~[can_i] ~[take] to finish?
  ~[what] ~[can_i] ~[take] to graduate?
  ~[what] ~[are] my ~[4yr]?
  ~[what] ~[are] a ~[4yr]?

%[prereqs]('training':'1000')
  ~[what] ~[are] the ~[prereqs] ~[for] ~[course]?
  ~[what] ~[are] ~[course] ~[prereqs]?
  ~[what] ~[must_i] ~[take] ~[for] ~[course]?

~[what]
  what
  which
  show me
  find

~[classes]
  classes
  courses
  sections

. (etc.)
```

Because there are many possible courses (CSCI141, CSCI142, MATH340, and so on), we do not wish to list all of these courses in the Rasa training data. Instead, we will extract the course from the query when we need it to pass to TAROT (just in the query that determines prerequisites). We take this alternative instead of using Rasa's entity extraction capabilities because we are not able to reasonably provide Rasa with all the training examples (all the courses) necessary for it to reliably extract the course as an entity.

But mentioning a course in a query is a good indicator that the query is about course prerequisites. Thus, we still want Rasa to learn about how courses are written. To do this, we use Rasa's regular expression matching feature. Chatito does not support regexes directly, so we need to create a JSON file of Rasa options that we provide to Chatito. This file contains the following information:

```
{
  "rasa_nlu_data": {
    "regex_features": [
      {
        "name": "course",
        "pattern": "[A-Za-z]{2,4}\\s*\\d{3}[A-Za-z]?"
      }
    ]
  }
}
```

This single regex tells Rasa what a course looks like (two to four letters followed by three digits, possibly also followed by a letter for general education courses). We tell Chatito to include this configuration in its Rasa output:

```
npx chatito training/tarot-training.chatito \
--format=rasa --formatOptions=training/tarot-rasa-options.json
```

Rasa's support for regular expressions is sometimes misunderstood. The regular expression's name (`course` in the preceding example) does not relate to any intents or entities in the Rasa training examples; it's just a name for the regex. Furthermore, in most Rasa configurations, a regex does not yield an entity even if the regex does match the input. In other words, regexes in Rasa do not create intents or entities. They are only helpful for *detecting* intents and entities. Whenever the regex matches one of the training examples, that training example records the fact the regex matched. If the regex matches in the input string (the user's query) as well, then Rasa looks for all examples, and the associated intents, that also matched the regex. Thus, regular expression in Rasa helps identify the intent and enables us to avoid creating a separate training example for every variation of the course names.

The last aspect to address in the TAROT example is NLG. Again, we use `SimpleNLG`. Our use of `SimpleNLG` is similar to the Pokémon example, but there is one interesting case. When listing a course's prerequisite, we have a few different possible scenarios:

- There are no prerequisites
- There is one set of prerequisite courses (a single course or multiple)
- There are multiple different prerequisites (each a single course or multiple), that is, CSCI211's prerequisites are either both CSCI141 and MATH125, *or* both CSCI141 and MATH141

For the first case, with no prerequisites, we just create a simple `String` that says, *CSCI111 has no prerequisites.* (where the course is whatever the user asked about). There is no benefit in using `SimpleNLG` to generate a simple statement that has no variation.

We handle the second and third cases with the same code. To do so, we use `CoordinatedPhraseElement`, with an *or* conjunction, for the different subsets of prerequisite courses. For each course in the subset, we use a new `CoordinatedPhraseElement` with an *and* conjunction (the default conjunction). If we ultimately only add a single course or a single subset to the respective `CoordinatedPhraseElement`, then `SimpleNLG` will simply not write the *and* or the *or*.

Lastly, if there are multiple subsets, we use plurals in the sentence, and if there are many subsets, we just stop after three and say how many more. At our university, the required senior research course (CSCI498) has complex prerequisites that can be realized in many different ways: two 300+ level CSCI courses and another 300+ level CSCI or CINF course:

```
public static String respondPrereqs(NLGFactory nlgFactory,
Realiser realiser, String course, List<String> prereqs) {

  // If no prereqs, return immediately
  if(prereqs.get(0).equals("[]")) {
    return course.toUpperCase() + " has no prerequisites.";
  }

  SPhraseSpec p = nlgFactory.createClause();
  NPPhraseSpec subject = nlgFactory.createNounPhrase("the",
"prerequisite");

  // if multiple prereq subsets, make sure "prerequisites"
  // is plural and the verb is "are" instead of "is"
  if(prereqs.size() > 1) {
    subject.setPlural(true);
    p.setPlural(true);
  }
  PPPhraseSpec prep = nlgFactory.createPrepositionPhrase(
"for", nlgFactory.createNounPhrase(course.toUpperCase()));

  // set the sentence subject to "the prerequisite",
  // and add a pre-modifier that says "for [course]",
  // resulting in "the prerequisite for [course]"
  p.setSubject(subject);
  p.addPreModifier(prep);
  p.setVerb("is");
```

```java
  // build a disjunction ("or") between subsets of courses
  CoordinatedPhraseElement prereqOptions =
new CoordinatedPhraseElement();
  prereqOptions.setFeature(Feature.CONJUNCTION, "or");

  // for each course mentioned in the subset
  // (extract with regexes due to how TAROT returns the data)
  Pattern coursePattern = Pattern.compile("([a-z]{4}[0-9]{3})");

  // show at most 3 subsets
  for(int i = 0; i < Math.min(prereqs.size(), 3); i++) {
    String pr = prereqs.get(i);

    // start a conjunction ("and") for the course list
    CoordinatedPhraseElement prereqsConj =
new CoordinatedPhraseElement();

    // extract each course
    Matcher prMatcher = coursePattern.matcher(pr);
    int count = 0;
    while(prMatcher.find()) {
      prereqsConj.addCoordinate(prMatcher.group(1).toUpperCase());
      count++;
    }

    // if we have multiple courses, say "all of ..."
    // or "both ..."
    if(count > 2) {
      prereqsConj.addPreModifier("all of");
    } else if(count == 2) {
      prereqsConj.addPreModifier("both");
    }
    prereqOptions.addCoordinate(prereqsConj);
  }

  // if we had lots of prereq subsets, just summarize the rest
  if(prereqs.size() > 3) {
    prereqOptions.addCoordinate(
nlgFactory.createNounPhrase((prereqs.size() - 3) +
" more options"));
  }

  // the object of the sentence is the list of courses
  p.setObject(prereqOptions);
```

```
        return realiser.realiseSentence(p);
}
```

Some examples of the output of our TAROT example can be seen in the following table:

Query	Response
what classes should I take next?	*In Fall 2018, you should take CSCI311, CSCI321, MATH142, and PHYS141.*
what do I need to take this semester?	*[Same response as previous.]*
what do I take next?	*[Same response as previous.]*
what's left?	*In Fall 2018, you should take CSCI311, CSCI321, MATH142, and PCB141. In Spring 2019, you should take PCB142, CSCI304, CSCI301, and CSCI331. In Fall 2019, you should take CSCI498 and 3 general eds. In Spring 2020, you should take CSCI499 and 3 general eds.*
what must I take to graduate?	*[Same response as previous.]*
what's left in my 4-year plan?	*[Same response as previous.]*
tell me the prereqs for csci211.	*The prerequisites for CSCI211 are both CSCI141 and MATH125 or both CSCI141 and MATH141.*
What must I take for comp sci 142?	*The prerequisite for CSCI142 is CSCI141.*
what are math 142's prereqs?	*The prerequisite for MATH142 is MATH141.*
what's required to take math 401?	*The prerequisite for MATH401 is all of MATH211, MATH221, and MATH243.*
What's required for computer science 498?	*The prerequisites for CSCI498 are all of CINF490, CSCI485, and CSCI490, all of CINF490, CSCI471 and CSCI490, all of CINF490, CSCI471 and CSCI485 or 1765 more options.*

Continuous evaluation

Now that we have developed some natural language query interfaces with natural language responses, we should address some techniques for evaluating whether the interfaces work.

First, we should note that developing good training examples for Rasa can be challenging due to the flexibility and ambiguity of natural language. For example, the question *What classes should I take?* might mean the student wants a schedule for the next semester or a schedule for their entire college career. Likewise, the question *What's needed for MATH442?* might mean the student wants to know just this course's prerequisites or the courses just this student needs to take before taking MATH442 or a complete multi-semester schedule that ends in the student taking MATH442.

Not only is language sometimes ambiguous, but it is typically far more varied than one expects. Chatbot developers might discover that after just a few minutes of interaction by users other than the developers themselves, a flurry of questions and phrases are fed into the system that bears little resemblance to the training examples.

For example, when asking about prerequisites, a student might ask *What's needed for MATH442?*, *What should I take before MATH442?*, *Does MATH442 have prereqs?*, *Are there any prereqs for MATH442?*, *What's required for MATH442?*, *Tell me MATH442's requirements*, and so on. The only practical way to discover so many variations is to place your query interface in front of users.

For this reason, we suggest that the training examples be generated in two phases: first, from the developers themselves; and second, from users. The first stage is probably required in order for the users to interact with a working (but incomplete) system. Without this interaction, users might not think of the same queries in a hypothetical brainstorming session as they would when actually working with the tool.

Continuous evaluation may be achieved by adding various monitoring and feedback mechanisms to a deployed system. We recommend at least the following additions:

- Log all queries and generated responses. This record is necessary for any analysis of the frequency of queries and discovering the variety of queries, as well as debugging whether the generated responses were appropriate.

- Highlight queries in the log that generated no response or the default *I don't know what you mean try asking...* response. These are a very important indicator that the user is not effectively using the system as they are typing what, presumably, they believe to be valid queries, but the system is unable to produce any response.

- Keep track of the number of queries or interactions per user per session. Longer interactions are not necessarily better interactions as the user may be struggling to find a way to ask the right question – the log would be able to show this. Likewise, short interactions may indicate the user gave up early.

- Keep track of user visits over time. If users stop returning, they might be dissatisfied with the interface.

- If the interface is presented in a website or other application, perhaps a feedback mechanism can be added that asks the user whether they are satisfied with the system's responses.

While natural language interfaces can be very challenging to get right, due to the wide variety of ways of asking the same thing, they offer a unique insight into the user's mindset. Normally, we are left tracking clicks or repeat visits to an app or website. It is difficult to tease out the user's intentions and feelings about using the app or website.

However, a natural language interface can easily expose the user's intentions and feelings: they will often provide exactly those facts in their queries. For example, when a user types *What are the prereqs for MATH442?*, we know exactly what they are trying to find out. We do not need to infer this from their pattern of clicks. When a user asks the same question a different way, we know they did not get their expected answer. We could even add natural language feedback to the system to explicitly acquire their reactions to using the system, and then use Rasa or sentiment analysis (as in *Chapter 3, A Blueprint for Making Sense of Feedback*) to gauge whether they are having a positive experience with the system.

Summary

This chapter demonstrated how to build a natural language interface for two different domains: breeding rules of the Pokémon game, and course advising for college students.

We developed a pipeline with three components: first, we determined what the user's question was about, known as its "intent," using the Rasa library. Then we computed the answer to the question by referring to domain-specific logic implemented in Prolog. Finally, we generated a natural language response using the data found by the logic backend.

As far as the user is concerned, they provided an English-language question and got an English-language response. It would be straightforward to handle voice input and speech output by using Google's Speech-to-Text and Text-to-Speech APIs. These two services would be added to the beginning and end of the pipeline, respectively, without requiring any changes to the existing three-stage pipeline. Finally, we also addressed a few issues related to evaluation to ensure the natural language interface works well for users. Since these kinds of interfaces engage users with regular language rather than code or an application-specific graphical interface, there are issues and insights unique to these kinds of interfaces that we would not normally find in common user tracking and feedback techniques.

In the next and final chapter, we'll discuss how AI is perceived by the public and how it suffers from hype cycles, that is, dramatic shifts in AI's popularity. We'll also offer advice for businesses who wish to make productive use of AI technology without becoming victims of the hype cycle. We conclude by looking at the near-term future of AI.

8
Preparing for Your Future and Surviving the Hype Cycle

Throughout our journey, we've demonstrated a variety of AI and ML projects, from being able to make sense of user feedback (*Chapter 3, A Blueprint for Making Sense of Feedback*), to detecting our products and logos in social media (*Chapter 7, A Blueprint for Understanding Queries and Generating Responses*). The projects that we've worked on were diverse, in order to see multiple different ways in which AI can help enrich applications. Throughout AI's relatively short history of just 60 years, many technologies have been developed to solve a wide variety of problems. These include symbolic reasoning (like our Prolog code in *Chapter 7, A Blueprint for Understanding Queries and Generating Responses*), heuristic search (*Chapter 2, A Blueprint for Planning Cloud Infrastructure*), neural networks (*Chapter 5, A Blueprint for Detecting Your Logo in Social Media*), and matrix factorization (*Chapter 4, A Blueprint for Recommending Products and Services*).

In this book, we've focused on some of the most popular and successful technologies. If we just look at a particular technology, such as neural networks, we might focus so closely on the details that we start to believe that *this isn't intelligence, it's just computer code!* AI has been subjected to numerous debates over the years on whether it is true intelligence or just clever programming. It's my opinion that if the application behaves intelligently, then we have AI. Over the course of the previous chapters, we've emphasized the importance of evaluating the success of the AI component of each application. Just using a particular technology does not automatically make the application intelligent. It needs to include the right domain knowledge or training data, it needs to be implemented correctly, and it needs to demonstrate that it actually solves the problem. How can a company be sure to use the right AI in the right places and for the right reasons?

In this chapter, we will be:

- Exploring what the state of the art is in several important application areas
- Understanding the "hype cycle" and what to expect as AI is hyped and then criticized
- Looking at the outlook on AI's near-term future and what to look for to stay ahead of the curve

Always one step ahead

AI repeatedly suffers from the hype cycle: the rise of intense interest in using AI for as many applications as possible, followed by disillusionment and claims that AI could never do what was promised. Even worse, AI has been misunderstood so often that there's even a name for it, the "AI effect." As described by its originator, Larry Tesler, *Intelligence is whatever machines haven't done yet* (http://www.nomodes.com/ Larry_Tesler_Consulting/Adages_and_Coinages.html). In other words, before the application is developed and deployed, it is called AI. Once it is generally available, the outcomes of this research and development are retroactively considered "just engineering" or "just software," and the allure of AI moves on to the next unrealized dream. For a classic example, A* search, used commonly in path-finding in games, was originally a novel AI technique in the 1960s. Now it's just a commonplace graph search algorithm.

In Pamela McCorduck's 1979 book, *Machines Who Think*, the AI effect is summarized as follows:

> *Practical AI successes, computational programs that actually achieved intelligent behavior, were soon assimilated into whatever application domain they were found to be useful and became silent partners alongside other problem-solving approaches, which left AI researchers to deal only with the "failures," the tough nuts that couldn't yet be cracked. [...] If you could see how it was done, people seemed to think, then it couldn't be intelligence.*

> *– Pamela McCorduck*

> *Machines Who Think : A personal inquiry into the history and prospects of artificial intelligence, AK Peters/CRC Press, 2004, pg. 423*

One might consider asking the general population about chess engines. Today, one can download an Android or iOS app and play chess against a grandmaster-level computer opponent. For example, the Pocket Fritz 4 app (`https://shop.chessbase.com/en/products/pocket_fritz_4`) running on an HTC Touch HD phone (released in 2008) achieved a 2898 performance rating on the Elo rating scale, while the current world champion Magnus Carlsen is ranked at 2882 (peak) (`https://en.wikipedia.org/wiki/Magnus_Carlsen`). Current open source chess software such as Stockfish (`http://www.computerchess.org.uk/ccrl/4040/rating_list_all.html`) is ranked at 3438 (`https://stockfishchess.org/`).

Is computer chess AI? Stockfish's own documentation does not use the terms "artificial intelligence" or "AI." The Wikipedia page on computer chess also doesn't use these terms, though the page is included in the "game artificial intelligence" category (`https://en.wikipedia.org/wiki/Computer_chess`). It seems that today, computer chess is just "clever algorithms" and lots of domain-specific information like large databases of opening chess moves. But in the late 1990s, humanity's position as the pinnacle of intelligence was undermined by the win of IBM's Deep Blue machine against then-world chess champion Garry Kasparov, who prior to this competition, had never lost a match (`https://www.nytimes.com/1997/05/12/nyregion/swift-and-slashing-computer-topples-kasparov.html`). Newsweek's cover headline on May 5, 1997, a week before the match, read *The Brain's Last Stand*. Yet, some do not consider Deep Blue's win as a triumph of AI nor do they consider it to shed any light on intelligence:

> *They're just overtaking humans in certain intellectual activities that we thought required intelligence. My God, I used to think chess required thought. Now, I realize it doesn't. It doesn't mean Kasparov isn't a deep thinker, just that you can bypass deep thinking in playing chess, the way you can fly without flapping your wings.*
>
> *– Douglas Hofstadter*
>
> *Mean Chess-Playing Computer Tears at Meaning of Thought, Bruce Weber, The New York Times, Feb 19, 1996*

(`http://besser.tsoa.nyu.edu/impact/w96/News/News7/0219weber.html`)

More recently, Google tackled the problem of beating the world's Go champion, Lee Sedol. In 2016, Google's AlphaGo system used deep reinforcement learning and Monte Carlo tree search to beat Sedol. Go is considerably more complicated than chess, which explains why 20 years passed between Deep Blue's win and AlphaGo's win. Perhaps AlphaGo and DL, in general, are models of a new kind of intelligence. Or perhaps they will soon be seen as "just statistics" or "just data processing."

The state of things

When starting a new AI application, we recommend using one or more of the following software tools and APIs. This section includes a selection of the most popular tools and does not attempt to be representative of every tool available. These tools facilitate the development of advanced, domain-specific applications, though they must be paired with some custom development to build a complete application.

Natural language processing

NLP refers to any processing that must work with normal human-written text or speech in everyday language (such as English, French, and so on), as opposed to text written in code or other structured forms. If your application must process natural language text or speech, NLP is usually required to extract relevant data before any further processing is done.

- **spaCy** (https://spacy.io/) and **CoreNLP** (https://stanfordnlp.github.io/CoreNLP/): Sentence parsing and part-of-speech tagging; entity extraction (for example, finding names of people, places, dates, and so on); document similarity measures. We used CoreNLP in *Chapter 3, A Blueprint for Making Sense of Feedback.*

- **Rasa** (https://rasa.com/): Support for building chatbots; uses spaCy internally. We used Rasa in *Chapter 7, A Blueprint for Understanding Queries and Generating Responses.*

- **Google Cloud Natural Language** (https://cloud.google.com/natural-language/): Sentiment analysis; entity extraction; content classification, that is, identify the topic or subject of a phrase or document.

- **Google Cloud Translation** (https://cloud.google.com/translate/): Translating text written in one language to another.

- **Google Text-to-Speech** (https://cloud.google.com/text-to-speech/) and **Speech-to-Text** (https://cloud.google.com/speech-to-text/): Converting recordings of speech to written text, and back again.

Computer vision

Computer vision covers just about any task that involves images or video, including detection, recognition, and tracking of objects, finding similar images, and repairing or enhancing images.

- **TensorFlow** (https://www.tensorflow.org/) and **PyTorch** (https://pytorch.org/): Neural networks and DL for object classification, image repair, image segmentation (for example, separating foreground from the background), and numerous other tasks; often used by other tools. We used `TensorFlow` in *Chapter 5, A Blueprint for Detecting Your Logo in Social Media*.

- **OpenCV** (https://opencv.org/): Image and video manipulation and conversion; camera interfaces and stereo reconstruction (that is, seeing 3D from a pair of cameras); feature detection (that is, for image classification purposes); object tracking.

- **Google Cloud Vision** (https://cloud.google.com/vision/): Optical character recognition (that is, converting scanned documents into text); object detection; face, landmark, and logo detection.

Expert systems and business rules

Expert systems were once virtually synonymous with AI, similar to how DL is today. They allow software to behave as a domain expert, such as a medical diagnostician, oil drilling expert, fraud detector, and so on. Today, expert systems shells, that is, the tools that allow one to build an expert system, are more commonly characterized as business rule engines and used to execute rules about a business's operations such as document workflows, issue tracking, and billing.

- **Drools** (https://www.drools.org/): Rule authoring and execution

Planning and scheduling

Some tasks require searching for a sequence or arrangement of activities or items to meet certain constraints. For example, finding an efficient route for parcel trucks to deliver all of their parcels is a planning problem, while finding an arrangement of teachers, students, classrooms, and times – so that each class is taught by some teacher and students are able to take the classes they need – is a scheduling problem.

- **OptaPlanner** (https://www.optaplanner.org/): Constraint satisfaction library for finding arrangements or sequences of items or actions that meet certain hard and soft constraints. We used OptaPlanner in *Chapter 2, A Blueprint for Planning Cloud Infrastructure*.

- **CPLEX** (https://www.ibm.com/analytics/cplex-optimizer) and **Gurobi** (http://www.gurobi.com/): Efficient constraint solvers for the subclass of problems that can be solved with integer linear programming (https://en.wikipedia.org/wiki/Integer_programming).

Robotics

Finally, we have the class of problems that require a physical entity, with motors and sensors, working in the real world. Robots may be used for many purposes, such as factory automation, self-driving vehicles, agriculture, personal companionship, and so on. Robots make use of many of the tools mentioned in the preceding sections since robots need to engage in planning, need to see with computer vision, need some sort of expertise like an expert system, and might even need to communicate with humans in natural language. However, there is a robot-specific platform worth mentioning:

- **Robot Operating System (ROS)** (http://www.ros.org/): Various libraries that handle specific tasks but are designed to work together to form a coherent integration; for example, various libraries will handle the sensors, while ROS helps integrate all those sensor values into a consistent description of the robot's world; likewise, ROS includes tools for coordinating motor commands across many kinds of motors

It is clear from this short list of software tools that many different kinds of problems may be solved with existing AI tools. Just knowing these tools exist may help a company tackle a complex problem without trying to implement their own AI from scratch or abandoning the effort from a false belief that the solution is out of reach. For example, if a company wishes to identify photos on social media that contain their logo, and engineers in this company are not aware of `TensorFlow` or our examples in *Chapter 5, A Blueprint for Detecting Your Logo in Social Media*, the task will seem impossible, and opportunities will be missed.

Our list of AI tools should be reassuring. There is a lot of support available for building AI solutions. But AI cannot solve all of our problems. As we have witnessed throughout the chapters of this book, while we might have the right algorithms, the effectiveness of our solutions often depends heavily on the quality and diversity of our training data, on the exhaustiveness of our patterns and rules, and the amount of time and effort we can expend writing code for special cases to handle the "long tail" of the real world, shown in the following figure:

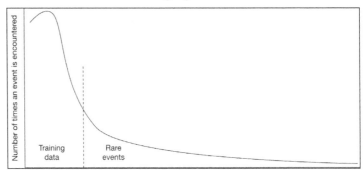

Figure 1: An example of the long tail problem: the training data happens to only include relatively frequent events, while the real world has many rare events that the AI system might not correctly handle

This long tail represents all of the kinds of things we see in real data, but which are not correctly handled by our software. Even with the best training data and most extensive ruleset, once deployed our software will inevitably encounter situations it has never seen and cannot handle correctly. And there will be a lot of variation in these situations, and they might be single events that never repeat. Hence the long tail: each case is virtually unique, but there are many of them. This is why we have emphasized continuous evaluation throughout this book in order to help detect these cases and handle them in the appropriate manner.

As we discussed in *Chapter 1, The AI Workflow*, building and deploying successful AI applications requires that engineers and project managers look at the whole software lifecycle, as they would with any software project: characterize the problem and find a business case, develop a solution, figure out a deployment strategy that integrates with existing workflows and infrastructure, and monitor the system after it is deployed to detect changes or surprises such as the long tail problem or unexpected changes in the kinds of data the system is processing. With this kind of strategy, building and deploying AI should be straightforward. However, this is not always the case. AI is exciting. AI is the future. But AI is sometimes overhyped, and this makes everything a little more difficult.

Understanding the hype cycle of AI

The CEO of Google, Sundar Pichai, said in January 2018, *AI is one of the most important things humanity is working on. It is more profound than electricity or fire* (`https://www.cnbc.com/2018/02/01/google-ceo-sundar-pichai-ai-is-more-important-than-fire-electricity.html`) Though Pichai was referring to useful pursuits such as cancer research and language translation, dramatic testaments such as these set an impossible standard for AI researchers and products and services enriched with AI technologies. AI is, indeed, making significant advancements in many application areas, and this book has shown just a small sampling of what can be done with AI with relatively little effort. But AI as a field and popular concern has witnessed these **springs** before – they always follow some kind of **AI winter**. An AI winter is a period of time when funding (often government funding) and venture capital available for AI research dwindles and the average person's optimism about AI's future sinks to the point that AI is seen as a fool's game. There have been a few AI winters in the past (`https://en.wikipedia.org/wiki/AI_winter`), but it is more important to keep in mind that AI research still progressed during these supposedly dry periods. David Brock, director of the Center for Software History at the Computer History Museum, summarized a recent panel discussion from researchers who have made significant contributions to AI since the 1960s (*Learning from Artificial Intelligence's Previous Awakenings: The History of Expert Systems, Brock, David C, AI Magazine, vol. 39, no. 3, 2018, pp. 3-15*, `https://aaai.org/ojs/index.php/aimagazine/article/view/2809`). Based on these panelists' comments, he made the following observation:

> *To date, a pronounced pattern in the history of artificial intelligence is that of oscillation. The communities of artificial intelligence have swung their attention to and from a core set of interests and approaches repeatedly: heuristic problem-solving, neural networks, logical reasoning, and perception. Each has fallen into and out of, then back into, favor for at least one cycle, some more. Yet many within the artificial intelligence community see steady advance. [...] Even so, outside the artificial intelligence community, the broader academic, commercial, governmental, and cultural interest in artificial intelligence has oscillated from almost-exhilaration to near-despair several times.*
>
> *Learning from Artificial Intelligence's Previous Awakenings: The History of Expert Systems, Brock, David C, AI Magazine 39, no. 3, 2018, pp. 3-15,*
>
> `https://aaai.org/ojs/index.php/aimagazine/article/view/2809`

In summary, while AI has advanced throughout the last half-century, popular opinion has oscillated. This phenomenon is not unique to AI. It is common in information technology. It is summarized by futurist Roy Amara: *We tend to overestimate the effect of a technology in the short run and underestimate the effect in the long run* (`https://en.wikipedia.org/wiki/Hype_cycle`). Michael Mullany documented a list of hyped technologies from the last few decades (*8 Lessons from 20 Years of Hype Cycles, Mullany, Michael,* `https://www.linkedin.com/pulse/8-lessons-from-20-years-hype-cycles-michael-mullany/`), including intelligent agents (for example, Microsoft's Clippy), speech recognition, evolutionary computing (for example, genetic algorithms), 3D printing, desktop Linux, quantum computing, and virtual reality.

The hype cycle may be visualized as in *Figure 2*. After an initial burst of interest, disillusionment sets in when the technology doesn't live up to expectations. Hopefully, the technology survives and continues to mature up to a point when it is ultimately appreciated again, and expectations are satisfied. The plot does not actually show a "cycle." While some technologies are hyped over and over again in different decades (such as virtual reality hype in the 1990s and 2010s), the hype cycle explains our tendency to repeat this curve for various technologies, over and over again. The only way out of the cycle is to learn to better identify the true capabilities and promise of new technologies:

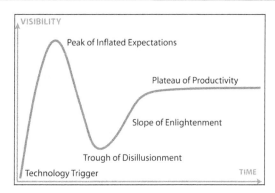

Figure 2: The hype cycle (https://en.wikipedia.org/wiki/Hype_cycle)

There is an advantage to riding the hype cycle. It is easy at this point in time to convince investors and granting agencies that AI, and DL, in particular, is the right approach to solve any number of problems. It is particularly easy if AI is being used to solve a challenging social problem such as detecting and removing fake news from social media, reducing the risk of cybersecurity attacks on individual consumers, detecting cancer earlier, and so on. There is a reason to believe AI can indeed play a significant role in solving these problems. But there is hype. Maybe too much hype. Maybe it is too early to tell.

One must be careful to set appropriate expectations for a company's software and services. Consider the case of IBM's Watson. In 2011, IBM demonstrated their new system's AI capabilities by beating *Jeopardy!* champions Ken Jennings and Brad Rutter in a televised game. Watson, at the time, used sophisticated document search techniques and a very large corpus of dictionaries, encyclopedia articles, and so on. Subsequent to that public display of AI, IBM has transitioned Watson into a kind of brand for their various AI offerings. Watson has since been tasked with diagnosing cancer, weather forecasting, tax preparation, fashion design, and so on (`https://en.wikipedia.org/wiki/Watson_(computer)`). Searching for news stories about these Watson ventures turns up mostly two kinds of stories:

1. Watson *will be* deployed for some application and promises significant advantages (for example, *Will IBM's Watson be an accountant killer?*, Marks, Gene, *The Washington Post*, February 6, 2017, `https://www.washingtonpost.com/news/on-small-business/wp/2017/02/06/will-ibms-watson-be-an-accountant-killer/`)

2. Watson *fails to* provide significant advantages (for example, *IBM's Watson recommended 'unsafe and incorrect' cancer treatments, Spitzer, Julie, STAT report finds, Becker's Health IT and CIO Report*, July 25, 2018, `https://www.beckershospitalreview.com/artificial-intelligence/ibm-s-watson-recommended-unsafe-and-incorrect-cancer-treatments-stat-report-finds.html`)

If IBM is hoping to avoid the trough of disillusionment in the hype cycle plot, they will need more news stories with positive outcomes (not just promises) to counteract the news stories with negative outcomes.

The hype cycle suggests that consumers and end-users will "continuously evaluate" your system's performance. You should, too. The product development stage, prior to deployment, is just promises, just hype. The proof is in the deployment. Does the system actually work? Does it do what was promised?

How do you avoid causing disillusionment in your customers? Keep expectations in-line with what is deployed. Be modest in your claims. For example, we could describe our course advising chatbot from *Chapter 7, A Blueprint for Understanding Queries and Generating Responses* in two ways:

1. Our bot can converse with students to make their college careers a success
2. Our bot can answer common questions about majors and course offerings to allow advisors to dedicate their time to more meaningful interactions

The first description seems to suggest that students can converse with the bot about just about anything relating to college; not only that, it suggests that conversations can be maintained across many questions and responses, requiring the bot to manage context in a way that it actually is not capable of doing. On the other hand, the second description narrows the range of suggested interactions to those that the bot is designed to support.

As much as possible (a marketing expert will push back on this), avoid using highly suggestive words like *learns, knows,* or *understands.* These words convey a kind of sophistication that is beyond most, or perhaps all, AI and ML tools. Even though "machine learning" has "learning" in the name, the "learning" that is meant in ML is usually not the same kind that is meant by people in normal conversation. ML techniques, like neural networks, are capable of learning about features and patterns and rules in the training data. But a neural network that learns to distinguish cats from dogs cannot be said to have learned what a cat is and what a dog is. If it is trained on photographs of cats and dogs, then it will likely be confused by a cartoon drawing of either. Yet we would expect a human (that is, a child) who learns about cats and dogs to be able to tell them apart with just a drawing. Researchers are always looking for ways to allow machines to learn these same kinds of abstractions that seem to come easy to humans, but a general-purpose learner in this sense is still unrealized.

Likewise, *knows* and *understands* implies the AI system will virtually never make a mistake. For example, a self-driving car that *understands road signs* would not run a stop sign on a clear day. But if this car does, in fact, run a stop sign because, perhaps, a tree cast a partial shadow on the sign, causing the computer vision system to mistake it for a yield sign (or whatever), it would be clear to everyone that, in fact, the car does not understand road signs. If road sign failures occur more than once, the car will be labeled *stupid*, an *AI failure*, and another example of the *false promise* of AI.

Of course, we do not suggest that your products be described in excruciating detail just for the sake of never over-promising. No marketing manager would allow that. We only wish to point out that people tend to remember the extreme cases rather than the norm. People remember when they won the lottery, not all the times they lost. They mostly remember when software fails, especially if it is catastrophic, less so all the other times when it did what it was supposed to do.

The next big thing

In conclusion, we now look ahead at what might be coming in the next few years. It is clear DL is here to stay, given its dramatic and broad successes in many application domains. In the near future, expect DL to be applied to even more applications, particularly in healthcare and medicine. There is also significant research interest in connecting data of different modalities together with DL. For example, building models that can create text descriptions of images, or creating images from text descriptions. This kind of research aims to put more logic and structure in DL architectures, so it's more sophisticated than simple "input/output" pairs (for example, input = image, output = "cat"). For example, Zhu and Jiang recently reported success in training a system to understand relations like *the person is next to the horse* just by looking at a photo (*Deep Structured Learning for Visual Relationship Detection, Zhu, Yaohui,* and *Shuqiang Jiang, Proceedings of the Thirty-Second AAAI Conference on Artificial Intelligence, 2018*).

It is not clear at the moment whether self-driving vehicles will be widely available to regular consumers. But the technologies developed to support the cars that are currently being tested will not disappear. It is likely that some sort of self-driving vehicles will be eventually used for industrial applications such as long-haul trucking on pre-defined routes. This does not necessarily directly impact software companies, but we should expect to see some new technologies from these efforts, just like the space program contributed LEDs for medical therapies and temper foam (`https://en.wikipedia.org/wiki/NASA_spinoff_technologies`). In particular, we might find self-driving vehicle research improves GPS, robotics and the ROS software, and computer vision software.

ML will continue to be available as a service via APIs, such as currently offered by Google (`https://cloud.google.com/products/ai/`), Microsoft (`https://azure.microsoft.com/en-us/services/cognitive-services/`), and Amazon (`https://aws.amazon.com/machine-learning/`). Expect these offerings to expand to include more AI techniques and easier methods for training the models on your own data. These companies will have so much data available for training, data that is not available to the public, and specialized hardware that it will be more economical for companies to use their APIs than attempt to build their own models and train from scratch.

To this end, expect these APIs to emphasize **transfer learning**, as we saw in *Chapter 5, A Blueprint for Detecting Your Logo in Social Media,* so that users can get high-quality AI models with little training data. Expect to find start up companies depending on these AI APIs, much like companies depend on cloud computing today.

Finally, it is likely we will find more benefits in working *with* machines rather than expecting to replace humans with machines. Consider the case of chess, which we examined at the beginning of this chapter. We showed how chess engines today are far better than chess champions. However, in 2005, two chess amateurs demonstrated that working with low-powered chess engines (a variety of them, simultaneously) allowed them to beat chess champions and other top chess engines at the time (*The cyborg chess players that can't be beaten, Baraniuk, Chris, BBC, December 4, 2015,* `http://www.bbc.com/future/story/20151201-the-cyborg-chess-players-that-cant-be-beaten`). A common explanation of this outcome is that the chess engines *can only search* for chess moves while humans *use their intuition,* something computers supposedly lack – and when a human's intuition is capable of critiquing the computer's output, performance is improved. We should expect to see more AI tools being used as cognitive apparatus rather than replacements. While it is possible that AI will be able to, say, automatically detect fraud with some acceptable degree of accuracy, would it not be better to have a human take a second look at the borderline cases? In this sense, AI can help us do our jobs better, can help us be more focused, more creative, and more productive. Computers, machines themselves, have played this role for decades, for centuries. AI is how we maximize this potential.

Summary

In summary, AI is hot stuff. Given the diversity of projects presented in this book, and keeping in mind the many kinds of projects we were not able to include, nearly every business can find a place for AI to enhance their processes, products, and services. We don't yet know the limitations of the current thrust of DL and ML generally. But even if some over-hyped expectations are not met, the software and techniques we develop and deploy along the way will still continue to solve business needs. AI winters, AI springs, and the hype cycle are mostly just media narratives to give dramatic arcs to otherwise complex and technical stories. But the excitement is real - the amount of AI and ML libraries, datasets, startups, jobs, courses, books, and videos are unparalleled in the history of the field. It's time to take advantage of it.

Other Books You May Enjoy

If you enjoyed this book, you may be interested in these other books by Packt:

Architects of Intelligence

Martin Ford

ISBN: 978-1-78913-151-2

- The state of modern AI
- How AI will evolve and the breakthroughs we can expect
- Insights into the minds of AI founders and leaders
- How and when we will achieve human-level AI
- The impact and risks associated with AI and its impact on society and the economy

Advanced Deep Learning with Keras

Rowel Atienza

ISBN: 978-1-78862-941-6

- Cutting-edge techniques in human-like AI performance
- Implement advanced deep learning models using Keras
- The building blocks for advanced techniques - MLPs, CNNs, and RNNs
- Deep neural networks – ResNet and DenseNet
- Autoencoders and Variational AutoEncoders (VAEs)
- Generative Adversarial Networks (GANs) and creative AI techniques
- Disentangled Representation GANs, and Cross-Domain GANs
- Deep Reinforcement Learning (DRL) methods and implementation
- Produce industry-standard applications using OpenAI gym
- Deep Q-Learning and Policy Gradient Methods

Deep Reinforcement Learning Hands-On

Maxim Lapan

ISBN: 978-1-78883-424-7

- Understand the DL context of RL and implement complex DL models
- Learn the foundation of RL: Markov decision processes
- Evaluate RL methods including Cross-entropy, DQN, Actor-Critic, TRPO, PPO, DDPG, D4PG and others
- Discover how to deal with discrete and continuous action spaces in various environments
- Defeat Atari arcade games using the value iteration method
- Create your own OpenAI Gym environment to train a stock trading agent
- Teach your agent to play Connect4 using AlphaGo Zero
- Explore the very latest deep RL research on topics including AI-driven chatbots

Leave a review - let other readers know what you think

Please share your thoughts on this book with others by leaving a review on the site that you bought it from. If you purchased the book from Amazon, please leave us an honest review on this book's Amazon page. This is vital so that other potential readers can see and use your unbiased opinion to make purchasing decisions, we can understand what our customers think about our products, and our authors can see your feedback on the title that they have worked with Packt to create. It will only take a few minutes of your time, but is valuable to other potential customers, our authors, and Packt. Thank you!

Index

www.ingramcontent.com/pod-product-compliance
Lightning Source LLC
LaVergne TN
LVHW081521050326
832903LV00025B/1580